A WELSH
WANDER

Praise for *A Welsh Wander*

For anyone planning to walk around Wales, the Offa's Dyke
Path or who just wants a good read about one person's
walking adventure, I would highly recommend that you
have a read of Tom's *A Welsh Wander*.

Rob Dingle – Offa's Dyke National Trail Office
(from the national trail website)

I've felt I was with you on your walk because of the
way you have with words and the wonderful pictures.

Anwen Hughes

What on earth are we going to read now? So enjoyed every
step along the way with you through your eloquent words.

Sue Patterson

This has made me laugh, cry, use an atlas! It is well-written,
brave, honest, funny, heartfelt, informative and descriptive.
Then there are the photos: so beautifully observed. I think all
of us feel we know Wales more now than we did! Dare I say
it, I believe that you have done more for Welsh tourism in 63
days than a well-organised and expensive campaign! You have
certainly enticed Dave and me to spend many more weeks in
Wales in years to come. Thank you and well done.

Denise Fleure

A WELSH WANDER

an epic trek
right around Wales

T O M   D A V I E S

First impression: 2017

© Copyright Tom Davies and Y Lolfa Cyf., 2017

The contents of this book are subject to copyright, and may
not be reproduced by any means, mechanical or electronic,
without the prior, written consent of the publishers.

Front cover photograph: Beth Clarkson
All other photos from author's collection
Cover design: Y Lolfa

ISBN: 978 1 78461 450 8

Published and printed in Wales
on paper from well-maintained forests by
Y Lolfa Cyf., Talybont, Ceredigion SY24 5HE
website www.ylolfa.com
e-mail ylolfa@ylolfa.com
tel 01970 832 304
fax 832 782

Contents

Foreword

I first heard about Tom and his Welsh Wander after his mum got in touch with me in August 2016. She told me all about her son's challenge to walk the whole perimeter of Wales and raise money for charity. My dad suffered from dementia, Tom's grandmother died of Alzheimer's and now his grandfather has developed the illness too. I decided to offer my support and join him on part of his trek of a lifetime, to help raise awareness of this terrible condition.

Tom is a proud Welshman who loves his country and is one of those people you can't fail to like. During his walk around Wales, Tom wrote a regular blog which kept his family, friends and followers up to date on his daily progress. I started to read it and enjoyed it so much that I suggested to him that it had the makings of a book. So off he went to work on it, and I am delighted that his first ever book has been published by Y Lolfa in Ceredigion.

A Welsh Wander tells his story as he treks around Wales with his faithful (but heavy!) rucksack, Wilson. During this emotional and sometimes exhausting journey along the Wales Coast Path and Offa's Dyke Path, there are highs and lows, with tales of blisters and frustrated tears mixed with smiles of joy and laughter.

His love of the Welsh countryside, its beauty, history and magical wildlife really shine through. He meets interesting characters and recounts heart-warming stories of the kindness he received along the way. And with the help of so many generous people Tom raised over £6,700 for the Alzheimer's Society, far exceeding his original target of £1,100 (a pound for each mile of his walk).

It has been a pleasure for me to get to know Tom and one day I hope to follow in his footsteps and complete my own Welsh Wander. Hopefully this book with its useful tips and advice will inspire you to do the same, and discover more of Wales – whatever the weather!

Pob hwyl!

Derek Brockway
April 2017

Author acknowledgements

My Welsh Wander wouldn't have been possible without the help of so many people. The encouragement and backing that I received along the way played a huge role in my overall success, and I would like to thank everybody involved. I dedicate *A Welsh Wander* to a few in particular.

Firstly, to my parents: Toinette and Edward Davies. You are the reason that I am who I am today and you instilled in me a love for the great outdoors from a young age. Without this, I wouldn't have had the motivation to even begin such a large trek. To my sister: Emily Davies. Growing up together and exploring far and wide inspired in me a sense of adventure that helped me find enjoyment in every day of wandering. To my Papa, Ian Bird, and my late Grandma, Mel Bird. Seeing your courage and determination through your battles with dementia and Alzheimer's gave me a reason to take on the 1,100 miles, and the conviction to see them through to the end. And lastly, to Grandma and Grandpa Davies: Frank and Pauline. Your unwavering support and your love of literature gave me the incentive to sit and write the blog each night, even when I was tired and aching, and your excitement at seeing it put into print has been a driving force in the creation of this book.

On my wander, I would always think of each of you reading every daily blog as I was writing it, so now that *A Welsh Wander* has become a reality, I hope that you enjoy revisiting the adventure that you helped me to write.

Tom Davies
April 2017

Introduction

On 1st October 2016 at about 1 p.m., I left Kington Golf Club to walk eight miles back to my home. Though not remarkable in terms of distance, terrain or challenge, this would be the most emotional walk of my life. I would shed tears on more than one occasion, see some feathers that would fill my heart with warmth, and arrive home to a welcome party that overwhelmed me with love and support. This may seem an overreaction for a three hour walk, but although the golf club is only eight miles from my front door, I had hiked 1,092 miles to get there.

After leaving my home in Presteigne near the English-Welsh border on 26th July, I had walked for 63 out of the last 68 days and circumnavigated my home country of Wales. Along the way, I had seen incredible views, discovered hidden gems, learned much of our nation's bloody and battle-scarred history, experienced magical wildlife encounters, had many 'laugh out loud' moments and met dozens of interesting and wonderful people to share in my journey. I had raised over £5,300 for Alzheimer's Society and made memories that I know will live with me long into my twilight years. I took on this challenge alone, but had wanted a way to keep my family and friends close as I walked and so my blog, *Tom's Welsh Wander*, was born. Each night, I would sit in a quiet corner of a pub, or a bedroom, or my tent, and pour my heart out onto the screen of my phone. I'd write about everything that had made that day memorable, as well as sharing my thoughts and feelings about the challenge.

This blog became very special to me as it was a friend to confide in throughout my solo miles, and that is why I have decided to share it with you now. I hope it will inspire you to explore the countryside on foot and to learn new things about the area you live in. I hope it will provide you with useful tips for long-distance walking, through the lessons I learned along the way. I hope it will make you laugh as much as I have while looking back on some of the brilliantly bizarre moments that made my wander so enjoyable. I hope it will make you want to visit corners of the incredible country that is Wales, as you see her through the eyes of somebody who fell head-over-heels in love with her as he walked. I hope that it will be half as helpful and as meaningful to you as it was to me.

The following 63 chapters are the 63 daily blogs that were published from many a small corner of Wales, where a smelly, bearded man sat quietly looking back at the day that had just passed. I have often added in later thoughts and reflections, but the majority of what you read is the original content of Tom's Welsh Wander, written every evening during my 1,100-mile journey.

Offa's Dyke:
Presteigne to Prestatyn

Day 1
Presteigne to Newcastle

Setting off this morning, I felt strangely numb. I'd been waiting for today since February, and now it was here. Walking out of the front door, I knew that the next time I set foot in my home I would have 1,100 miles in my legs.

After giving Dad a goodbye hug so he could go and do the farm chores, it was lovely to have Mum walk with me a little way, waving goodbye as I began to climb the slopes of the Slough Road. On reaching Evenjobb, I touched my first acorn waymarker and took my first steps on the Offa's Dyke Path. The acorns will eventually take me to the North Wales coast in about a week's time. For now, I was treated to views of the rolling, green hills that the borderlands are so well known for. Beautiful. Peaceful. Home.

Following a short rest on a bench in Dolley Green, I made short work of the climb up to the Knighton Road, stopping only to take photos of Presteigne and our farm in the distance – the last time I'll see them until I've walked back home the long way. The dyke is really impressive in places between Dolley Green and Knighton! The ditch and raised banks are still easily visible (in places, I'd guess it was at least 30 feet from ditch to top) and it seemed to snake away into the distance like a garden hose laid out in front of me, showing me the route ahead. I'm looking forward to seeing and learning more about its history in the days to come.

In Knighton, I was stopped by a few people who had either recognised me from the local paper, or were interested in my large backpack. It seems I've become a bit of a local celebrity! I had a lovely chat with a couple who had walked nearly every major trail in Britain in their younger days, and they had many interesting stories to share. The half-hour conversation ended in a donation, as did a shout of 'Aren't you the guy in the paper?' Thank you all for your generosity!

The afternoon saw the arrival of rain and even steeper hills than those this morning. It was challenging! My legs were beginning to feel the extra 20 kg I was carrying and the constant 'waterproof on, waterproof off' was a little irritating. Still, a couple of nice chats with people tackling Offa's Dyke in the opposite direction kept morale up, as did my bag of Haribo!

All day, I'd been following the acorn waymarkers and it didn't take long to notice that the majority of them had a bird's feather stuck into the top. Sometimes blackbird, sometimes magpie, sometimes buzzard. It became a bit of a game trying to spot them all, so I was a little sad when they seemed to stop at Knighton. It had been at least two miles since I'd seen one, and 90% of those two miles had been uphill. My morale was dropping as rapidly as the path was climbing. And then I spotted a feather sticking out of the next fence post. My avian friend was back! It was at this moment that a thought crossed my mind. My grandad's surname is Bird, and so obviously my grandma's was too. I'm not normally one who believes in supernatural occurrences of any sort, but it was a heart-warming and comforting feeling that on what would have been my grandma's 88th birthday, the pair of them were helping me along on my journey. From then on, whenever I started to doubt whether my legs would make it to the end target of the day or if I was on the right track, a feather would pop up stuck in a waymarker or fence post, just to reassure me that I was still going well.

I'm now sitting comfortably in the Quarry House B & B in Newcastle with my legs up, having had a soak in a hot bath and a cup of tea. Heaven! I decided I'd save camping out in the rain for another night, and my hosts, Simon and Michelle, were both so kind to clear out the room that they usually use for storage so I could stay. I can't thank them enough!

Sorry for rambling on so much – excuse the pun, it was totally intentional. It's probably taken you as long to read this as it did for me to walk today's 20 miles! I'll try to be briefer tomorrow. Promise! Nos da, pawb.

Postscript The night before I'd started, I'd suddenly been hit by a wall of worry. Throughout my months of planning, all I'd thought about was the freedom that the trail would offer and how different that would be to my very structured life in teaching. However, as I sat there wanting to get excited, the only emotion that came over me was anxiety. I was now seeing the huge distances I'd be covering and the large weight I'd be carrying, the minimal training that I'd had time to do and how isolated parts of the challenge would be. I already had over £1,100 of sponsorship, and I feared failure. How would I ever explain it to those who had been kind enough to donate?

Needing two rest stops before I even hit the Offa's Dyke Path didn't help to ease this worry the following morning, and as I began my circuit, the hills that this section of the ODP is famous for were taking their toll. I eventually made it to Newcastle, over 20 miles from my start point, but I was tired and nearly broken. Although I apologise at the end of this blog for being too long-winded, I hadn't yet realised its importance in my emotional state. As I walked on, the blogs would not become 'briefer', but instead far more personal and open, and far more detailed.

Day 2
Newcastle to Forden

Day 2 began with a tasty breakfast cooked by Michelle and Simon at the B & B. They also made me sandwiches to take for lunch on my hike today... Such lovely people and a real lucky find to happen across them yesterday while on my way to a pub in the village of Newcastle, which was a mile further out of my way and apparently much more expensive. I guess the lucky duck that Grandma and Grandpa Davies bought for me while on holiday in Whitby is working its magic already!

I'd had no fewer than five people warn me about how tough

the first five miles of today's route would be, so it was with a slight feeling of trepidation that I set off this morning with already stiff legs. I was pleasantly surprised that I seemed to loosen up on the first climb, and found the first few miles relatively easy going, despite the constant alternation of steep ascents and descents.

I reached Churchtown feeling pleased with progress so far, but in need of ditching the bag for a bit. The name 'town' is stretching it a bit here. The only buildings in sight were a pretty little church, a caravan and one lonely house. While sheltering from the rain inside the church, a Swiss duo joined me. They were walking Offa's Dyke in the other direction as far as Knighton, before hopefully catching a train to the airport in a couple of days' time... I wished them luck with both of their aims, knowing how few and far between trains in Knighton are! After nearly an hour spent sharing stories of hiking and teaching (the younger woman was a year 5/6 teacher too!) we parted ways and set off up steep climbs on opposite sides of the valley.

The weather was typical of a British summer – I stripped off my waterproofs and had to put sun cream on near the top of the steep climb from Churchtown, walked for 300 m to crest the hill, saw another bank of rain rolling in and quickly had to layer up again. This pattern continued all morning. My legs were also starting to feel the pace. I'd liken those five miles to laying out five basketballs in a line on a table. Now imagine you're a fifth the size of an ant and have to walk over all of them. It was draining! At least the beautiful views and impressive sections of the dyke earthworks offered a distraction from the pain in my legs, back and feet.

I actually shouted out in joy when I topped out on the Kerry Ridgeway, apparently one of the oldest roads in Britain, and saw flat ground below me stretching for miles into the distance. The afternoon was going to be a lot easier, as will the next couple of days' walking.

With flatter ground came greater pace, and I was eating

up the miles with the aid of my iPod. The flat fields near Montgomery were the location of one of the bloodiest battles in the English Civil War in the 1640s – a huge victory for the Parliamentarians as they lost only 40 men, compared to the 500 Royalist soldiers killed and 1,500 taken prisoner. It's impossible to imagine that sort of violence taking place in fields which now look like a scene from a postcard, with their golden crops, scarlet poppies and ancient oaks.

I ended the day in a small hamlet called Kingswood, which is just past Forden. Tent pitched and my first blister dealt with – on the sole of my left foot (ouch!) – I'm now sitting in the local pub enjoying a burger, a coke, an electrical socket and free Wi-Fi! The staff at The Cock are extremely friendly and have offered to share my blog and Just Giving page with their Facebook group. This trip is already restoring my faith in humanity!

I'm only five miles away from Welshpool now, so I'm ahead of where I hoped to be after two days and looking forward to a day of flat walking tomorrow. Hopefully I'll make an even bigger dent in the 1,100-mile target!

Nos da, pawb!

PS The feathers continued today, if a little less frequently. I always smile when I see one.

Day 3
Forden to Llanymynech

Today did not start well. I'd noticed the chickens roaming around the grounds of the B & B that I was camping at when I arrived last night, but didn't think any more of it. Until 3.45 a.m. that is, when the roosters (there were two) starting sounding the morning call. They sounded it again at 4.30 a.m. And again at 5.10 a.m. And again at 6 a.m. And just to make sure that I didn't go back to sleep for too long, they kindly woke me up again at 7 a.m. by having a morning call conversation with a rooster across the valley. I've never craved chicken for breakfast before, but I came mighty close to jumping out of my tent in the early hours to give it a try. Note to self: if you notice chickens anywhere near your chosen camping spot, choose a different camping spot.

After far too little sleep, I crawled out of my tent and packed up everything as quickly as I could to stop it getting soaked in the newly-arrived rainstorm. Breakfast was provided by Mary and John in the B & B and we spent a happy hour chatting afterwards. I left a little later than planned, despite the roosters' best efforts, and headed for the highest point of my walk so far – Beacon Ring.

Three miles of trudging uphill through never-ending rain later, I arrived at a place steeped in history. Built back in the BC years as an Iron Age fort, the Beacon Ring has played roles in many battles since, including providing a gathering point for Henry Tudor's troops on the eve of the Battle of Bosworth in 1485. As I walked through the still-clear entrance in between the high protective banks of earth, the mist creeping through the trees gave the place an eerie feel. I could sense the soldiers of years past nervously awaiting orders and preparing weapons, in the full knowledge that not everyone gathered in this small copse of trees would live to see many more days.

The soggy slog back down the hill to Buttington was miserable. My feet were hurting, my legs weakening, my back beginning to ache and I was feeling tired after the disturbed night. It was the first time since the very beginning that I've doubted whether my body can cope with this challenge, and it was definitely the lowest I've felt in the three days so far. I was even considering stopping for the night in Welshpool, having covered less than 7 miles.

But how things can change with a target met and a full belly! I arrived in Buttington half an hour earlier than I thought I would and had a tasty meal of fish and chips. Looking at the guidebook, I decided to try and head for Llanymynech tonight;

a further 11 miles of walking after 6.5 hilly ones this morning! However, these 11 would be flat. Very flat! It seems this trip is already changing me. I've always been excited by lots of contour lines on a map, showing steep and mountainous ground, but as I sat in the shelter of the pub I was overjoyed to see that there were hardly any contours crossing my route for the rest of the day (only three in fact!).

The weather had also decided to play ball and so away went the waterproofs, out came the sun cream and the miles started to tumble. It isn't the most spectacular or interesting section of the Offa's Dyke Path, but as I followed the banks of the River Severn and the towpath of the Montgomery Canal, I felt a million times happier than this morning. Progress was being made and my body had stopped complaining. I met a few nice people hiking the ODP in the other direction, and we had brief but lovely chats about our experiences so far and what was to come. I also met many fields of cows and had more one-sided conversations with them too.

Feeling positive again, and having covered more ground than expected today, I'm ready to take on the hills again tomorrow after a hopefully rooster-free sleep. Fingers crossed!

Nos da, pawb!

Postscript

This really was a day of two halves. Firstly, I'll say the uphill miles to Beacon Ring had a lot of interest, with wooded sections of dyke and lots of local history leading up to the fantastically-preserved earthworks atop the hill fort. However, the fact that it was both raining and humid meant that I was rather unhappy in my coat and waterproof trousers for the duration of the climb, and this was compounded on the descent by the fact that my boots were too small. Every step sent my toes crashing into the ends of my Scarpas and at one point, I sat down and contemplated changing into the lightweight sandals that I was wearing in the evenings. I phoned home from this spot, and Mum immediately got onto the internet to order the larger pair of boots that I so desperately needed.

Buoyed by the knowledge that I had no more than a few days left in these boots, I hauled my bag onto my back again and continued the painful journey downhill to Buttington Bridge. The afternoon lifted my spirits tenfold. Flat walking meant that the boots were bearable and although I had trouble finding anywhere to camp at my end point and had to resort to another B & B, the comfortable room completed my day in happiness. That morning had been my first major struggle of the walk, and the fact that I had come through to the other side smiling gave me renewed belief in my ability to complete this challenge.

Day 4
Llanymynech to Froncysyllte

This morning couldn't have been more different from yesterday morning. The sun was shining, and my legs were feeling great as I tackled the hill out of Llanymynech. I reached the old quarry in no time at all and caught a glimpse of a peregrine falcon, the fastest animal on Earth, in the distance. The views all around were spectacular, so I had high hopes for the day.

After dropping down into the valley, I met a man walking the other way. During a nice chat, he showed me his map and I noticed a campsite near Chirk, which was just outside the reach of the narrow map in my guidebook. This became my destination for the end of the day. 18 hilly miles away from Llanymynech was a big ask, but my legs felt good so I was confident I'd make it.

The next people I met were a family of four from Montgomery, atop a 280 m summit near Trefonen. They had spent the school holidays for many years walking sections of the Offa's Dyke Path, and now that the children had reached 11 and 14, they only had one small section remaining: between the summit they stood on and home in Montgomery. The children were keen to share stories from their time on the path, telling me all about funny navigational errors committed by Dad, and being chased by cows. It was lovely to see two children so into the outdoors and their hiking, especially in an age where for children the word 'fun' seems to mean sitting in front of a computer game. I instantly thought back to my own childhood and our weekly Sunday-morning walks that would happen rain or shine. I guess that's where my love for the outdoors began, and I hoped that these two would keep their love for it as they got older too. After a while sharing stories, they kindly gave me a donation towards my fundraising and we wished each other luck with the rain that was forecast for later.

My pub lunch in Trefonen was the first let-down of the day. The pub only opens in the evenings, so I was left eating my sandwiches five hours earlier than I'd hoped and on the roadside. Feeling a little miffed, I went into the local shop to buy more food for later, and came out feeling much happier after two more donations! One from the owner after asking about my bag, and one from the customer who was behind me in the queue. Thank you both! This instantly improved my mood again and I was ready for a long and hilly afternoon.

The rain came and went, as did the miles and hills. My legs were now feeling the pace, but I was confident still of getting to Chirk in good time. Something I've found while hiking is that everybody talks to you. I've not passed a single person with a rucksack in four days of trekking without chatting with them for at least five minutes. I thought this streak might be broken when I saw two lads eating a snack a good way off the path. I waved, they waved and then they shouted over to ask where I was headed today. We had a great chat for a good few minutes before they took the name of my blog, promised a donation and warned me about an overgrown section of the path ahead. Streak still intact! I hope they found somewhere to camp in Trefonen and managed to get into the pub too. If so, they'd be more successful than I was!

Arriving at the road into Chirk, I came across a man waiting for the bus. He was local, and told me that he'd never heard of a campsite anywhere nearby. Worrying! I decided to wait for the bus with him to see if there was a B & B in town that I could stay at. No bus showed. The poor bloke had to walk two miles on a sore leg to get into Chirk, and I had only one option left. Continue along the Offa's Dyke Path until I found a suitable place to stop for the night. Another four miles on top of my hilly 18 already completed today.

After climbing the hill to Chirk Castle, I snapped a couple of pics, put my head down and went into quick-march mode. The four miles were my quickest of the day by far and my legs held up remarkably well. On arrival in Froncysyllte, I knocked on the door of a B & B, whose owner very kindly let me pitch my tent in his field free of charge. I guess I must have looked so rough that he took pity on me! He was even kind enough to give me a lift into the village .

So now I'm sitting in a pub with a belly full of steak and chips, feeling rather pleased with the end result of a tricky day! 22 hilly miles completed and the prospect of three much shorter days taking me to the North Wales coast a day earlier than planned. I'm thankful to everybody that I met today, because they undoubtedly kept my spirits up much higher than they might have been with the few disappointments I had to face. The people that I'm meeting on this hike are as good for morale as any beautiful view, and I'm looking forward to meeting many more in the weeks to come.

Nos da, pawb! I'll see you tomorrow after a hopefully more straightforward day.

Postscript On returning to the B & B that night, I knocked on the door to thank the owners and was invited inside for a drink. After helping them move a new sofa into their lounge, I sat down with the man who had let me camp for free, me with a water and him with a pint. We discussed many things across the dining room table, including some of the conspiracy videos that he liked to watch online. This is where the conversation grew interesting! He told me about a theory he'd seen that had convinced him the world was flat! He provided many arguments to support this, including horizons and plane tracking websites, before explaining that it meant the world must be a disc shape. Antarctica forms a ring around the disc, with all of the countries arranged around a centre point. He asked how I thought the gases stayed in, and my answer of 'Gravity?' was clearly not correct. There is a place in Antarctica which 40 countries have signed a treaty never to go to (I didn't ask about the other 160+ countries). This is where the dome touches the ground.

Deciding against arguing the case of a spherical Earth with satellites, astronauts, day and night and various other counterpoints, I just listened, fascinated by his points of view. Though I didn't, and will never, think that what he was telling me was accurate, it was genuinely interesting to learn what another person can believe in, and how totally different that can be from anything you'd expect. After he told me about the blank-shotgun-cartridge booby-trapped signs that he'd placed on the road to convince people to vote leave in the Brexit referendum, and the watchtower that he'd created to watch over them to find out who had been tampering, I went back to my tent wondering if I would wake up again the next morning or be murdered in my sleep!

As the many remaining pages in the book will suggest, I did wake up the following day and got on my way early, after using the nearby wood as a washroom and leaving the address of my blog with a thank you. Did I feel relieved to still be alive? Yes! Did I regret knocking on the door of that B & B? No! The family were kind enough to let me stay for free and I had got to know a truly fascinating individual through a conversation that I will never forget. Wales was already surprising me with the friendly, giving, and sometimes downright bizarre people that call her home.

Day 5
Froncysyllte to Llandegla

Today has been a great day! Starting nice and early, I had lots to look forward to. Some sights that I'd been interested in seeing since I received the guidebook in April, and a welcome visit from Mum at the end of the day with some boots that are hopefully a better fit for my feet.

A mile after leaving my camp, I was walking alongside the canal heading towards the Pontcysyllte Aqueduct. Built by Thomas Telford in 1805, it stands 126 ft above the River Dee at its highest point and is still the largest aqueduct in Britain. Crossing the Dee so high up provided an excellent viewpoint for miles around, and I was glad the weather was dry enough to enjoy it. I was shocked at the lack of a railing on the canal side of the walkway though, imagining travelling across on a narrow boat. It would not be a place to lose your balance!

After climbing through woodland for a few miles, I topped out on the Panorama Walk above Llangollen and gasped at the view in front of me. The town was sitting in the bright sunshine far below, and the Dee was sparkling as it meandered its way past the golf course. Ahead lay Castell Dinas Brân, a ruined thirteenth-century castle on the top of a steep-sided hill, and above me were steep crags of rock. It was by far my favourite view of the hike so far, and will take some beating in the 1,020 miles still to come!

I made the detour to Castell Dinas Brân, almost instantly

regretting the decision to climb the steep path to its top as my legs and feet began to ache. It was worth the pain though! There isn't much left of the building, and it's hard to imagine that in that beautiful and peaceful spot, a formidable castle once stood. It was home to the Princes of Powys Fadog and was completed in 1260. You'd imagine that such an impressive castle stood for centuries, but it was abandoned and torched in 1277, a mere 17 years after it was completed! All that remains today are a few small parts of the keep, hall, gatehouse and Welsh Tower, but it is still a special place to wander around. It felt like I was in the times of King Arthur, and the views all around were spectacular. The weather certainly picked a good day to brighten up.

The ODP takes you underneath sheer crags of rock for the next three miles, and at times it was very narrow. It was like being back in the mountains of Snowdonia again, with steep drops on one side and towering cliffs on the other. I loved it! After dropping to the rather dramatically-named World's End, a steep 300 m climb lies ahead to take you up onto a bleak moorland landscape at 500 m above sea level. I put my head down, went into donkey mode and plodded along. I was surprised at how easily my legs coped with the climb – maybe they are finally starting to understand that this is their lot for the foreseeable future – and at the top I met two cyclists who were climbing a total of 4,500 ft in 40 miles. I honestly think I'd find that harder than my 1,100 miles of walking! We wished each other luck and began to track across the moors.

Half a mile later, I met Sharon and Leigh, two teachers from the north of England who are hiking the Offa's Dyke Path from Knighton to Prestatyn and had coincidentally started on the same day that I did. They were the first people I've met who are walking north in four days, and they could only have been about 8 miles ahead for the 80 miles that we'd already covered. We walked together for the remaining three miles into Llandegla while sharing stories of our time on the path so far, teaching, family, previous adventures and much more!

The miles passed more quickly than any on the trip so far and it was soon time for me to head to the campsite, while Sharon and Leigh continued on for another six miles. I hope they made it to their B & B in good time!

In the hour walking together, I was reminded how much easier it is walking with other people. Having somebody to talk to makes you forget all about sore legs and blisters and how far you have to go. You just enjoy chatting, laughing and spending time with somebody else. I'm looking forward to days to come where friends have said they'll join me, because I know those will be huge high points of this challenge. This afternoon certainly was.

I managed to beat Mum to the campsite by a mere 2 minutes and was talking to the owner when she arrived. £7.50 became £5 with a £2.50 donation to my fundraising (thank you!) and then I was able to pitch my tent before we headed into Llangollen. It was lovely to catch up on how things are going at home, and it felt like an afternoon of normality as we sat in a café eating a good hot meal. Plus, the new boots that mum had brought up felt much more comfortable on my feet. Happy days! Walking 83 miles in five days in boots that have turned out to be half a size too small has not been kind to my feet. I had a blister yesterday that stretched from level with the ball of my left foot, through the gap between my big and second toe and onto the top of my foot. Not pretty, and not particularly comfortable to walk 22 miles on either. I'm hoping these boots will fit me better. Thank you Dad for buying them for me, and thank you Mum for driving two and a half hours to deliver them to my canvas front door! I can't tell you how grateful I am, and how lovely it was to see you for a few hours.

Sitting in the local pub with a diet coke in hand, knowing that I am now only 28 miles from dipping my feet in the sea, is a fantastic feeling, especially after such a good day. A beautiful and interesting variety of scenery and historic sites, some new friends who I may well meet up with again tomorrow when we all reach Bodfari, and seeing one of my two first and best friends in the world with a wonderful gift too. Just the morale boost that I need before tackling the Clwydian Mountains.

Nos da, pawb. I hope everyone has a good evening and I'll see you tomorrow!

Day 6
Llandegla to Bodfari

I'll start today's blog with a confession. When I skimmed through future sections of the Offa's Dyke Path guidebook a few days ago, I saw the Clwydian Mountains as an 8¾-mile section before the final stretch to Prestatyn. Two easy days of walking to finish my first stint on the ODP. However, when I read these sections properly last night, I realised I'd made a bit of an error. The 8¾-mile Clwydian section is actually two 8¾-mile Clwydian sections! Oops. Two options then: take the three sections as three days and arrive at Prestatyn eight days after leaving home, or take on both 8¾-mile mountainous sections today and still arrive in Prestatyn tomorrow. Those of you that know me probably won't be surprised that I went with the latter option!

At 8 a.m. this morning, I was sitting in a charming little community shop and café in Llandegla eating a steak slice and a scone, those traditional breakfast foods, before tackling what was sure to be my toughest day so far. My legs felt good and my size 11 boots were so much more comfortable than the 10½ ones. Thanks again, Mum and Dad! I felt confident that I would get to Bodfari, but knew that my lack of careful reading would probably lead to a very long day and a rather late finish.

About half an hour into the first climb, my legs seemed to remember something from a few years ago. They were rather good at mountains! I arrived at Clwyd Gate (6 miles into the day) in great time after singing lots of different motivational songs to myself and the sheep along the way (I apologise to the sheep!). The miles and mountains continued to tumble and my spirits were as high as the peaks I was climbing.

The highest point of the walk came at Moel Famau, and the car park at the bottom marked the halfway point too. Reaching this point at midday was a real boost as I certainly wouldn't be finishing as late as I thought. Legs still feeling great, I covered the uphill mile in less than 20 minutes and was soon coming over the horizon with the Jubilee Tower just ahead. It was then that I spotted two familiar faces waving at me a short distance away. Sharon and Leigh, my hiking partners of yesterday afternoon, were about to leave the summit, having taken in the spectacular views. We arranged to meet later for a drink unless I caught them up on the way down, and I climbed the final steps to the remains of the Jubilee Tower. It was originally designed like a three-tiered Egyptian obelisk to celebrate the golden jubilee of George III in 1810, but was never completed. A violent storm brought down the unfinished top of the tower and the remaining ruins were demolished for safety reasons. All that remains now is the base, but this is still a fantastic platform from which to observe the surrounding panorama of views. And quite some views they are!

Yesterday's favourite view was seriously challenged! To the west you could see the mountains of Snowdonia, to the north lay Prestatyn and the coastline I have been heading towards since leaving home on Tuesday, to the east was Liverpool and the Wirral (and even Blackpool Tower if you strained your eyes) and to the south was an excellent view of the ODP sections that I have been hiking for the past couple of days. It was, quite simply, breathtaking!

It was a hard spot to leave, but with the draw of the sea to the north, I motored on down the hill towards the next climb. It wasn't long before I bumped into Sharon and Leigh having lunch, so we walked together for the remainder of the day – a further 6 miles. They have done so many hiking trips together and to hear them talking about these with such happiness inspires me to take on many more trips like this in the future.

27

Once this one is completed of course – there is still a very long way to go!

Once again sitting in a pub and with my tent pitched in the beer garden, I'm looking back fondly on a day where my love of hills was rekindled. I'm also looking forward to arriving in Prestatyn after 12 miles of walking tomorrow, and dipping my feet in the sea for the first time of many during this adventure. I'll now be walking on or near the coast for about 9 weeks. I can't wait to find out what secrets and surprises the Wales Coast Path has waiting to be discovered.

Nos da, pawb. Have a lovely evening. I'll see you at the seaside tomorrow!

Postscript Day 6 was the first day that my body felt truly comfortable while walking, and I was on a real high at the end! The road ahead looked far less painful, and I foolishly let myself think that it would be easy from that point onwards. I was in blissful ignorance of some of the physical challenges that were yet to come, but as a naïve, novice long distance walker, I got carried away with being impressed at my body's strength that day. Despite the mountainous terrain, my legs had stopped complaining on uphills and my back felt better after ditching 2 kg of things I had been carrying, but didn't need. Mum had taken these home for me when she had brought the new boots to my camp the previous afternoon. Despite the weight only having dropped from 20 kg to 18, it felt like my bag, Wilson, had been on a crash diet and lost half of his weight!

The knowledge that I wasn't using some of what I was carrying had made Wilson feel twice as heavy as he actually was. Before I started, I'd had romantic images of me sitting outside my tent by a stream every evening, reading a good book. In reality, my blog was taking nearly an hour to write each night, and by the time I had sourced food and a place to sleep, I was more than ready to drift into the land of nod. A book is a fairly heavy thing to carry anyway, but a book that I wasn't reading felt like an elephant on my shoulders. As did the fourth T-shirt, the fourth and fifth pairs of boxers, the second pair of shorts, the numerous unnecessary items in my first aid kit, my cheque book and even the pen. The lesson I learned – don't take it unless you will definitely use it!

Day 7
Bodfari to Prestatyn

My roll mat and tent must have been very comfortable this morning, because I managed to sleep through my 7 a.m. alarm and didn't wake until an hour and a half later. There went my early start and early finish. I walked the first four miles at a very quick pace to make up time, and soon reached my first 100-mile mark in Rhuallt. It was a good boost to get me up the steep climb out of the village and towards the Prestatyn hills.

At the top of the first hill, I passed a group of four ladies who were on their last section of the ODP. They've been hiking the trail one weekend every year, starting from Chepstow six or seven years ago, and were making good progress towards the finish. I hope they made it there before it started raining. They were interested in the size of my backpack and after hearing about my challenge, they kindly donated £15. The generosity that I am receiving from complete strangers on this hike is incredible, from sponsorship to upgrading my room (as has just happened in the hotel in Chester), or letting me camp for free. It's reminding me that although the news we see on TV is usually bad, most people in this world are still kind and good at heart.

The path wasn't particularly special today, with lots of irritating windy sections that made it feel a lot longer than it might have done, and had it not been for the fact that the sea was getting ever closer, it could have been a really miserable 12 miles. Having not lost the waymarkers once in 100 miles, I was annoyed at losing them twice between Rhuallt and Prestatyn. Whether they were hidden or my observational skills took a snooze I'm not sure, but the end result was an extra mile of walking when I wasn't in the cheeriest frame of mind anyway.

The inland cliffs of the Prestatyn Hills soon blew away any negativity from my thoughts. The end of the ODP was quite literally in sight, and the views across to Snowdonia and the Great Orme were very pretty. After dropping steeply into Prestatyn, a corridor of golden acorn ODP signs lies in front of you. A mile and a half of navigating bustling streets with my wide backpack brought me to the seafront and the steel sculpture that symbolises hikers' efforts on the trail. Even though I've not finished my challenge, it was a special moment to touch it and take a seat at its base to wait for Sharon and Leigh, who I knew were only 20 minutes or so behind me.

When they arrived, I was introduced to Allan, who they had met while walking a few miles back and who had walked all the way from Knighton too. It's funny how we've all been walking the same trail at the same time, but haven't met until near, or at, the end. Many photos were taken as we dipped our feet in the sea to mark the end of the trail, and we went for a celebratory cup of coffee to reminisce about the week and discuss future walking plans.

All too soon, it was time to go our separate ways. I was sad to say goodbye to Sharon and Leigh as they have made my last three afternoons of walking so much more enjoyable. I hope they have a safe trip back to the north of England and I'm sure we'll stay in contact. Allan and I were able to continue chatting on the train to Chester, where it was great hearing his experiences of walking many different trails and mountains. He has summited every British Munro (mountain over 3000 ft high), which is quite some achievement!

Now I am sitting in a very nice room in a hotel in Chester enjoying an evening of relaxation and television! Tomorrow, I am going to attempt to walk the 32 miles back to Prestatyn, so it'll be an early start and long day of walking. Thankfully it is flat – only 30 m of ascent in 30 miles – so the going will be as easy as it could possibly be... hopefully!

Nos da, all. I'll see you after my first day of many on the Wales Coast Path.

Postscript Since returning home, I've realised how much of a disservice I did to some of my early Offa's Dyke Path sections. This one in particular stands out as falling victim to my tunnel vision. Still having over 900 miles to walk by the time I woke up on day 7, my focus had been entirely taken up by reaching the coast. No longer interested in any of the pretty, green views around me, I only wanted the blue sea and the golden sand. I'm going to return to this part of the dyke and walk it as I walked my later sections; totally immersing myself in the moment and enjoying every little thing that makes this such a special trail.

The sense of pride and relief I had upon reaching the sea was huge considering how far I still had to go on my challenge. I put this down to my first section of walking being completed and to sharing in Sharon, Leigh and Allan's happiness at completing their hikes. The latter of these influences, however, instilled a small but deep sadness in me as well. As I said in the blog, Sharon and Leigh had been such good company during the previous three afternoons and had stopped me feeling lonely at times when the isolation could have got to me. Now I would have to continue without them.

I had decided early in the planning phase of my Wander that I would take the train to Chester. The ODP ends on the Wales Coast Path in Prestatyn, so it would have been easier just to turn left and keep walking, but ever the pedantic perfectionist, I wanted to walk the whole WCP, and that meant starting it in Chester. The walk back to Prestatyn would be a dull one, but at least I wouldn't be feeling like I'd missed anything out. As I lay in my comfy hotel bed, I was worried about how I would cope with the monotonous 80 miles of tarmac walking ahead without Sharon and Leigh to keep me company. This, combined with my body growing used to sleeping on my roll mat, meant that I struggled to get any sleep at all on the night when I most needed it. I was already worried that I'd bitten off more than I could chew for the following day, and now I would have to do it while physically tired too.

North Wales Coast Path

Day 8
Chester to Prestatyn

Today has been an epic. Not in terms of enjoyment, but in terms of mileage, time and pace. I started in Chester at 8.30 a.m., knowing that it was a mile and a half to the start of the coast path and that I intended to complete the first two sections today: a 12¾-mile stretch to Flint, and an 18-mile stretch to Prestatyn. A total of over 32 miles of walking. I've always wanted to do a marathon, but didn't ever imagine that my first one would be in walking boots with 18 kg on my back! Thankfully, it was all going to be flat and there would be lots of places to refill water and food along the coast.

Chester is a genuinely lovely city, and I enjoyed seeing the cathedral, town hall and city walls as I walked at pace towards my starting point. Arriving at the first Wales Coast Path sign at nine, I took the obligatory selfie with the dragon shell symbol that will guide me for many hundreds of miles to come, then set off along the River Dee towards its estuary.

The first two hours were torture. The mist made it incredibly hard to judge distances and the path was a perfectly straight line for mile after mile. Features on the river bank that looked 50 metres away would take five minutes to reach, and the bridge in the distance never seemed to get any closer. Then there was the heartbreaking moment when I looked back to see if I could still see the bridge that I had passed 15 minutes earlier, and it looked like it was only 100 m behind me and at least five times closer than the one up ahead. I started to wonder if I was moving at all, or if the whole path was just a giant conveyer belt keeping me walking on the same spot.

Eventually, the sound of the cars became audible, the graffiti on the bridge became legible and it was possible to read the road signs. I'd arrived at my crossing point! Seven miles in two hours – I knew I would make it to Prestatyn in plenty of time for the 9 p.m. closing of the campsite gates. The five miles to Flint passed without significant event, apart from meeting Jack on the main road into the town. Jack was laying cables for BT and I was striding out with my iPod. I nodded hello and he asked where I was going. Conversation started, I chatted at length with him and his colleague, and as I was about to go, Jack dived for his wallet and pulled out a £10 note to put towards my fundraising. My first boost of many today created by the extraordinary generosity of people who I've only just met. Thank you, Jack. By 1 p.m., I was sitting eating a tasty meal, having completed section one of my two-section day.

After 12 tedious and mentally-draining miles in the morning, my first few minutes of afternoon walking took me past Flint Castle. I allowed myself two minutes to pop in and look around the remains of what was once a great statement of power from King Edward I in 1277, to keep the wild Welsh in check. Parts of all four towers are still intact and it was nice to be able to climb the original steps that King Edward himself might once have climbed. The expansive views over the estuary and its settlements hint at why this location was chosen as a perfect defensive position.

Another huge section of uninteresting path followed as I drew ever closer to the mouth of the Dee. The derelict *Duke of Lancaster* was the next interesting sight. The ship (not a person!) was originally a luxury vessel and later a car ferry, before being moored in the spot it still stands in today to be used as a 'fun ship'. However, the plans never came to anything and the ship was left to decay. It now stands rusting and covered in graffiti, making for an eerie sight as you walk by.

Apart from a beacon in the shape of a dragon, there was then nothing overly interesting for the next umpteen miles. My legs and feet were painful, I was hot, sticky and being plagued by flies of all sizes and my mood was worse than it had been all day – and it hadn't been great from mile two onwards! I was severely doubting my ability to make it to mile 32 and was just trudging on miserably at as quick a pace as I could manage.

As I reached my marathon mark (26 miles), I bumped into a group of four people. They asked about my hike and one lady noticed the rather sore rash on my arms and legs which has been with me since Day 4, suggesting various causes and expressing concern. I waved it off as heat rash, and on hearing the details of my challenge, all four proceeded to empty pockets, coin trays in cars and even give me the prize money that the two ladies had won in a flower show that day! My mood was instantly lifted and I found the next couple of miles easier going again. It's amazing how a moment of kindness from a stranger (or four) can lift your spirits and how that can affect your outlook on a challenge.

Feeling positive about reaching Prestatyn once more, I made good time to Talacre and finally turned west to head along the North Wales coast. This came with a new challenge though. The Wales Coast Path was now following the beach, and as if walking on soft sand wasn't hard enough, the wind was straight into my face as well. Belief soon started dipping again. There was the minor distraction of a disused lighthouse, but my focus now was almost entirely on my watch and the pain in my feet and legs. After a couple of miles, beach walking became salt marsh walking and salt marsh walking became dune walking. I was cursing whoever had decided to take the path this way, and was feeling thoroughly fed up.

The last few miles are a bit of a blur. I know my whole body ached, I know the soles of my feet felt bruised and know I was in a right grump. The view was nice, but as far as I was concerned, the whole 32 miles of path had had four interesting sights and 31½ miles of rubbish.

Feet dragging, I arrived at the campsite behind a car turning in, and didn't know whether I had the energy to climb the very short, very slight hill to the reception. There was no sense of achievement or happiness, just overwhelming tiredness and soreness. A lady had hopped out of the car and

I felt awful that in my zombie-like state, I hadn't recognised her. She was one of the group of four who I'd chatted to earlier. Introducing herself as Anwen, she explained that she had been worried about my rash in case it was a knotweed reaction, and had gone to buy some tablets and cream for me! She'd waited at the campsite for a bit, even asking at reception if I'd arrived yet, and had then driven around looking for me. I was staggered. I didn't know this lady, apart from a five minute chat at the roadside, and she had gone to all that trouble to help a complete stranger. Some people really are incredible! Wishing I hadn't already booked the campsite, I sadly had to turn down Anwen's offer of the spare room at her and her husband's house, but her pure kindness had already given me a much-needed lift at the end of a very tricky day. I can't begin thank her enough. To top it off, the campsite owner, who I'd spoken to first thing in the morning to explain my aims for the day and book a spot, refused to take any money for the pitch and instead told me to donate the £10 fee to my charity. Another act of kindness from a total stranger that ended my day on a high.

So it was a day of two very different sides. The path was awful. I wished for most of the day that the Welsh had let the English have that section of estuary and coast so that I would never have had to walk it. It's boring, long, mostly featureless and not waymarked particularly well either (thankfully the guidebook was spot on). But on the other hand, the generosity and amazingly kind nature of a few people I met brightened the day at the moments I needed it most. That will be my overriding memory of Day 8. Not the pain or the boredom. Not the dull nature of the start of the Wales Coast Path. Not even the 32¼ miles that I've completed in 11 hours of walking time. But the fact that the generosity of everybody who has donated, both on my walk and back at home, gave me the strength to get to the end of the day.

Thank you to all of you, and sleep well. I know I will! Nos da, pawb.

Postscript

Day 8 was one of my most memorable days of walking for many good and bad reasons. It was the longest day of my whole Welsh Wander, both in terms of mileage and time. Would I recommend taking on a 32-mile day near the beginning of a 1,100-mile hike? Never. Would I do it again? Probably not! Am I glad that I did it? Now, yes. At the time, the pain in my feet was excruciating. As comfy as my new Scarpa Mistrals were, no true mountain boot is designed to be comfortable on tarmac, and 28 of my 32 miles were on roads and pavements. By the last mile, my walking poles were taking as much of my weight as my legs and my breath was coming in short gasps. I was totally exhausted. It took 20 minutes of lying on the grass in the newly-arrived drizzle before I could move to pitch my tent, and after an hour and a half of effort to have a shower and write my blog, I fell asleep genuinely hoping that I wouldn't pass away in the night. My body felt strange, with random tremors cropping up all over the place and a persistent light-headedness. I had drunk 4 litres of liquids that day and so was sure I couldn't be dehydrated. I just let my eyes close and hoped for the best when the morning arrived.

Despite my physical state, there was a glimmer of light in the growing darkness that had been rekindled by the kindness of a caring person at the end of the day. Her gesture with the cream and tablets is a story that I continued to tell people for the remainder of my walk, so people all over Wales now know of this wonderful lady called Anwen who went for a walk in Talacre on 2nd August 2016, and helped a stranger more than she could ever know. Eventually, as my body recovered and I realised that I hadn't jeopardised the overall success of my journey by taking on too much at the start, as I so often do, I began to feel proud of the 32 miles I walked on Day 8. By pushing my limits to the very edge and reaching a goal that I'd feared was beyond my abilities, I'd proved that my body could handle this challenge. I didn't dream of covering that distance in one go on this wander again, but I eventually became glad that I had done it on that hot and sticky day.

Day 9
Prestatyn to Colwyn Bay

I allowed myself a lazy start to Day 9. My body was not happy with me after yesterday, so I wanted to take some time just to relax in my little canvas home. Reading the guidebook, I decided to try and reach Colwyn Bay which, with walks to and from campsites included, would add up to about 18 miles. I thought that as the going was still flat, my legs would just about hold up.

After a hearty Tesco breakfast, I hit the promenade at the same point the Offa's Dyke Path finishes and headed at good pace towards Rhyl. Already, I was enjoying today more than yesterday. Yes, I had a strong headwind which made the going a little harder, but two things were making me happy. I felt that I was now making progress again, rather than walking 32 miles back to a place I had been in the day before, and I felt like I was on the proper coast now. The waves were crashing against the promenade and sand from the dunes was whipping around my legs as I was looking far out to sea and across the bay to the Great Orme.

Rhyl and Prestatyn were once booming holiday destinations. From Victorian times onwards, people from Liverpool and further afield had flocked to the beach resorts in their thousands. Now, the once famously popular towns are a little past their best. There is still a good tourist industry being headed up by the endless caravan parks that line the left-hand side of the coast path for mile after mile, and the money that has been put into restoring the seafronts has certainly made them feel less run down, but there just isn't the hustle and bustle that I imagine there used to be. They feel a little sleepier today.

The WCP followed promenades or cycle paths for the entire day, passing through the equally caravan-dominated towns of Towyn, Abergele and Pensarn. I spent the afternoon hopping between cafés and enjoying cups of tea in most of the towns I

39

passed through, determined to take it easy and not get carried away after yesterday. At Llanddulas there was the interesting sight of a honeycomb reef, which is formed very quickly by honeycomb worms. Because of the efficiency of its master craftsmen, the reefs can change shape from month to month. They are apparently quite rare in Wales, and are usually found much further south.

Arriving in Colwyn Bay, I recognised two people wearing wetsuits and fiddling with ropes, sails and boards – Gareth and Rachel, two of my old mountain-walking friends from university. It was nice to stand and have a catch up, however brief, especially as I'd not really had a full conversation with anybody else all day. Most people were holidaymakers and had just shot me inquisitive stares as I walked along the perfectly flat prom looking like I was on my way to climb Kilimanjaro.

Now I'm sitting in a pub in Rhos-On-Sea before going to find my campsite for the night. Tomorrow will be a more interesting day (so hopefully a more interesting blog!), passing Llandudno, the Great Orme and Conwy Castle. The day after, I'll arrive in Bangor and get to spend some much-needed time with friends. I knew that walking with people was easier, but the last two days have shown me how the isolation is as much a part of this challenge as the distance I'm walking. I really am looking forward to days when friends and family can join me, so if you want a day of coastal walking with a tired and probably slightly smelly guy, keep an eye on my blog and let me know when I'm close to you! It'll be nice to have your company.

For now, I'm off to find my campsite. 50 miles walked in the last two days is definitely a good enough reason for an early night, I think.

Nos da, pawb! Have a good evening.

Postscript Shortly before arriving in Rhos-On-Sea, I'd had an encounter that would make me wary of dogs for the remainder of the trip. I decided not to include the story in my original blog for two reasons. One, at the time of writing, my blood was still boiling and I didn't want to say something that I would later regret. Two, I didn't want to worry my family with so much of my journey still to go!

I had been walking along, minding my own business, and had noticed a German Shepherd being called down to the beach to his owners. The large dog was clearly nervous and didn't want to clamber over the rocks, so as it came running towards me, I asked calmly if he was having a little trouble finding a way down (it had become my custom to talk to animals on days where I was wandering alone with nobody else to converse with!). This particular animal, however, clearly didn't appreciate my large rucksack, walking poles and reflective sunglasses. Baring his teeth, he came charging at me, growling and barking with his hackles raised. When within range, he started snapping viciously at me as I frantically used my poles to keep him at a distance where he was unable to take a chunk out of my leg. The owners, by this point, had realised something was wrong and the man came charging towards the dog, yelling at the top of his voice. The beast eventually took off, and I stood rooted to the spot feeling very shaken. Had I not had my sticks, I felt sure that the dog would have torn into me.

The owner walked by without stopping and instead of checking to see if I was OK, he produced the line, 'I'm sorry, but he never would have bitten you.' In my tense state, this meagre attempt at an apology was a red rag to a bull and I wheeled around to reply with a heated stream of 'what ifs' and my opinions on dog owners who cannot control their animals. I waited for his response as he grabbed his dog, but he simply turned and shouted 'Well, go then!' Deciding against launching into another tirade, I turned and headed towards Rhos with trembling hands, thumping heart and a head full of anger. I probably hadn't dealt with the situation in the most composed way, but after being attacked by a large German

Shepherd, I wasn't exactly in the most composed frame of mind. I've never been overly comfortable around dogs that I don't know, and the memory of those few minutes would stay with me for the entire walk, causing my heart rate to rise each time a large dog came over the horizon.

Day 10
Colwyn Bay to Penmaenmawr

Day 10's blog starts with the end of Day 9. I was tired and trying to put my tent up in what felt like a hurricane. During the process of trying to turn a kite into a tent by fixing it to the ground, I managed to cut my hand quite nastily on a tent peg. I'm not one to fuss about pain, and so wrapped it in a tissue and carried on, eventually fixing my tent up into a sturdy position. Soon after diving inside out of the elements to sort my temporary home into order, I heard a voice outside. They asked me how my hand was and when I unzipped my tent to reply, my camping neighbour plonked a plate containing a sausage bap, a banana and some digestives inside and asked if I'd like tea or coffee! Once again, I was overwhelmed by the kindness of a complete stranger. We hadn't even said a word to each other, and he'd gone to the effort to provide food and a cuppa for a fellow camper who was clearly having a spot of bother. In discussion later, he said he sympathised with me as he had once climbed Everest! He got within 4,000 ft of the summit before altitude sickness turned his group around. His stories were fascinating! Coupled with the fact that the campsite owner had told me my stay was free as a 'well done' for my charity work, what could have been a miserable evening was actually rather pleasant.

This morning made yesterday's 'hurricane' look like a bit of drizzle in a light breeze. As I trudged over the Little Orme towards Llandudno, I was so drenched that I thought it may have been drier to swim around the coast rather than walk it. I was cold, looking like a drowned rat and very hungry. Then, out of the rain, a purple sign emerged. A Premier Inn with a Brewer's Fayre restaurant – dry, warm, cooked breakfast – the three things I wanted most in the world at that moment. I spent the next half hour making the most of the all-you-can-eat buffet and when it came to 11 a.m., I asked the waitress where I should pay. She told me not to worry about it and to go and enjoy my walk. I would have paid the £8.99 cost of the breakfast just to stand inside the door for five minutes of shelter, but she'd given me the whole thing for free! The lady on the table next to mine then leaned over and gave me £10, telling me that her mum had died of Alzheimer's and that she hoped I raised loads of money. Two more examples of the amazing generosity of complete strangers.

Walking along the prom in Llandudno, I was feeling buoyant and more at home than I have since leaving Presteigne. I'm now in the part of North Wales that I'm familiar with, and it's great to be back in my old university haunts. As I was reminiscing about times spent here with friends and family, I heard a shout from behind. I turned around to see Sam, a friend from Presteigne, running after me. He'd been sitting in a window across the road and is in town to play a concert in Venue Cymru before his big trip out to Argentina later this month. We walked together for the next 20 minutes or so up onto the Great Orme, and parted shortly after Sam had pointed out my first seal of the walk. It was so nice to catch up, and I hope the concert is going well!

The Great Orme is a spot that I have loved for many years. It's a beautiful outcrop of limestone that juts a couple of miles out into the Irish Sea. The cliffs are not only dramatic, they also provide a haven for bird life, so I was enjoying spotting choughs, cormorants and gannets perched high and low. Around the point, you're met with a stunning panorama stretching from Conwy with its castle, across the mountains of

Snowdonia to the start of the Menai Straits and the expansive coastline of Anglesey. I could see my next three or four days of walking from this one spot, and I took a moment to take it all in. It wasn't just across the water where there were interesting sights. Below me were the concrete bases of a WW2 artillery school. The cadets used to train by firing shells out to sea at floating targets, and at its peak in 1942, the school was training 710 soldiers of mixed ranks.

The path takes you through dunes, small towns and marinas until you reach Conwy. Here, walking over the bridge towards the castle, I began to wish that I had booked a place to stay in town so that I had time to take a tour. The still mostly-intact castle is hugely impressive, and the quaint town is encircled by medieval city walls. I hope to come back and visit properly soon, when I haven't set myself a challenging mileage target!

Striding out along the beautiful sands of Conwy Morfa, I had to take a minute to sit and admire the views back over my day's walking. In complete contrast to the filthy weather of this morning, the Orme was shining in the sun and the waters around it were sparkling. The odd boat was sailing back into Conwy Marina and the seabirds were lazily floating around overhead. It really was breathtaking.

The next bit of walking had two very different sides. On the left was the noise and excitement of the A55 dual carriageway with all manner of vehicles speeding along towards their journeys' end, and on the right was the peace and serenity of the perfectly flat sea, the Great Orme sitting proudly in the distance, and the empty sands of the beaches of Penmaenmawr and Conwy Morfa. Whichever way you decided to look, there was always something interesting to see.

So today has been a good one! That 20 minutes with a friend and the kindness of complete strangers has kept me in good spirits, and the stunning views and variety of interesting sights have kept me from feeling bored. After nearly 20 miles today, tomorrow's ten will take me to a place that feels like my second home, with good friends, favourite places and the prospect of my first rest day on Saturday.

Nos da, pawb! I'll see you in Bangor tomorrow.

Postscript At the end of Day 10, my feet were once again growing very sore. I'd been walking on tarmac for the majority of the day and had set a challenging mileage target by booking into a bunkhouse in Llanfairfechan. By the time I reached Penmaenmawr, I was hungry, tired and really struggling to put one foot in front of the other. After wandering around the town unsuccessfully trying to find somewhere to eat, a man offered me a lift to a good local pub that he knew of in Llanfairfechan. Quickly deciding that it would be easy enough to take the bus back to Penmaenmawr in the morning, I accepted his kind offer and was soon sitting in the pub tucking into some much-needed hot food.

After eating, I began to write my blog, but got chatting to a tough-looking middle-aged man at the bar. Will was an ex-soldier and told me fascinating stories about his time in the army. One in particular has stayed with me. On 8th June 1982, he was aboard a landing ship in the Falkland Islands. The ship was called the *RFA Sir Galahad*. At approximately two in the afternoon, three Argentinian jets flew overhead and the *Galahad* was hit by two or three 500 lb bombs. 48 Welsh Guards and crewmen perished in the explosions and subsequent fires. Will himself was standing next to his friend Simon Weston. While Will escaped unharmed, Simon suffered 46% burns. He pleaded with Will to put him out of his misery, but his friend just couldn't bring himself to do it; instead helping Simon to safety. Simon's story was widely covered in the news and he is still a very well-known face of the Falklands War today. Will now drives a taxi in North Wales. He said that he still attends reunions and enjoys the humour and camaraderie that bonds the old Welsh Guards together. He regularly jokes with Simon that he should have killed him that afternoon in 1982!

Fascinated by Will's stories of his time in the army, some horrific but others beautiful and moving, and being regularly interrupted by an incredibly drunk local at the table opposite, I found it hard to write a sentence of my blog without getting distracted. This may explain the rather stunted end to Day 10's writings. At the time, I was far more interested in learning about the past life of this quiet Welsh taxi driver, whose eyes had seen so much more in his early years than mine will in a lifetime.

Day 11
Penmaenmawr to Bangor

Setting off this morning, my spirits were high. I had a little over ten miles of walking (12 according to the sign on the path) and then I would be putting my feet up, catching up with a good friend and not picking up my 18 kg bag again until Sunday morning. Bliss! As much as I am enjoying daily hikes, my feet in particular are feeling the miles now.

The views for the first hour were the same as the last hour yesterday: peaceful seascape on the right, busy dual carriageway and railway on the left. With the sun shining, I enjoyed my time on the path, weaving over and under the road and train line, with Anglesey and Bangor looking closer with every bend I rounded. The path climbs above the road tunnels and weaves across the cliff face until you've been through Llanfairfechan, a town that I know fairly well, having launched many walks from its higher reaches with the University Mountain Walking Club. The inland views were becoming as nice as the sea ones, so I had high hopes for my last nine miles on the North Wales stretch of the Coast Path.

After pounding the streets of Llanfairfechan, the WCP then returns to true coastal walking – my feet were no more than a couple of metres from the sea for the next three miles. Walking along sand and pebble beaches towards Bangor, I soon arrived at the Spinnies nature reserve. Here, the air was full of birdsong and I could count at least ten different varieties of seabirds intermingling on the soft sand that is revealed at low tide. Penrhyn Castle and its grounds up ahead and the mountains of Snowdonia behind me ensured that I was never without a beautiful view, whichever way I looked.

Penrhyn Castle was soon to be in my bad books though. The path is not allowed to go through its grounds, so just as I felt that I was within touching distance of the place that feels like my second home, I was walking away from it again. Following a country lane away from Bangor and away from the sea, the big detour takes you to Tal-y-bont and finds scraps of just about every footpath in the area to touch for a few metres before veering off somewhere different again. I like to think I have a pretty good sense of direction, but after following this winding trail to nowhere for 40 minutes, I was feeling totally disorientated and rather irritable. This is a part of the world I know very well. I lived here for three years and have visited regularly ever since. I have been to Penrhyn Castle and walked back to Bangor in half an hour. And yet after an hour of seemingly endless flitting between paths and roads, under the railway then back over it, the place that felt so tantalisingly close was still not even in sight. I was ranting out loud about the path planners and wondering why on earth they'd chosen such an awful route to end the North Wales Coast Path.

To add to my frustration, the mother of all rain showers arrived completely without warning on this hot and sunny day, forcing me to dive for the waterproof bag cover and my coat. Momentum disrupted, the shower disappeared as soon as it came and I had to stop a minute after layering up to layer down again. And then again two minutes later to find my sunglasses and hat. It felt like the path and weather were conspiring to keep me from the rest I needed so very much, and I was feeling more annoyed than I have done since I left home.

It was such a disappointing end to a path that had been

improving day on day after such a poor start. I'd have preferred it if it had just joined the A5 and followed the pavement for a mile into Bangor, rather than taking the long-winded, back-of-beyond way that it did. There was nothing to gain, no interesting sights out there. Just prolonging the walk for an extra few miles, after 78 had already been covered in three and a half days. Thankfully, I eventually arrived in Bangor and was greeted by Siân. It was so nice to catch up, and my mood was lifted again in no time at all. It's funny how moods and emotions can swing so wildly from one extreme to the other when your body is aching and tired and you've been pushing yourself to the limit for so long.

I'm taking a much-needed rest day tomorrow to give my legs and feet a little time to recover before hitting the Anglesey Coast. I'm excited to see what beauty she has to show me, as I'm sure it'll be a big step up from the majority of the North Wales Coast Path. I'll also be joined by Siân and Rob for a day or two each, which will be a fantastic change from solo walking. Fingers crossed the weather stays nice!

I won't see you tomorrow as I'm sure nobody would be interested in reading about my time with my feet up, so I will see you on Sunday after my first day of Ynys Môn walking!

Penwythnos da, pawb! Have a good weekend!

Postscript My feelings at the end of the first section of Wales Coast Path were mixed. I was pleased to be on the coast as I felt like the main bulk of my challenge had now begun. However, I'd not really enjoyed the four days of walking. The planners of the WCP did the best they could with the terrain they had. I had not expected much of the 80-mile section of path, and, apart from a short stretch between Colwyn Bay and Penmaenmawr, my expectations had been quite accurate. North Wales is a place where the mountains meet the sea. It is beautiful, but the coast path has very little option other than to hug the cycle path and A55 dual carriageway that are sandwiched between the sheer cliffs and the turquoise-blue waters. There is an option of a high coast route, which crosses the mountains of Eastern Snowdonia and the Carneddau, and normally I'd have taken this far more interesting option, but having planned a perimeter-of-Wales walk, I felt that I should stick as close to the edge of the land as possible. Things were due to look up though. I knew of many beautiful spots on the Anglesey coast, and I was sure that I'd find many more gems during the next week of walking.

Anglesey Coast Path

Day 12
Bangor to Red Wharf Bay

After my rest day yesterday, I was feeling relaxed and refreshed. No aches, no pains apart from the lingering blisters, and the prospect of starting Anglesey's pretty coastline with a great friend. This would be a step up from the North Wales Coast Path, for sure!

Setting off after a bit of a lie-in, Siân and I discussed the day's mileage and decided that if we cracked on, we could probably make the 23-mile trek to Red Wharf Bay in time for the bus at 8.30 p.m. From the outset, the day was good. The coast path took us to a place in Bangor that we'd never found before, and crossing the Menai Bridge is always beautiful. In what felt like no time at all, we'd reached Beaumaris with its famous castle. The ruins are rather impressive and it's clear to see the concentric design, with the inner and outer walls and moat. To penetrate the heart of this fortress would have been very tricky indeed!

After chips and a sorbet by the sea, we set off along the beach towards Penmon Point. Faced with a low-tide option (more beach walking) and a high-tide option (inland roads) we decided that we could see enough beach to continue along it. This hasty choice presented us with an interesting dilemma when faced with a dead end a couple of bays along: to climb the very steep bank and find a way back down to the beach on the other side of the big, sea-surrounded rock face in front of us, or to walk back on ourselves and take the dull-looking high-tide route? Naturally, we took the former option and made the scramble up to a field and then back down to the beach about 50 m later. It was a fun momentary return to mountaineering.

The weather was stunning and we enjoyed a happy half hour skimming stones while sitting on the beach, looking across the sea to a beautiful panorama of the Great Orme and Snowdonia. Anglesey was already delivering on its promises of spectacular scenery and the views continued most of the way to Penmon Priory. A historical place of pilgrimage, the thirteenth-century Augustinian Priory was built around a sixth-century monastery. In the sixteenth century, it was privately-bought and a dovecote was added to the site. There are still large parts of all the buildings intact, with some having been turned into a modern church and house. The dovecote is still largely undamaged, and stepping inside to see the thousands of perches makes you imagine what the place would have felt (and smelled) like when full to the ceiling with birds. It's certainly an interesting place, so I hope I get the chance to go back and spend more time exploring the history that surrounds it. For now though, there were miles still to cover!

Penmon Point is another spot of outstanding beauty. Views across the lighthouse, Puffin Island and mainland North Wales stretch out before your eyes and seabirds soar overhead. There's also a nice little café, which we took full advantage of! Refuelled and refreshed, we pushed on to an inland section of path, making great time through the 20-mile mark to Llanddona. On arrival at the expansive sands of Red Wharf Bay, we decided to hug the coast and follow the beach all the way to the village that shares its name on the other side. Here, Siân told me about a fantastic pub that we could finish at. Target in sight, we hit the windswept bay and made a beeline for the other side. Battling the gale-force crosswind was tiring and an earlier calf twinge was nagging me a little, but because of Siân's company, what could have been a miserable hour of walking was great fun.

Tired and aching, we were within touching distance of the Ship Inn when a river seemed to emerge out of nowhere to give us one last test before we were allowed to have a much-needed sit down. Finding a sandbank across it, we confidently strode out only to find that within a few metres, Siân had sunk to her ankles and me to my bootlaces. Quicksand! Beating a hasty retreat with the whole ground moving beneath us, we hit safer sand and reassessed. The resulting extra ten minutes of

53

walking towards the sea brought us to a narrow point where we decided to wade across. With sharp, mussel-covered rocks on the riverbed and the water freezing cold, the barefoot crossing was not fun, but we were soon on the other side and arriving at the comfort of the Ship.

We drew some funny looks immediately and after a chat with the tables next to us that Siân initiated, the details of my challenge and the impressive mileage covered by us both today prompted no less than three donations from various tables within earshot! Totally humbled after our 15 minutes of comfort, kindness and conversations with lovely people, we made the bus we'd hoped to and parted for separate flats after a fantastic day.

I know I've said it before, but walking with people is so much easier than solo walking. Siân and I walked 23 miles today and every single step (apart from the ones through the quicksand and freezing river!) was a pleasure. Walking in the company of such a good friend keeps spirits high and aches and pains to a minimum. I hope she enjoyed the day as much as I did, and that the blisters aren't too bad!

I'm now sitting in a nice restaurant in Menai Bridge before walking to another friend's flat down the road, which will be my base for my week of Anglesey walking. Rob and Siân's kind offers of beds, showers and washing machines means that this week will be a comfortable one, and I know that Anglesey has so much more beauty to reveal in the days to come. I can't wait to see what I find!

Nos da, pawb. I'll see you tomorrow, when I'm nearing the most northerly point of my entire trek.

Day 13
Red Wharf Bay to Amlwch

Waking up to a sunny day, I knew it would be another good one. Just like yesterday, I had a good friend to keep me company and I knew there were some very pretty spots along the stretch of coast we planned to walk. Also, the fact that I'm based at Rob's house in Menai Bridge for all of my Anglesey walking means that I have been able to shed some weight from my pack.

After catching the bus out to Red Wharf Bay, where Siân and I finished yesterday, Rob and I set a very fast pace all the way to Moelfre. This is a small place with a lot of historic and scenic interest. The beautiful cliffs, which were a scene of peace and serenity today, were once the site of one of the worst maritime disasters in British history. In 1859, a large ship – the *Royal Charter* – encountered hurricane force winds off the Anglesey coast. Attempts to keep the ship off the rocks failed and she slowly began to break apart as she was battered by the weather onto the rugged coastline. Although it was only 30 m offshore, rescue attempts were mostly unsuccessful, and the crew and cargo (including many millions of pounds' worth of gold) were plunged into the rough seas. A handful of passengers and crew made it to shore, but some 450 lives were lost, most being smashed onto the rocks by the raging waves rather than drowning. A horrific scene met the townspeople in the morning as the bay was littered with debris, cargo and corpses that had washed up overnight. A memorial now stands close to the spot where the ship was wrecked, and it's a very sombre place.

Walking on from Moelfre Point, we hit the beaches of Traeth Lligwy, Traeth Penrhyn and Traeth Yr Ora. All three are beautiful, but the latter is really special. Described as the hidden gem of Anglesey's east coast, there were a total of only four families on the soft, golden sand that day. The waves from the crystal-clear, turquoise-blue sea were gently lapping onto the shore and you got the sense that the beach is never any busier than it was in that moment. You could have picked the scene up, dropped it in the middle of the Caribbean and it would have fitted right in. It's certainly a place I'll be returning to for a relaxing summer's day in the future.

Around the point, we were met with an obstacle. We'd been following beaches and rocks just below the coastal path all day, as it kept us right next to the sea and was more interesting than the campsites above. We'd made a bit of an error though. Dulas Bay happens to have a large river running through it and unlike yesterday, there was no chance of paddling across this one. Our only option was to trek around the edge of the inlet, avoiding patches of quicksand and sticky sludge in the salt marshes and follow the tree line as best as we could until we hit the path again. This time it was Rob's turn to wander into quicksand, but he developed a unique style of getting out. We'll call it a stylish, wide-based waddle. It worked well!

Upon meeting the coastal path again, we followed it inland through a wealthy-looking estate and back to the sea near the north coast. The heat was beginning to slow us down, so we reassessed our target of Cemaes Bay, still a further 13 miles away, and instead set our sights on the more achievable Amlwch. While stopping for a rest from the afternoon sun, our gaze was drawn by a seal floating in the bay below us. In quick succession, seals two, three and four popped up in a line next to our original one, and we enjoyed watching them bob about in the millpond-like sea until our legs felt ready to journey on.

Ending the day in Amlwch, and after a much-needed coke with ice, we had a nice chat with Ian and Gary, who we'd met earlier on the path, and travelled back towards our reward: an evening in Dylan's restaurant in Menai Bridge. The delicious three-course meal will be perfect preparation for 23 miles of very undulating, but apparently spectacular coastal walking tomorrow. I'll reach the most northerly point of my entire walk, hopefully see plenty more marine life, and begin the long walk south!

I'll see you all tomorrow, when I am heading towards home for the first time since leaving. Nos da, pawb!

Postscript Rob and I have walked together in the mountains for a good few years now, and usually match each other stride for stride. The pace he'd set while leading early that morning had been punishing, so after walking through the heat of the day, taking a long time to navigate our way through the sticky sludge of the Dulas Estuary and climbing some steep hills on the inland section of path, we were both flagging. My hat and sun cream had kept the worst of the sun away, but Rob had turned down the offer of sharing these, probably selflessly deciding that I needed them more as I had to carry on the next day (as is Rob's way). As we closed in on Amlwch, Rob began to feel rather ill with heatstroke and while taking a rest in the shade, he fell asleep. Deciding the snooze would probably do him good, I wrote the majority of Day 13's blog while sitting next to him, looking out to sea. It was a truly beautiful spot to write in, so I didn't mind reducing our target mileage for the day and soaking up the peace and serenity of that little corner of Wales whilst Rob recovered. I would find out the following day that I probably wouldn't have made it to Cemaes either – I had hugely underestimated how far from Amlwch it was. I guess everything happens for a reason.

Day 14
Amlwch to Church Bay

Leaving Amlwch in the sunshine, I was looking forward to a day which promised spectacular coastline and many potential wildlife sightings. Without any proper mileage tables in the guidebook, or any scales on the small sketched maps that are included, I estimated it would take about an hour to reach

Cemaes. During that time, I'd pass Porth Wen and the most northerly point in Wales before cracking on to the 18¾-mile section between Cemaes and Llanfachraeth that the guidebook suggests you can cover in a long day of walking. Easy!

An hour in, I had just passed the pretty little village of Bull Bay and was not even in sight of Porth Wen. Time for a rethink! If I made it to Cemaes by 11 a.m., I should still have time to get to Llanfachraeth before the last bus at 6.30 p.m. The day was now looking slightly more challenging, but still manageable.

By 11 a.m., I had reached Porth Wen and it was absolutely beautiful! The red, ruined buildings of the old brickworks stand on ledges built out from the cliff on the far side of the bay and the waves were lapping gently into the numerous caves and rock formations. The mostly pebbly beach was completely deserted, and had I not had a big worry about time on my mind, I'd have certainly stayed an hour to explore the cove fully and relax at the clear water's edge. As it was, I was stressing that I was nowhere near Cemaes yet and had realised that the section I'd thought would be short was actually rather long. I took a moment at the headland near Llanbadrig to enjoy standing at the most northerly point of my entire 1,100 miles, before taking my first slightly southbound steps. After singing many Welsh hymns to myself to keep spirits high, I arrived in Cemaes at 12.30 p.m. Time to reassess my goal for the day.

Deciding on a more realistic destination – Church Bay – over a burger and chips, I set off towards Wylfa Nuclear Power Station. This dominates the views across Cemaes Bay and the coast path is meant to take you up close to the buildings, which I was quite looking forward to. It would be interesting to get a sense of how the plant worked. However, still with an ambitious target in mind, I was met with a big fence and a 'temporary diversion' sign. This diversion (around the proposed site for a new nuclear power station) was a long one and by the time it had finally taken me back to the coast, my mood had deteriorated. The scenery here wasn't as pretty as the morning and the whole landscape looked bleak, especially in the grey of this afternoon. There seemed to be more derelict buildings than in-use ones.

After crossing the causeway at Cemlyn, the bleakness seemed to intensify. There were no other walkers, no spectacular views and no recognisable buildings anywhere. For the first time this trip, I felt lonely. I'd had the company of friends for the last two days and even when I'd been walking alone in the days before, I'd still seen other people or even buildings that I knew had people in. But out here, there was very little evidence of human habitation at all. I was just starting to feel really down when I heard a noise in the water. I looked over the low cliff edge to see a seal bobbing around close to land. A few photos and a thank you later, I left for the next cove and the seal was there again. In the next bay, she popped her head up as I arrived and her friend appeared alongside. After splashing around for five minutes, they swam back towards Cemlyn and I headed around Carmel Head to hit a long southerly section that would take me to Church Bay. Had it not been for the brief company of those seals this afternoon, I know I would have been feeling very lonely indeed, so I am very grateful that they were there.

The coast path started to get more beautiful again towards the end of my day. The tidal island just south of Carmel Head is only cut off for a few minutes either side of high tide, and the shape of the pebble beach with the backdrop of rugged cliffs made it look like a scene from a postcard. After snapping a few photos, I strode out to reach Church Bay at 5.30 p.m.

Upon reaching the pub, the only local taxi company told me that they couldn't pick me up until seven, and I needed to get eight miles further down the coast within an hour. Oh dear! I decided my best bet was to walk along the road trying to hitch a lift with somebody. Despite numerous cars stopping, no-one was going to Llanfachraeth. Beginning to wonder if I would ever get back to Menai Bridge, I came across a lady sitting in a van who was on the phone. After some awkward, through-the-windscreen smiles and a plea from me for a lift, she told me she'd just arrived home but was happy to take me where

I needed to go anyway. It seems that I am being surprised by the kindness of strangers most days on this walk now. I hope it continues!

40 minutes later, after Alawn had refused to take any petrol money, I was sitting on the bus that I had panicked about catching all day. I watched through the windows as we slowly but surely made our way back north, and stared in disbelief as we came within a mile of Church Bay to stop at a bus stop. I could have walked from the bay and waited here comfortably for the bus instead of making poor Alawn drive an extra 16-mile round trip after her busy day. I just prayed we wouldn't go past her house!

So today has been a mix of stunning scenery, kind people, a change of direction and overly-ambitious targets. Through it all, I've learned some lessons:

1. Don't set targets without an accurate estimation of the distance between start and end.

2. Always carry a tent, whether you've got a permanent base or not. I'd have felt less pressure with timings if I'd had mine on my back today.

3. Always check bus stops before your target destination. You might just need them!

After an evening socialising with two great friends, I'm off to bed before an early start tomorrow which will see me arrive on Holy Island. Nos da, pawb!

Postscript
That evening, I downloaded the distance charts for the WCP to my phone. I was fed up of missing targets and wanted to be able to plan more accurately where I would be at the end of each day. They were a daily guide for the rest of my trek, being particularly useful as they gave mileages between every settlement, not just the recommended start and end in the guidebook. Being able to accurately work out where I would be at lunchtimes and bedtimes made my life on the trail so much easier, and I wished I'd had those handy little charts on my phone from the outset.

Day 15
Church Bay to Holyhead

After learning lots of lessons yesterday, I learned one this morning too. Don't assume that just because there are lots of early buses from Bangor and Amlwch, they will all be stopping at the place you want to go to. After being a little too late to catch the 7.20 a.m. bus from Menai Bridge, I realised the scale of my mistake. The next bus from Amlwch to Rhydwyn (a mile from where I finished yesterday) was at 12.45 p.m. Oops! I was forced to take a relaxing morning at Rob's flat, which was actually rather nice.

Making sure I arrived in Amlwch early, I had an hour and a half to kill before the 12.45 bus. I spotted a little café not far away and decided a cup of tea was exactly what the moment called for. After noticing my bag and hearing a little about my challenge, the owner of the café told the girl behind the counter to give me a breakfast and tea for free for all my charity work. Completely touched but having already eaten, I explained that the tea would be fine and was then offered a free sandwich for later to keep me going. Needless to say I snapped up that generous offer! While drinking my tea I got talking to Bill, who has cycled many tour routes all over the world. He's even raced Chris Boardman, and beat him thanks to a well-timed puncture. During our conversation, Bill gave me a kind donation, as did two other couples who had overheard us. I left Caffi Pen Yr Dref with a huge smile on my face put there by the kindness of the staff and customers. Thank you all!

After arriving in Rhydwyn four hours later than intended, I followed a footpath towards Church Bay, right up until the point where it stopped in the middle of a field. I was thankful therefore, to see two walkers hiking purposefully in the opposite direction. I thought this must be a sign that I was on the right track. Until we got talking that is. It turns out that Paul and Karen were also looking for Church Bay!

We teamed up to navigate our way through fields and back lanes while chatting happily all the way. Paul and Karen are on their honeymoon, having got married at the weekend. Instead of seeking out tropical sunshine, they have opted for rain, coast paths and blisters while hiking the entire Anglesey Coast Path. I couldn't be more impressed! They got married in the Lake District and put a big banner high up on one of the mountains on their wedding night while still dressed for the big occasion. It sounded brilliant! I think we're probably carved out of the same mountain stone. After successfully finding the coast path, we parted to walk in opposite directions, but not before Paul and Karen had given me a hugely-generous donation and a bag of fruit pastilles to keep me going today. I cannot thank them enough as both gifts had that very effect. I hope we'll bump into each other again in the south of the island.

If the Little Orme still holds the title for the worst weather of my walk, today has taken the title for the longest period of bad weather. Apart from a few brief dry spells, it has rained all day. However, this wasn't too upsetting as I'd already done the most spectacular parts of the coast yesterday and with 14 miles to cover and a start time of 2.30 p.m., I needed to put my head down and get shifting anyway. So that is what I did. With my body feeling strong despite returning to full 18 kg pack weight today, I ate up the miles without stopping for a rest all day. I paused to eat the sandwiches that I had so kindly been given earlier, but other than that I just kept walking. The first seven miles were completed in two and a half hours and the second seven in two hours dead. The coastline was flat and apart from the few beaches I walked along, there was nothing overly interesting to distract me from the task in hand. Walking over the Stanley Embankment to Holy Island, I knew that my target of finishing by 8 p.m. would be easily met, and so pushed on through the rain.

The route into Holyhead is not particularly pleasant. Arriving in the evening and being dragged through back alleys and neglected playing fields, I felt a little on edge. I've never particularly liked the town, and today didn't help its cause. The path does stick rigidly to the sea, so there can be no arguments that it has taken the true coastal route, even if it is a little ugly. The surroundings only served to drive my legs faster and before I knew it, the station was in front of me. Every green man worked in my favour at the busy road crossings and on arrival at the ticket machine, I saw that I had five minutes until the next train back to Bangor. It was like Holyhead was working hard to get me on the earlier train and not leave me sitting on the platform for an hour and a half before the next one. I warmed to the town a little bit in that moment!

So now I am sitting in Wetherspoons in Bangor before heading back to Siân's house for a relaxed evening. A day that could have been miserable with a dull coastline and poor weather was actually rather enjoyable. I have the kind people that I met early on and the improving stamina in my legs to thank for that!

Nos da, pawb. I'll see you tomorrow after hopefully completing Holy Island with more good company.

Day 16
Holyhead to Four Mile Bridge

Today I had the prospect of walking 21 miles between two places that are about 7 miles apart! That is the beauty of following the coast path around Holy Island. However, two things would make this enjoyable rather than an irritant. The coast path would take me to North and South Stack, which are both absolutely beautiful, and I would be walking with good company all day. I'd only met Bethan a couple of times before. The first time I had dangled from the end of The Cantilever, a huge, balancing, seesaw-like rock near the summit of Glyder Fach, to photobomb a University Mountain Walking Club group picture, and the second time had been a day later on a trip to Caernarfon Fun Centre. Despite this, she had kindly offered to spend her day off from her job as a staff nurse in the Bangor A & E department walking with me, and had picked a potentially good one!

We left Holyhead at around nine and soon after leaving the town outskirts, we were on the flanks of Holyhead Mountain. More hillock than mountain in reality, the 220 m peak still provides stunning views over the whole of Anglesey and Northern Snowdonia on a clear day, as well as great climbing routes and scrambles for more adventurous types. Today though, the coast path was our goal and it took us around the side of the 'mountain' to a very windy North Stack and soon to South Stack. Here, over 100 steps can take you down to a beautiful spot near the lighthouse. Sightings of a variety of seabirds are guaranteed and if you're lucky, you could be treated to porpoises, seals and a few types of dolphin too. I've spent many a happy hour relaxing there with friends in the past, but today we had a target of 15 more miles to meet before 8 p.m. Suddenly, the steps didn't seem so appealing! A brief sighting of a grey seal allowed us to tick this off on the daily sightings board in the RSPB centre at Ellin's Tower and after a cup of tea in the café, we hit the trail, aiming to reach Trearddur Bay by two.

The coast path along this stretch is really pretty. I was pleasantly surprised, as I've always driven by without a second glance on my way to South Stack and honestly wasn't expecting much from it today. There are lots of rocky outcrops in the sea and choughs swoop gracefully over the steep and often very high cliffs. A couple of beaches are tucked away in quiet coves and with the sun coming out, it was hard for us to resist the calling of the crystal-clear waters. However nice the swim would be though, the remaining 12 miles of walking with sand-filled socks would create many new blisters to add to my existing five.

At Trearddur Bay, Beth kindly treated me to lunch in The

Black Seal. Despite us feeling rather out of place in our walking gear, the staff couldn't have been more welcoming and the food was amazing – though neither of us could finish our chips after the 8 oz burgers. With five hours until the bus that we needed to catch back to the car in Holyhead, we knew the nine miles of afternoon walking would be fairly relaxed so long as we kept a steady pace.

The coastline south of Trearddur remained beautiful, with a couple of natural arches in the cliffs and a few more quiet coves. We had a nice chat with a couple who had spotted another seal and they gave me £5 to put towards my fundraising shortly before we parted. Another kind donation from total strangers – this is becoming a regular occurrence! Beth developed a blister on each foot, so I got to play nurse to the nurse with my abundant supply of Compeed blister plasters before we pushed on to the last miles of the day. Rounding the southern tip of Holy Island after finding a couple more nice beaches, we made decent time on an inland section and reached Four Mile Bridge an hour early. Thankfully, there was a comfy bench at the bus stop for us to take the weight off our feet.

It was lovely to get to know Beth better today; yet more proof that walking with friends is easier than walking alone. My feet and legs hardly ached once in the 21 miles despite the undulating terrain at the start. If long-distance trekking was seen as a human lifespan, I think I'm entering my late teens now. I've got over 270 miles in my legs and am starting to feel confident in my abilities. I still overestimate how much ground I can cover sometimes, but most days are smooth. I've learnt lots from lots of different people, and from myself, and am settling into my life on the path rather comfortably. My body is almost completely used to the daily mileage – only my feet need to catch up – and though my emotions still hit huge highs and some rather deep lows, the wild mood swings of the early teen years happen far less frequently than they did in the first couple of weeks. I'm loving life, and have a long and bright future on my journey around Wales, where I have loads of exciting prospects and possibilities to look forward to. I just hope it lives up to my expectations!

Nos da, pawb! I'll see you after my penultimate day of Anglesey walking.

Day 17
Four Mile Bridge to Malltraeth

Yesterday, I said that I was in my late teen years of long-distance-walking maturity. This morning, I proved that part of being in your late teens is still making big errors in judgement every once in a while! 200 m into my 20-mile day, I was faced with a dilemma. My guidebook disagreed with the waymarkers for the first time in 270 miles of walking. So which should I follow? I decided to go with the guidebook, then almost instantly turned around and went for the waymarker. It looked like a longer route and after everybody's generous sponsorship, I didn't want to take an accidental shortcut. The path took me further and further from the guidebook route and I wasn't best pleased when I arrived back at the Stanley Embankment, which I'd crossed to get to Holyhead two days ago. Deciding that the waymarkers were just going to take me in endless loops of Holy Island, I walked through Valley and straight back along the road to within a few hundred metres of where I'd decided against following my faithful guidebook in the first place. I had gained a few pretty views, a nice chat with a local teacher and about four miles to add to my day's total, but I had lost an hour's walking time and I still had the same amount of ground to cover that I'd had when I woke up this morning.

My displeasure continued when I joined the correct route. The waymarkers seemed to take you into huge fields and then leave you to guess how to get out. It was also the most winding bit of path since the last section of Offa's Dyke, so although

I was covering great distance on the ground, I wasn't getting very far as the crow flies. The tracks between fields and around their edges were overgrown and my bare lower legs took a battering from nettles, briars, bracken and gorse. I have the war wounds to prove it. The straw that broke the proverbial camel's back was the number of fiddly little kissing gates I had to negotiate with my huge backpack. The gates where there was enough room to pass were full of nettles, and the gates where there wasn't enough room required some clambering just to be able to continue along the path. If the WCP is to be turned into an official national trail, they need to consider those of us carrying more than a day pack. My temper hit its peak when a kissing gate that I was forced to climb violently swung open as I was stepping off and threw me into a gorse bush. I directed some coarse words at the offending gate, and stormed off towards RAF Valley.

20 minutes of grumpy walking later, I was cheered up by the sight of the long, golden beach at Cymyran and Rhosneigr in the distance. After my detour, I had hoped to reach Rhosneigr by two to have lunch, but after a speedy few miles along the sand, I arrived an hour earlier than expected and in much better spirits. A windy walk on a pretty beach would cheer anyone up, I think. A hot meal in a local pub where the owner gave me a J²O on the house was the cherry on top, and by the time I set off for my 12-mile section this afternoon, I had a big smile on my face again.

The coast got prettier again this afternoon too. South of Rhosneigr, the cliffs slowly began to get bigger and on the summit of a little hill, I came across a Neolithic burial chamber, Barclodiad y Gawres (Apronful of the Giantess). The rocks at the entrance still bore the artwork that had been carved over 4,500 years ago by settlers from Europe! When the mound was excavated, they found cremated remains and signs of various mysterious rituals which had included limpets, farm animals and crops. Standing alone inside the entrance tunnel looking through the bars at the strange arrangement of boulders inside was a very uneasy feeling, so although I was fascinated, I was pleased to get back out into the sunshine.

The coast grew ever more beautiful, with secluded coves and rocky outcrops, and after walking around the outside of the Anglesey Circuit with the noise of engines tearing the air, I was thrilled to reach St Cwyfan's Church while the tide was still out. This tiny whitewashed building is nothing special to look at in itself, but it stands on a tiny green island atop stone walls that gets completely cut off at high tide. It's a beautiful sight to be met with on rounding the corner after a mile of inland track walking, and I was pleased to get to explore one of the places I was most excited about seeing on the Anglesey coast. The 'Church in the Sea' only has services once a month, but it is a very peaceful place to sit and take in the views of the coastline and beach.

Knowing the last bus back to Menai Bridge was just before 8 p.m., I hit speed-walking mode and soon swallowed up the soft-sanded beach at Aberffraw. The wind was getting ever stronger and my legs added sandblasting to their list of abuse today, but at least the route was clear and the sea was a beautiful turquoise-blue. After a mile walking through the vast, empty dunes to a little road, it was inland tarmac walking nearly all the way to Malltraeth. This provided no interesting sights or pretty views, and so meant that I could crack on with my head down and make it to the bus stop in plenty of time.

After another day of two very different halves, I'm glad to have ended on a high. Tomorrow will be my last day of Anglesey walking, so I'll save my final assessments until its completion, but I know of at least one more stunning place that I'll reach early on in my 23 miles. I'm sure I'll find many more surprises along the way too.

Nos da, pawb. I'll see you when I'm back on the mainland!

Day 18
Malltraeth to Menai Bridge

Waking up, I knew that today would take me to a few parts of Anglesey that I know really well. In particular, I was looking forward to Ynys Llanddwyn (Llanddwyn Island) near the start of my day and the section of path along the Straits between the bridges at the very end. I'd visited both many times while at university and they are still to this day two of my favourite places to while away a few hours. Knowing I had about 25 miles to walk, I set off nice and early.

The path from Malltraeth begins over an estuary causeway, and the waters around it were teeming with wading birds of all varieties in the early-morning light. Their songs filled the air and I felt completely relaxed, despite this being the second-longest distance I'd planned to cover in a day on my Welsh wander. After winding through the tall pines of Newborough Forest for an hour, sadly without a red squirrel sighting, I made a beeline for the sound of waves. Climbing the steep dunes, I was treated to a view of Llanddwyn Island glowing in the sun over the calm sea, with the mountains of the Llŷn Peninsula providing a gorgeous backdrop. I stopped and took a moment to drink in the beauty in front of me.

Llanddwyn Island has everything you could ask for in a small jut of land poking into the sea! There's history, folklore, wildlife, secluded sandy coves, interesting geology and incredible scenery. This combination meant that it took me well over an hour to walk the half mile around its sights. The whitewashed lighthouse stands proudly on the rocks at the very end of the island, and set back from it on a little hillock is a huge cross. Further back again, is the ruin of the church of Saint Dwynwen and just across from this is a stone celtic cross. All of this is squeezed into a few hundred square metres with a backdrop of sea and mountains. Wow! Saint Dwynwen is the Welsh patron saint of love and has a day dedicated to her (25th January) just as St Valentine does in England. When a love triangle turned nasty, ending with her true love being frozen into ice, Dwynwen ran away and met an angel. She asked for three things; for the man she loved to be unfrozen, to be allowed to help all those who are unhappy in love, and to never want to marry anyone for the rest of her life. After her wishes were granted, Dwynwen settled on Ynys Llanddwyn and became a nun. The church was built in her memory, and was a place of pilgrimage until King Henry VIII split from the Catholic Church.

Leaving the history and folklore behind, I passed a bay where Siân and I had once seen a seal and pup. I glanced across thinking it unlikely that I'd be so lucky again, but I was proved very wrong! On the rocks, about 20 m off the beach, were four seals sunbathing. They were lolling about on their backs with round, speckled bellies proudly pointing skywards. Occasionally flicking flippers or rolling around, they began to have a conversation in groans, grunts and tuneful calls. I sat entranced for at least half an hour, feeling incredibly privileged to have been allowed to enter their world for a short time. It was hard to drag myself away, but after a nice chat with a local family I decided that the 19 miles ahead of me couldn't wait forever (and it seemed the seals could!). It's said that 'neither sickness nor sorrow will follow a man from Llanddwyn'. This was certainly true in my case today, as I left feeling peaceful, happy and very lucky.

The walk along the sands of Traeth Llanddwyn is a treat too, as you have dunes and pine forest on one side with the mountains and sea on the other. I was enjoying myself so much that I almost missed the turn inland. In fact I would have, had I not decided to take a photo at exactly the right moment! A few miles of walking later and I arrived at the 23 huge stepping stones over the Afon Braint. These had gathered a bit of a crowd, and I had a long chat with another nice family. They have holidayed on Anglesey every year for the past 12 years and say they still haven't discovered all it has to offer, which doesn't surprise me at all after my seven days of coastal walking. We shared a few tips, and headed off in separate directions.

The path spends the next 15 or so miles darting inland, then returning to pretty parts of the coast. Had it not been for the stunning views across the Menai Straits to Caernarfon with its castle, Y Felinheli with its sailboats and the mountains of Snowdonia, I may have become a little tired of this. Thankfully, the pretty views were there often enough to keep me smiling. During its longest inland stretch, the path passes close to the burial chamber at Bryn Celli Ddu (Mound in the Dark Grove). This, like Barclodiad y Gawres, is Neolithic and well over 4,500 years old. The mound is very pronounced and the entrance is open to the public. Inside, the chamber felt very claustrophobic, but less eerie than Barclodiad y Gawres – maybe because of the light coming in from the other side, where a decorated vertical stone stands guard over the souls of the ancient dead. I was still glad I'd taken a detour to see it, though, as it is very interesting.

After passing beneath Llanfairpwllgwyngyllgogerychwy rndrobwllllantysiliogogogoch (or Llanfair PG to locals!), the track leads you under the Britannia Bridge, which carries the railway and the A55. Here, two huge stone lions stand almost in secret beneath the road. It's a shame they're not more visible, although I suppose the sight of two lions ahead might distract drivers on the dual carriageway! Continuing down the path to the water's edge, I ambled along the Straits enjoying the sights and sounds of the wading birds just as I had this morning in Malltraeth. Knowing that the only walking I had remaining would take me to two of my favourite university haunts (Church Island with the celtic cross war memorial, and the Belgian Promenade that was built by Belgian refugees in 1914 as a thank you to the people of Menai Bridge for being so welcoming) I found an old bird hide that we used to visit in university and sat down to think back on my seven days of Anglesey walking. The coastline is beautiful. The mix of sheer cliffs, dramatic rock formations, vast expanses of sand

and beautiful little coves surrounded by a turquoise-blue sea is breathtaking. The quieter sections are a haven for a wide variety of wildlife and there are amazing stories and remnants from the past dotted all around the island. Put simply, Anglesey is incredible, and to enjoy all of her coastal brilliance in mostly sunny weather while being joined by good friends on three days has been fantastic. I'm genuinely sad that this week has come to an end.

Diolch yn fawr iawn, Anglesey! It's been a pleasure to walk your coastline. I hope the Llŷn Peninsula provides just as many fantastic memories. Nos da, pawb.

Postscript When people ask me today what my favourite section of walking was, I find it impossible to answer. Instead, I give them a top three, with each one having a different reason that makes it the best. Anglesey is always one of these three. So many things made that week special, from beautiful scenery to close friends, wildlife encounters to sunny weather. The tern waymarkers of the Anglesey Coast Path are a must-follow for anybody who enjoys a week-long hike. I already knew of a few special places around the coast before my Wander, but I left the island with a whole host of new favourite spots to return to in the future. In total contrast to the rather irritable end of my first section on the WCP, as I walked under the Menai Bridge with the sun setting on Day 18, I felt uplifted by my experiences on the trail. Though I was sad to be leaving Ynys Môn, I was excited for what the rest of my journey would bring.

Llŷn Peninsula Coast Path

Day 19
Menai Bridge to Caernarfon

After walking 133½ miles in seven days, I decided that a lie-in was in order. Siân was going to be walking with me again and the buses back to Bangor would be a lot easier to catch from Caernarfon, which is only 11 miles away. I'd been considering a rest day anyway, so a chilled-out morning followed by my shortest day so far on this trip would be a good compromise. At 11 a.m., we set off back over the Menai Bridge knowing that today would consist of mostly flat walking on cycle paths. Not the most interesting, but it would be 11 more miles ticked off and at least I'd have Siân to chat to all day.

I'd explored Treborth Botanic Gardens a little at university, so walking through the woods this morning was like a trip down memory lane. We soon passed through an ornate metal gate into the Vaynol Estate, where neither Siân nor I had been before, and the beautiful woodland scenery continued. It wasn't long before we came across a tree-house-style bird hide with a comfy bench and a terrific view over the Straits. Time for a rest! Along the next couple of miles, we came across various other pristine pieces of woodwork: high benches, tables and hides that were all positioned in perfect places to observe activity in the water. The surprises continued as we left the estate. Round a corner in the track, we were met with the sight of a fallow deer in the woodlands. She'd spotted us too and did her best to hide, but we caught a glimpse of her fawn as the pair disappeared into the trees. A really special goodbye from a quirky little estate that neither of us had expected much from.

Following a tea in a café in Y Felinheli, we cracked on up a steep hill to where a cyclist was repairing a puncture. Pleased to have the excuse to take a break, we got chatting to Roy, who is 82 and still cycling regularly, as well as running a cycling website and keeping his Facebook followers up to date with his travels and people he meets. He told us that he measures his day not in miles or hours, but in 'gossip minutes', which we both thought was fantastic! Going out and talking to most people you meet is something that I'm trying my hardest to do on this hike, and Roy is an expert at it. He told us that he learns something new from people every day, and introduced us to some vocabulary he'd learned that morning. After Roy took a picture of us for his Facebook group when he discovered we both share his love of whistling, we sadly had to leave him mending his puncture and continue along our way. Siân and I both agreed that if we are half as active and confident as Roy is when we reach 82, we'll be very happy!

The cycle path made for easy walking and after spending some time with a couple of horses just outside of Caernarfon who took a keen interest in Siân's camera, we completed the day's hike and caught a bus back to Bangor. Much to my delight, Yr Hen Glan (our chosen pub for the evening) had the Olympics on multiple screens and we spent a brilliant three hours watching no fewer than five Team GB medals – four golds and a silver. Perfect timing for our biggest medal rush of the games! My urge to see some of the action was quenched a little as we shouted, cheered and crept closer to the edge of our seats, much to the amusement of people nearby.

So today's potentially dull 11 miles were made brilliant by quirky discoveries, brief wildlife surprises, interesting people and great company throughout. Tomorrow I'll begin the most beautiful and isolated miles of Llŷn Peninsula walking, where I'm looking forward to discovering many of her hidden gems.

Nos da, pawb. I hope you're enjoying the Olympics as much as we did tonight!

Postscript Those of you who know me even a little will know of my love for all things sport! It was at least a month after setting up my Just Giving page that I realised I'd be walking through the duration of the Rio Olympics, and I briefly toyed with the idea of delaying my start so that I wouldn't miss it! Four years previously, while living in a shared house in Hereford, we'd had four screens set up in front of our two sofas showing a wide variety of sports. This year, I wouldn't even have one. During this phase of my walk, I often joked that the hardest part of my entire challenge was not being by a TV all day! This made the night of Day 19 so special. Being able to get excited watching so many Team GB triumphs with a great friend is one of my happiest memories from the walk!

Day 20
Caernarfon to Trefor

Last night, Siân and I stayed up very late to see Andy Murray become the first man ever to defend an Olympic singles title. We also stayed up for the medal ceremony for good measure. It was an amazing match and I had no regrets about staying up... until 8.30 a.m. this morning when my alarm rudely woke me up. I silenced it quickly, thinking that my 18 flat miles would be easy to cover in a little over half a day. The tennis was worth walking a bit faster for!

After eventually bidding farewell to Siân, I caught a mid-morning bus to Caernarfon and enjoyed a nice chat with a lady in the next seat. As I went to get off, she gave me a £5 donation and said that I was inspirational. I left with a big smile, and a fried breakfast in Morrisons added to my good mood!

Caernarfon is a town full of history, with the old town walls and very intact castle dominating its appearance. It was a major part of the 'Iron Ring' that Edward I created to show his power over Wales. I snapped a few photos and, as in Conwy, vowed to come back and explore the town in greater depth. We had been into Caernarfon Castle on a family holiday when I was younger, but it would be nice to refresh my faded memories and take in more of the history, rather than just being impressed by how high up we were on the walls! While walking away along the coastal road towards the Llŷn Peninsula, I was hit by a sudden wave of sadness. Bangor is like a second home to me. I know the area like the back of my hand and have a couple of very close friends there. While walking around Anglesey, I'd been familiar with places most days and had always returned back to either Rob's or Siân's flat. I'd quickly grown used to being in homely surroundings again and spending time with people that I know and care about, and I was sad that it was at an end. The next time I'll be somewhere that I feel so at home will be when I arrive back in Presteigne in seven weeks' time, and this morning, that seemed an awfully long way away.

What I've found on this challenge so far is that minor things have big effects on your mood, whether positive or negative. After about half an hour of feeling miserable, I came across another hiker, who was at the side of the path looking at the view. I instigated a conversation, hoping to cheer myself up, and after sharing hiking stories and our love of this way of life, I was reminded of all the good things about this trip. The freedom, the scenery, the wildlife, the hidden treasures and perhaps most of all, the people you meet. I left feeling a lot happier, but after an hour of the same view and increasing temperatures, I was starting to sink again. At this exact point, I spotted something that made me exclaim my surprise out loud. A feather was sticking out of a road sign underneath a WCP waymarker. Countless feathers stuck deliberately into posts had kept me going in tough times on Offa's Dyke, and I knew full well that they would have been left by someone hiking that path. This meant I wasn't surprised at all when they stopped as soon as I hit the coast. And yet here, over 200 miles since I'd last seen a feather marker like this, one had appeared just as I was on a low day. After taking a couple of pictures, I was ready to move on when a lovely couple came around the corner and we had a good chat for a while, further raising my spirits. It felt as though my grandma was looking down on me, knowing that I needed a little help today, and had sent some signs to guide me through. I looked up to the heavens and whispered a thank you.

The next few miles were dull and the heat of the day was really slowing me down. I was struggling and I wasn't even halfway to Trefor yet. Barring a nice conversation with a man and his son outside their house which resulted in a very generous £10 donation, there was nothing to break the monotonous plodding on along the tarmac. I stopped for a bite to eat in Caernarfon Airport (actually a seven-mile walk from the town itself) and passed through Dinas Dinlle at about 4 p.m. This meant eight miles had been covered, and nine were remaining. I was cursing myself for sleeping the extra hour this morning, and with the temperature showing no sign of dropping, I knuckled down to what I knew would be a pretty unpleasant few hours of hot, sticky walking along a busy road with only a distant sea view.

I can only assume there were issues with land owners when plotting the path's route between Dinas Dinlle and Trefor, as it was appalling. Half an hour spent dodging cars up a busy, narrow lane was followed by mile after mile of pavement walking. The air was humid and oppressive and after four miles, I was desperately searching for shade. Finding a stone bus shelter with a bench, I pretty much collapsed onto it and just closed my eyes. Today didn't involve huge mileage, but it was becoming my hardest day since I tackled the 32 miles from Chester to Prestatyn in one go. I needed a boost of some sort, so I phoned home. After nearly an hour spent chatting with Mum and Dad, and arranging a potential visit for Saturday, I felt ready to take on the last five miles. The air was a little cooler and the next village I arrived in had an interesting church, and a well that was said in medieval times to cure children with epilepsy (or 'falling sickness'). The mental stimulation was a welcome change from the drone of cars and it provided me with enough energy to complete the final few miles into Trefor.

Arriving at the campsite, the owner kindly told me to donate the pitching fee to my charity and before I could even set my tent up, my neighbours in a static caravan came out to chat. Stu and Clare (and their young children Jim and Heather – who is celebrating her third birthday today!) were kind enough to give me a pint of orange juice and a comfy seat in front of the Olympics while we chatted. They made me feel so welcome and offered basically anything I could ever want! The soft armchair, the juice and the company was everything I could have hoped for though, and they ended my day on a really big high that I didn't think would be possible when I left Caernarfon this morning.

Today for me was a real illustration of how people enrich our lives. Although I could see the mountains in the distance, the view didn't really change all day and the path was dull. I started happy, but was soon feeling really down and the heat was making every step draining. But the variety of conversations that I had with the people I met, and the generous and unexpected acts of kindness that they performed for me, have sent me to my tent smiling.

Nos da, pawb. I'll see you after my first of five apparently beautiful days of coastal walking!

Day 21
Trefor to Porth Towyn

I started a little earlier today as it was meant to be hot and I knew that the first few miles would be steep and uphill. At Trefor, the mountains meet the sea at steep cliffs and there is no way around, so naturally, you have to go over them. The climb was the toughest I've done on my trek since the Clwydian section of Offa's Dyke, but my legs coped fairly well and I was soon standing at the highest point on the whole Wales Coast Path. I cannot even begin to describe how beautiful the views were. The weather was incredible and the sea was a hundred different striking shades of blue. The heather-covered mountains were bright purple and the green fields below were stretched out like a patchwork quilt. Turning around, I could see a large portion of the Llŷn Peninsula, which will make up my next few days of walking.

The descent from this spot was mostly on a road that winds down the cliffs with a gradient of 25%. It wouldn't have looked out of place in the Alps with the riders of the Tour de France powering up it. The views remained beautiful and the final hairpin pointed me towards Nant Gwrtheyrn; a little mining village that has been restored into a heritage centre. The café was my main point of interest though! The sun's heat was becoming intense and I had had to work hard to pull myself and my 18 kg backpack up to 330 m above sea level, so a cold drink and a rest in the shade was definitely deserved.

Leaving the café, I knew that I still had about 14 miles to go and that the day was going to get hotter. After dropping to sea level, the path had to climb over another hill and just as I hit low-level ground the other side, up it went again. The heat was getting to me so much that sweat was trickling down my sunglasses and I was feeling light-headed. To keep myself focused until Nefyn, I started singing songs from *Les Miserables*. It's been a family favourite for as long as I can remember, so my sister Emily and I are almost word perfect now. Just as I was hitting the crescendo notes in 'One Day More', I noticed a dog run across the path in front of me and looked left to see his owner standing not ten metres away on the side of the hill with a big, cheesy grin on his face. Suddenly very self-conscious, I had three options: carry on belting out the rest of the song proudly and look like I'd escaped from the asylum; suddenly stop and look embarrassed; or tone down the volume but carry on to disguise my embarrassment. I chose the latter, but didn't look back to see his reaction for fear of turning an even deeper shade of red! I hope he enjoyed the surprise, out-of-breath and probably out-of-tune performance of the Boublil and Schönberg classics!

Mercifully, the path flattened out after Nefyn and I was able to make good time to the Tŷ Coch Inn on the beach. A quick drink later, I was back moving at pace around the headland and along the golf course. The weather was still roasting, but the views were gorgeous enough to make me pleased it wasn't cloudy. Unfortunately, the hot weather was having an effect on an annual animal event too. I've learned up at our local golf course in Kington that on a few days every year, queen ants emerge from the ground and fly around, evilly attacking anything that moves before they migrate to start a nest of their own. I've learned this the hard way, as I've been the moving thing that gets attacked more than my fair share of times! Today, it happened again. Every few minutes, I'd walk through another swarm and have to wage war on the miniature monsters before I was stung red raw. I must have made quite a sight from a distance, apparently slapping my entire body viciously before calmly strolling on, only to repeat the wild thrashing further down the path.

I'd entertained the idea of extending today's 18 miles to 22, which would take me to a campsite where my old housemate and good friend Kate is staying. However, on arrival at Porth Towyn, I felt very light-headed and nearly hit the deck. My body was telling me it was time to stop and I was in no state to disobey it. I rapidly pitched my tent and headed to the nearest pub for a hot meal and many cold drinks. And that's where I'm sitting now, with a pint of water in hand, following my J²O and pint of coke! My day is not over though. For 18 extremely hot and often hilly miles, I've been looking longingly at the crystal-clear, turquoise sea on my right. The thought of diving into it has kept me going even when sweat has been pouring down my face, so I vowed that once I'd pitched my tent, I'd go for a swim. I needed food and Wi-Fi first, but as it's nearly a full moon tonight and the sky is clear, I'm going to have a moonlight dip before my shower!

Nos da, pawb! I'll see you tomorrow when I've rounded the tip of the peninsula and am heading towards home again.

Day 22
Porth Towyn to Aberdaron

Last night at about quarter past ten, I made my way down to the sea at Porth Towyn in the bright moonlight. I reached the beach, leaving my towel and fleece on a rock, and waded into the inky blackness. Counting to three, I took the plunge and started swimming around to warm up before lying back and looking up to a clear night's sky. The stars have always fascinated me and as I bobbed about in the moonlight, I was able to pick out a few of the better-known constellations. The beam from the lighthouse at South Stack was visible as it warned any boats off the cliffs on the north-west tip of Anglesey, and the only sound was the gentle lapping of the waves on the beach. It was everything I'd hoped it would be. Peaceful, refreshing and a really special moment on my trek.

All this came at a price though. Despite my best efforts in the shower, I still took a load of sand back to the tent on my feet, and my sandals, towel, shorts and fleece were all wet. I've managed to dry a freshly-washed pair of socks or boxers on my bag while walking, but this would be a whole different story! I don't regret my moonlight swim for a moment – it was magical – but it won't be happening too often whilst I'm camping!

This morning, I had a good long chat with John in the tent next door, which allowed time for everything except my sandals to dry on the outside of my tent. Result! Sandals strapped to the outside of my bag, I set off. The air was humid and with yesterday's efforts still fresh in my body, I felt like I was wading through treacle and didn't manage to cover much ground at all in the first couple of hours. The promise of a café at Porth Oer kept me going though, and despite finding the going tough all morning, I made it there in time for a late lunch. Stepping onto the shore, I was reminded how its nickname of Whistling Sands came about. The beach was singing to me as I crunched along in my boots! As pretty as the cove is though, it was rather busy today so I had no urges to take another dip in the crystal-clear waters.

I thought this morning's path had been very up and down, but I was in for a wake-up call this afternoon. The end of the Llŷn Peninsula is dominated by hills and as there is no way around, the path goes over each one. It reminded me of my first couple of days on Offa's Dyke. Steep ups followed by steep downs and then another steep up again almost instantly. At least the views back over the colourful gorse and heather to the peninsula were beautiful enough to keep half of my mind away from the pain and tiredness in my legs. A couple of seal sightings also provided good excuses for rests!

The final summit is home to an old coastguard watch post, and gives you a full view of Bardsey Island. This small, shell-shaped bit of land has been a major place of pilgrimage throughout history, with the bodies of '20,000 saints' said to be buried there. Unless the hill is hollow, I can't see there being enough room, but it's a nice Welsh folk tale and while gazing out over the water to the island, it's easy to understand why it became such a spiritual place.

The walking remained quite demanding to reach the tip of the peninsula, and then I turned for home. The northernmost parts of the expansive Cardigan Bay were visible through the mist, and I could see a lot of my next week and a half of walking. It was a slightly daunting sight with my legs feeling as tired as they were, but the knowledge that I have now covered over 350 miles in 22 days of walking spurred me on.

With a renewed spring in my step, I headed into Aberdaron, where I was due to finish today and meet Kate. It's crazy to think we've only seen each other a handful of times since sharing a house for two years at university, and it was great to have a good catch up on the way to the campsite that Kate, her fiancée Sian, and Kate's family and friends were staying at in an excellent village-style tent set-up. It was nice to see Sian again on arriving at the campsite and I was quickly introduced to nearly a dozen different people, every one of them lovely! We spent a happy evening enjoying barbecue foods and sharing stories before retiring to tents as the rain began to fall. I was reminded how nice it is to be among a group of happy people. With everyone laughing and joking, it's hard not to smile. Conversations have been few and far between on this isolated stretch of the Llŷn, so tonight was a real treat. The rain has started to fall heavily now that I am back in my little canvas home, so I have a feeling I'll be packing away a very wet tent tomorrow morning.

I hope everyone has had an enjoyable an evening as I've had. I'll see you tomorrow after a day of hopefully beautiful Llŷn walking. Nos da, pawb.

Day 23
Aberdaron to Abersoch

Today started well, hanging out with Kate and Sian and the gang while enjoying sausages for breakfast. Kate was also kind enough to make me a packed lunch and drive me back to Aberdaron, where I finished yesterday. It was lovely spending some time together again, so I hope we don't leave it as long as we did this time before we next meet up!

Leaving Aberdaron, the mist was thick and the air was sticky. I had been hoping last night's rain would have cleared it, but the humidity and visibility seemed to be even worse than over the last two days. After negotiating five undulating miles to Y Rhiw in the morning, I enjoyed a cup of tea in the café at Plas yn Rhiw before tackling the 15 miles of this afternoon.

While there, a lady overheard my conversation with the women behind the counter about my walk and came over to my table to give me £10. It was a really generous gesture and cheered me up ready for the task ahead.

The first five miles of the 15 were along a vast beach called Hell's Mouth. Here, the cliffs were made of a thick clay with loads of different types of rock embedded inside. I had to tear myself away from the interesting geology, with the thought that I'd ask Dad about it later, and continued the seemingly endless trek along the sand. On reaching the other side of the bay, the path begins to rise and fall again as it rounds two pretty headlands. Unfortunately, the mist stopped me seeing the promised views of Snowdonia and Cardigan Bay, but the islands of St Tudwal were some consolation.

At around the 15-mile mark of the day, an old blister (now rather large hole) on the sole of my left foot started to hurt. The pain got worse and worse and eventually reduced me to a slow limp/waddle along the cliff path. I'm sure I made for a funny sight, but inside I was struggling. My body felt weak because of the humidity and with the new foot issues, I severely doubted whether I could make it to Abersoch. If I walked normally, I feared doing more damage to whatever was causing the pain, and if I walked on the side of the foot, my ankle hurt and I feared long-term joint trouble which could end my walk.

In the end, it was a mixture of grit and determination that got me to the pub I am now sitting in. My foot is throbbing and I'm slightly concerned about what I'll find when I take my boot off, so wish me luck! Today has not been the greatest, but I have the promise of a bed and a shower after a very kind offer from Gareth and Menai, who live locally. I'm extremely grateful, especially after the trials of today. The pub landlady gave me a kind donation too, which has put a little smile on my face once again.

Nos da, pawb. I'll see you tomorrow when my foot has hopefully made a miraculous recovery!

Postscript There is a lot that I could have written about Day 23 that evening, but decided that the time was not right. I wrote this blog while in a rather sorry state, physically and mentally, and I think that writing about all the challenges of the day might have just finished me off. It was the lowest I'd felt in the whole three and a half weeks of walking, but I didn't want to worry everybody back at home by telling them quite how down I was feeling. I just went through the motions of describing the bare bones of the day and tried to force some food into my rather sick-feeling stomach – the pain in my foot was making me nauseous. Now however, the slightly scary and very bizarre tale of certain parts of the day can be told in full!

Within a mile of leaving Aberdaron, I was just about to walk through a kissing gate into a field when I noticed a very hormonal bull rampaging up and down the fence that the WCP followed. He was trying to get to a field of cows on the other side of an embankment, and was frothing at the mouth in frustration. To enter the field would have been incredibly stupid, so I climbed the barbed wire and walked along the fenced-off embankment instead. I was secretly praying for the farmer to catch me and question me about my trespassing, as I was itching to voice my opinions on his negligent attitude towards the footpath. Having lived on a farm for nearly all of my life, I am fully aware of what is allowed on a public footpath and what isn't, and that bull should certainly not have been where it was. However, I passed through without confrontation and so didn't get a chance to vent my early irritations. Still, I wasn't going to let it spoil my day, and soon walked on happily at a fast pace.

After stopping for lunch, I shed my waterproofs and a middle-aged man caught me up, with an older lady lagging behind. I'd noticed them below the path as I'd left the bull's field, and he clearly recognised me as he told me how impressed he was that I'd stayed ahead of them for so long. Deciding against telling him that I'd just had a 20-minute lunch stop, I made small talk and we discovered we were headed in the same direction for the next 15 miles. He offered to walk with me, sympathising with my isolation, and I thought it strange when he set off and left the woman. He said she would catch up later though, so I fell into step behind him.

It only took a few minutes for the conversation to start concerning me. The man told me that he'd been tasered by the police a few years back and put in prison, despite the fact that in his mind, he'd done nothing wrong. He was adamant that they'd singled him out for no reason, and got quite agitated as he recounted his story. He told me about how he'd hit rock bottom in prison, but since coming out, he'd designed tents for people like Ben Fogle and Ray Mears. Beginning to wonder about the credibility (and sanity) of the man I was alone on a high clifftop with, I asked if his tent business had a website. He told me that it didn't as he'd gone to a lot of effort to erase all evidence of himself online, 'for obvious reasons.'

My alarm bells were now ringing, but I couldn't see a polite way of telling the guy that I'd rather walk alone. He handed me my opportunity a minute later though, when he suggested that I take the lead and set the pace. I'm not trying to be rude, but the man didn't look like he was in the best shape, so I set an extremely quick pace for the next 15 minutes. Now dripping with sweat and struggling to speak through his gasps for breath, the man told me that he was going to wait for his friend, shook my hand and leaned on a nearby gate. Needless to say I continued with that half-walk, half-jog pace for the next few miles to put a considerable distance between us. I was running on pure adrenaline.

The combination of this fast pace followed by many miles of walking on sand probably created the excruciating pain in my left foot later in the day. Finding nowhere to stay in Abersoch due to the fact there was a big wakeboarding competition in the town that night, I ended up sitting in a pub, picturing myself wild-camping in the forecast storms while feeling more down than I had done in any of my previous 22 days of walking. I wasn't looking forward to it. I'll leave it to Day 24's blog to tell you just how differently the day actually did end after Gareth and Menai arrived at the St Tudwal's Inn to pick me up.

Day 24
Abersoch to Criccieth

Last night, I was feeling very low. My left foot was agony, I was drained after another hot day and I hadn't worked out where I was going to sleep that night. Heavy rain was forecast and my tent was already soaked. While I was trying to force some food down despite my lack of appetite, Mum phoned the nearest campsite to me but couldn't get a response. She then phoned some local family friends, Gareth and Menai. After asking for some local knowledge on where to stay, Gareth said he knew a good place: their home in Llanbedrog. Half an hour later, they'd driven to Abersoch to pick me up and I was in a warm car on my way to a warm bath and a warm bed. How things had looked up in such a short space of time.

After telling me to take full advantage of their home, Gareth helped me put my tent up in the garage to dry and Menai washed my clothes while I was soaking my aching feet in the bath. Once I felt human again, we spent a lovely evening chatting about the Wales Coast Path. Gareth and Menai have spent a large part of the last year hiking different sections of the path to raise money for three different charities in memory of their son Robin. Their aim was to complete the whole path before his 21st birthday, and they succeeded last Friday. I'm in awe of their efforts and they are so inspiring; turning something so tragic into an opportunity to do something so positive. Their incredible fundraising total now stands at nearly £12,000! On top of all this, Gareth, Menai and their son Guto are genuinely some of the nicest people in the world! I left the Evans home this morning with clean clothes, a dry tent, a well-rested body, signs that Menai had made for me to strap to my bag to promote my fundraising, sandwiches, cream for my sore foot, a full belly and an even fuller heart. The perfect fuel for a day of rainy walking.

Gareth drove me back to last night's finishing point in

Abersoch and within a couple of minutes of leaving the car, two people had already stopped me to ask about my challenge and I'd received a kind donation. The signs that Menai has made for me are going to be amazing for my fundraising! After an hour and a half of rainy walking, I stopped at a café in Llanbedrog, texted Gareth to let him know I'd arrived back in town and put my bag down with the sign facing outwards. A man immediately gave me a donation and as I went to leave, the occupants of the two tables closest to me jumped up with money in hand too. Thank you all! After a chat with one of the tables, I turned to leave and Gareth and Menai were standing in front of me. It was lovely to see them again and chat for a little while before I had to get going. I hope we meet again sometime soon.

The path from Llanbedrog to Llanystumdwy follows a couple of huge beaches. Each one took over an hour to walk, but my painful left foot was glad of the soft ground. The beaches were separated by the town of Pwllheli, where I enjoyed lunch in a Wetherspoons. With the heat of the past few days, my appetite has not been good and so I've struggled to finish a meal. I think this is part of why I've felt so drained this week. Today was cooler and I was determined to pack in the calories again!

The beach in the afternoon was almost completely deserted. I walked for over an hour along the sand without seeing another soul. I never felt lonely though. I felt peaceful and happier than I've felt while walking for a good few days. I think being looked after so well last night and the knowledge that I'd be seeing my friend Rob this evening and my parents tomorrow was enough to keep me upbeat, and so I merrily sang my way along the breezy shore in the afternoon sunshine. Thankfully there were no onlookers this time!

On rounding the point near Llanystumdwy, I was met with a sight that took my breath away. The promised views of the mountains had been a disappointment all day because of the wet weather, but before my eyes now was a panorama of Southern Snowdonia with the beginnings of Cardigan Bay in the foreground. Sandwiched between mountains and sea were the towns of Criccieth and Harlech, with their respective castles catching the light just enough to make them stand out. I sat down and simply looked for ten minutes, taking it all in.

The remainder of the walk to Criccieth was hard to dress for! Hot sunshine turned to torrential downpour in seconds and just as the waterproofs had been applied, the storm would disappear as suddenly as it had arrived. I also missed storms that passed well within a mile of my location, without ever feeling a drop in the spot where I was standing. The localisation of the weather was amazing and it was interesting watching different parts of the landscape get obliterated by curtains of rain, only to reappear a minute later in brilliant sunshine. The constant layer changes were delaying the end of my day though.

My only slight disappointment was Criccieth Castle. It was built by the Welsh so was the only castle in King Edward I's 'Iron Ring' that his world-leading architect, James of St George, didn't design. Owain Glyndŵr, leader of the Welsh rebel army, tried twice to destroy the castle and succeeded on his second attempt, with the once-great Welsh fortress being abandoned and left to ruin. I'd been looking forward to exploring the remains, despite knowing there wasn't much left to see, so I was surprised to see the path up to the castle blocked by a closed gate and a sign saying that it is only open during certain hours to paying customers. Still, today had been an enjoyable one so I didn't linger on such a minor thing.

I've finished the day at Dylan's in Criccieth, waiting for Rob to finish work while having a tasty second hot meal in the space of an afternoon! Menai's sign has received more attention, resulting in another £15 in sponsorship from two lovely groups of people who I got talking to. I continue to be amazed by the generosity of strangers. Tomorrow, I'll walk nine miles to meet Mum and Dad in Portmeirion before finishing with another two miles once they've gone home. I'm so excited to see my parents as it's been over three weeks and over 300 miles since I've seen either of them! Today has been made fantastic by the kindness and generosity of so many people, and I know tomorrow will be made brilliant by people too. I'm doing most of this trek on my own, but in 400 miles I've only felt alone for about half an hour. The people I meet along the way make my days happy, and the thought that so many of you back home have donated or are following my progress on this blog spurs me on when I'm feeling low. Thank you all!

Nos da, pawb. I'll see you tomorrow once I've finished the Llŷn Peninsula section of my challenge!

Postscript This was the day where the future of my face was decided! One of the two people who had come over to my table in Dylan's to ask about my challenge was called Richard. During our conversation, he asked if I was keeping my beard for the whole Wander. I hadn't shaved it since Day 5 and was still undecided on whether to shave it off when Mum and Dad brought my trimmer to Portmeirion the following day, so Richard made my mind up for me. He held out a £10 note, and said that he would sponsor me if I promised to keep growing the beard for the remainder of my walk. I was only too pleased to accept his kind sponsorship and turn down the trimmer the following afternoon!

Day 25
Criccieth to Penrhyndeudraeth

Last night, the weather was horrific: howling gales and torrential rain. It would have been horrendous weather for camping, but I was lucky enough to be in Rob's mum Bridget's caravan watching the Olympics in the warm. I couldn't have been more grateful to them both! Spending the evening in good company and out of the elements was just what I needed at the end of a long day.

This morning, I had a nice chat with Bridget and she gave a hugely generous donation to my fundraising – thank you so much! Combined with the sandwich for lunch and the promise of a lift back to the caravan tonight as well, I was sent off with an enormous smile on my face. I was also happy because at mile nine, I would be seeing Mum and Dad.

This morning's weather made the 'hurricane' on the Little Orme two weeks ago seem like a beautiful summer's day. In all my years of mountain walking, I've never hiked through anything like it! The wind was so strong that each raindrop hitting my face felt like a small rock, and I couldn't walk three steps in a straight line without being knocked sideways. The tide was a high one and with the added power of the gales, waves were tearing up the beach and into the dunes that I was walking through. I stood on a sandbank to film a particularly strong surge of waves and it was swept from beneath my feet, dunking me into the water. Thankfully, my Scarpa boots are amazingly waterproof. The force of less than a foot of water moving inland at speed made me imagine how terrifying a 20-foot tsunami must be. The power that Mother Nature was displaying was awesome and I was loving every minute of the battle to keep walking. It was exhilarating!

Despite the windy conditions, I made excellent time to Porthmadog, and then to Portmeirion, where I was due to meet my parents. It was amazing to see them both as a lot has happened for us all since I last saw them. It was like a piece of home and a few hours of normality had come to the Llŷn to find me, and their visit has given me a huge emotional boost for the weeks to come. It's funny how the simple things in life can be taken so much for granted. I've never really thought about how wonderful it is just to sit and chat with your parents, but as we sat in a café eating and talking, I was filled with a deep happiness that can only come from spending time with people you love. I guess you don't really appreciate these simple things until you are away from them.

Portmeirion was a hugely interesting place too. It's like a slice of traditional Italy has accidentally been dropped in North Wales. The ornate buildings are painted a variety of bright colours and are surrounded by winding paths and immaculately-kept gardens. The whole village was designed by Sir Bertram Clough Williams-Ellis and is an explosion of different architectural styles. There are ornate little statues everywhere and the attention to detail means that there are surprises around every corner. To explore the sights with my parents made it even more special.

After stocking up on supplies and saying goodbye until I reach New Quay, I was back on the path for the final two miles of the day. Bridget was kind enough to come and pick me up from Penrhyndeudraeth and we've spent a nice evening chatting in the caravan. She also cooked me a tasty pasta bolognaise! A night in front of the Olympics with Rob lies ahead, followed by another good sleep in a proper bed. Perfect!

The care of Gareth, Menai and Guto, and now Bridget and Rob too, has been so fantastic over the last three days that I feel refreshed again after a week of feeling quite jaded and tired. The Llŷn Peninsula section of path has been challenging, partly due to the weather, but I have still appreciated its beauty. There were plenty of surprises on the north coast, with the incredible 360° of stunning scenery from the highest point on the WCP being a stand-out moment. Bardsey Island and Whistling Sands are very pretty too and the Pilgrims' Trail has lots of little historic spots to discover. The sea is often littered with outcrops of jagged rock which are viewed from steep cliffs or soft, sandy beaches. For a small peninsula, there is plenty of interest and it's an area that I hope to explore more in the years to come, when I can stop and appreciate the surroundings more fully.

Diolch, Llŷn and your residents. You've given me an amazing six days!

Nos da, pawb. I'll see you tomorrow once I've started the short Meirionnydd section of path.

Meirionydd Coast Path

Day 26
Penrhyndeudraeth to Talybont

Today started well, with plenty of fuss from Colin the cat to make sure I didn't go back to sleep! Bridget kindly gave me breakfast, a packed lunch and a lift back to Penrhyndeudraeth, where within a couple miles of starting walking, a man and a lady – who manages the Pines Care Home in Criccieth – came running out of their front door to ask which charity I was walking for, having seen the sign on my bag. The conversation ended in a very kind £10 donation and maintained my good mood. The views across the salt marshes to Portmeirion were pretty and for a few miles, I played cat and mouse with a lovely family who are up here on holiday. Our conversations grew longer each time we passed, and we passed a good few times!

By the time I reached Harlech, I was in a very good mood. The sun was out, the morning's walking had been good and I was about to go and explore Harlech Castle. Had I known how my day would end, I would have cracked on with walking and visited the castle another time, but at this point I was living in blissful ignorance of what lay ahead.

The castle was another of King Edward I's displays of power in North Wales. Designed by the 'Master of the King's works in Wales' – Master James of St George – and built in only six years (1283–1289), the castle sits on top of a high cliff that would have made it tricky to get at even without the towering walls and concentric design (walls within walls). When it was built, the sea was at the bottom of the cliff, which meant that supplies could reach the castle even when it was under siege. Nowadays, the estuary has built up nearly a kilometre of sand dunes and beach between the castle and the Irish Sea. During its active lifespan, the castle endured five sieges, resisting one and falling to four. One of these defeats was to Owain Glyndŵr in 1404. He made the castle his Royal Court and lived there for five years, before his defences were breached and his

Day 1: Setting off from Presteigne on 26th July 2016

Day 1: ODP sign above Whitton, plus feather

Day 3: Canalside walking near Pool Quay

Day 3: Flood banks of the River Severn near Pool Quay

Day 5: Panoramic walk above Llangollen

Day 6: Looking ahead to Moel Famau

Day 7: Allan, myself, Sharon and Leigh at ODP end in Prestatyn

Day 8: Arrow-straight walking alongside the River Dee near Chester

Day 9: Looking back to the seafront at Rhyl

Day 10: Dune walking away from the Great Orme

Day 10: The Great Orme from Morfa Conwy

Day 11: My coastal footprints near Llanfairfechan

Day 12: Siân and me near Penmon

Day 13: Rob and me near Moelfre

Day 13: Traeth Yr Ora

Day 14: Porth Wen

Day 16: Bethan and me nearing North Stack

Day 16: Natural arch south of Trearddur Bay

Day 17: St Cwyfan's Church

Day 18: Ynys Llanddwyn in front of Llŷn Peninsula

Day 18: Afon Braint stepping stones

Day 20: Caernarfon Castle

Day 20: Feather by waymarker near Caernarfon

Day 21: Starting the Llŷn in Trefor

Day 21: Highest point on the WCP – looking towards the Llŷn Peninsula

Day 21: Highest point on the WCP – looking towards Caernarfon

Day 21: Views from Nefyn Golf Club

Day 22: Looking back to Bardsey Island

Day 25: Portmeirion

Day 26: Harlech Castle

Day 26: View from Harlech Castle

Day 28: Beautiful Mawddach estuary views

Day 28: Barmouth and the Mawddach estuary

Day 28: Sunset on arrival in Tywyn

Day 29: 800 m to Ynyslas – 30 miles to walk there

Day 29: Hiking inland towards Machynlleth

Day 30: Arriving into Aberystwyth with Matt

Day 30: Sunset on arrival in Aberystwyth

family taken to the tower of London. Glyndŵr's subsequent disappearance remains a mystery. The final battle at the castle was during the English Civil War, when Harlech was the last Royalist fortress that remained standing. Much of the castle is still intact and I spent a good hour exploring all there is to see, from rounded boulders that were used in attacks on the castle, to walking on top of the walls and towers marvelling at the views both inside and out. It was nice to learn more about its history too.

After enjoying the food and Wi-Fi at a nearby pub and receiving more kind donations, I went outside into what I thought would only be a shower of rain. However, this shower lasted for the remaining six hours of walking. To say it was raining cats and dogs doesn't do it justice. I think raining elephants and hippos would be a more accurate representation. A few people stopped to offer me lifts, but despite the temptation of travelling under a roof, I battled on through the onslaught of Mother Nature. After following the waymarkers and walking pointlessly for nearly a mile through the Shell Island campsite to turn round a hairpin and come back along the beach 20 m away, I phoned mum to see if she could find any B & Bs in the area. I didn't fancy a night under canvas in the Welsh monsoon, and I thought enviously of my sister Emily who is working at the tennis in Cincinnati in the warm weather!

While on the phone, I must have missed a waymarker because I found myself beside a river at the point where it crashed into the waves. I could see a campsite just the other side and it was already after 8 p.m., so I decided to improvise! Walking inland, I couldn't find a way across and so I decided to wade through the point where fresh water met salt. It looked fairly shallow, but I went barefoot anyway to avoid the chance of soaking the inside of my boots as well as the outside. Boots and sticks in hand, I walked painfully over the rocky bed until the halfway point, where I realised that there was no chance of getting across safely. The first half had come up to mid-shin depth and was fast flowing. The second half was faster and deeper still. Cursing my decision, the river, the weather and just about everything else I could, I angrily put my socks and boots back on to sandy and sore feet, knowing that I'd have to backtrack until I found the path. With the combination of the weather, the river, a sore ankle that kept twisting with every uneven bit of path and the inevitably growing darkness, I felt angrier and more down than I have done in a long, long time. The night was only growing darker and wetter and I hit the lowest emotional point of my trek so far. I felt like everything was conspiring to stop me settling for the night, and considered just sitting down in the dunes and waiting until morning.

Thankfully, I've always been far too competitive and I was not going to be beaten by Mother Nature today. I put on a burst of speed, found the path (which wasn't waymarked off the beach anyway) and made it to Talybont just before half nine. Finding a caravan site, I spotted tents and made a beeline for them – tripping over a low wire fence that was invisible in the low light. It hurt, but never mind: I'd still beaten the elements and would be warm and dry once I managed to pitch my tent in the dark. This was surprisingly easy and I was soon unpacking, feeling annoyed but victorious. Mother Nature was to have the last say though. Her constant assault from the sky had soaked through Wilson's waterproof cover, leaving me with a sopping wet sleeping bag and pillow. My illusion of a comfortable, warm night had been popped, and I was left trying to stay warm by putting on all three t shirts that I'm carrying as well as my fleece. Still, at least the tent was holding up well so I'd be dry, and my stomach was full thanks to the sandwich that Bridget had made me that morning. My mood would have been horrendous had it not been for the kind offer of spending the next two nights in a holiday cottage owned by Clare and her family. As I drifted off to sleep with my wet sleeping bag beside me, I was thankful that I'd have a chance to dry it, and all of my other kit, after tomorrow's short walk.

Throughout the walk, I tried to be as honest and open as possible about how I was feeling so that the blog would be a true representation of the highs and lows of long-distance walking. However, at the time of writing this blog, I was embarrassed at how I'd acted following the failed river crossing, and so held back a little. The weather had gradually worn me down all afternoon and the carrot at the end of the stick was visible a mere few hundred metres away. I was desperate to reach that campsite, and this desperation led to me foolishly attempting to cross a river that was raging as a result of the sudden deluge of run-off water. I twisted my ankle while trying to cross with my bare feet on jagged rocks, before I realised that I would be swept away if I attempted to go any further. This moment was heartbreaking. I could see the end of my day, but couldn't get to it. My already painful feet were covered with sand, and I had no idea how much further I would have to walk. The sun had already set and the rain was continuing to fall so hard that it was bouncing off the rocks at the river's edge.

Having had my spirit weakened so much since leaving the castle, tears of frustration left my eyes and I broke into a torrent of abuse and curse words directed at the sky, and shouted as loudly as I possibly could. I'd completely lost control. I threw my rucksack to the ground and screamed a challenge to Mother Nature to keep throwing more obstacles in my way, then collapsed down onto a boulder with my head in hands, tears streaming down my face and gasping for breath. It was a tantrum worthy of a toddler who had learned a lot of bad words far too early in life, and with the way that my screams and shouts were instantly carried away by the wind along the vast, empty beach, that's exactly how big I felt. I'd hit rock bottom. After taking a while to calm down, I found a little scrap of my dogged and competitive nature still alive somewhere deep inside, determined that I wouldn't be beaten. I sent a text to Mum telling her that I was pitched up and in the dry, not wanting her to worry, and then set about retracing my footsteps to find where I'd missed the path to civilisation.

It is a moment in my walk that I am both really proud of and horrendously embarrassed by. I haven't lost control like that for as long as I can remember. The elements and circumstances had worn me down to a point where I didn't feel like me any more. But the fact that I found the inner strength somewhere to get up off that boulder, walk for another hour with a twisted ankle and bruised, sandy feet, pitch my tent in a downpour by the light of my tiny torch, survive the cold night without a sleeping bag and get up to walk the next morning after a very disturbed sleep is perhaps my greatest personal victory of the entire walk.

Day 27
Talybont to Barmouth

Last night wasn't overly fun. My lack of sleeping bag meant that I woke up cold a few times, but thankfully I eventually slept so deeply that even two alarms and a phone call failed to wake me. Oops! Finally dragging myself out of my tent at around nine, my camping neighbour Pete invited me over for a tea and a bacon sandwich. Already, today had started a lot better than yesterday ended. My kit was still wet, so I decided that rather than walking 22 miles to Tywyn and getting to Clare and Carl's family's cottage late, I would do a short walk to Barmouth and have the afternoon to dry my kit out and rest my legs. It would be as good as a rest day, but I'd still be further along in my challenge. Perfect!

The miles this morning were not interesting ones. The height and force of the river was impressive, and I was relieved I'd decided not to try and push on with wading across last night, but other than that there wasn't much to look at. The path wound through fields without many directional waymarkers, and at one point I looped around to a spot that I had been standing in ten minutes earlier, to have another go at finding the correct way. It was a bit like a guessing game, but I'm getting better at picking likely routes now and am making fewer daft decisions – with the exception of last night! For someone who is used to navigating with an OS map, using a guidebook and waymarkers has taken some getting used to. Eventually, I reached the road that the path would follow all the way to Barmouth, and put my head down to eat up the miles quickly.

The Barmouth promenade was another chance for nature's awesome power to be on show. The waves were crashing over the walls and soaking anybody within range. The sand strewn across the road and path was testament to the fact that the sea had been wild for some time! Turning left, I walked into Barmouth town centre and felt like I was arriving in Birmingham. Aside from the fact that everybody I spoke to seemed to have a Brummie accent, the streets were heaving and trying to navigate through them with my big backpack was interesting to say the least. Eventually finding a pub to eat in, I got chatting to a large family group who gave me a few donations before I left. Thank you!

On the train to Tywyn, I was excited about spending an afternoon in front of a television while my sleeping bag dried and my clothes got washed. My only issue was going to be the potential hour-and-40-minute wait for the bus. However, on arrival at the station I was met by Carl with his car, ready to give me a lift back to the cottage before they went home to Knighton. I couldn't have been happier to see him and after a short drive to the cottage, it was lovely to see Clare, Josie (who I taught for two years) and her younger sister Erin (who I also taught in the occasional lesson when at Whitton School!). It was great to see the family again as it was like being close to home, and I can't thank them enough for their kindness. The knowledge that I'll have another two nights in the warm and dry kept me going through a very tricky day yesterday. The girls had left me a couple of motivational notes too, which made me smile as I settled in for an afternoon of relaxation and comfort.

Tomorrow, I'll walk from Barmouth to Tywyn and then

return for another night in the cottage. The next few days are certainly going to be better than the last two have been, and I'm looking forward to getting back into the groove of enjoying the walking in this adventure. I always knew there would be high points and low points, and I'm lucky that I'm having so many more high points along the way to make the low points a less important rarity. Thank you to everyone who is adding to that pile of good things. You're all amazing!

Nos da, pawb. I'll see you after a night in the warm, and a hopefully drier day of walking.

Day 28
Barmouth to Tywyn

I was a little disorganised this morning and managed to catch the bus that got me into Tywyn just after the 9.39 train to Barmouth. The next train wouldn't get me there until just after midday. Today's planned 18 relaxed miles had become 18 rather quick ones. After killing time with a cooked breakfast, I enjoyed the train journey along the coast and stepped off into a crowd that was similar to a London tube station in rush hour! Barmouth had been busy yesterday, but it felt like the sunshine had sent everybody within a 50-mile radius to the seaside there today! I was pleased to get onto the railway bridge that spans the estuary, and away from the chaos.

I'll admit that I hadn't expected much from this stretch of coastline. Knowing that Barmouth seafront is very touristy, I didn't think that the scenery would be very interesting. I was to be proven hugely wrong though! While crossing the bridge over the Mawddach Estuary, the views were spectacular. On the right was Barmouth shining in the sun and across the shimmering sea, I could see the entire Llŷn Peninsula reaching out to Bardsey Island. On the left, the river stretched widely to fill the valley between steep-sided, towering mountains. I stood in awe for a few minutes before kicking into gear and making tracks to Fairbourne.

It was on arrival in Fairbourne that I became a fool for a few seconds. I decided to walk along the wall so I'd have a nicer view of the sea, and then got distracted by that view while stepping onto the aforementioned wall. The result? I underestimated its height and kicked the wall about an inch from the top with all my weight going forward expecting to find flat ground. Now totally off-balance, I fell forwards over the wall before I could get a hand down to steady myself. My right shin, knee and lower thigh scraped down the concrete edge, my ribs hit the top and my head gently rested on the ground the other side, bag on top, leaving my bottom pointed to the sky. I was in considerable pain, but jumped up and looked around to see if anyone had noticed my ridiculous attempt at climbing a two-foot-high wall. I thought I'd got away with it, until I saw a sympathetic look from an elderly couple walking towards me. I thought their restraint was incredible, because despite the pain from my leg and ribs, even I found it hard not to laugh, and I hadn't seen the whole thing happen! No lasting damage though. Just a grazed shin, thigh and wrist, cut knee and a bruised ego!

My second attempt at scaling the North Face of the Two-Foot Wall was more successful, and I walked along Fairbourne Beach taking interest in the huge concrete blocks spaced about 2 m apart for the entire length of the bay. A board next to a ruined lookout post informed me that they were 'Dragon's Teeth' tank traps, erected in World War II to stop a potential D-Day-style beach landing.

The path then climbs from sea level to 300 m in a short space of time. Most of the climb takes you inland, so although you are a lot higher than you were an hour earlier in Fairbourne, you're actually no closer to your destination. If anything, you're further away. I wanted so much to hate this section, and expected to rant about a stupid route in this blog, but I honestly couldn't bring myself to do it. The views were quite simply stunning.

103

The Llŷn Peninsula was visible in the distance, clear enough to pick out towns such as Criccieth, the Mawddach Estuary was glinting in the bright sunlight, Barmouth and Fairbourne were crawling with ant-like people enjoying the beaches and the dramatic mountains dominated the scene inland before plunging steeply to the river.

After a while admiring the views, the path drops to sea level again and into the village of Llwyngwril. Bridget had told me about the 'yarn bombing' here, so I was expecting to see the odd bit of knitting in the streets. What I got, however, was far beyond anything I'd imagined! Every fence had knitted bunting and many signs had been turned into walking sticks, or given colourful socks. The first major centrepiece was Gwril the giant. He pokes his huge head over the village bridge to watch over everyone who crosses. His wife, the mermaid, was sitting on a bench next to a shepherd with sheep and sheepdogs at their feet. This yarn bombing is to celebrate the National Sheepdog Trials being held in the village, and it looked like every resident had spent an entire year knitting! Even my coast path signs weren't safe, as a clown dangled off the one that pointed me back up into the hills.

On reaching the high point of the second inland section (only 200 m above sea level this time), I bumped into a Gold Duke of Edinburgh group. They had come all the way from Cambridge and were on Day 1 of a four-day expedition. We got chatting and when they showed me their route, I realised we were going the same way for a short while. We walked together and discussed our challenges, as well as finding out a little more about each other. Everyone in the group was a pleasure to chat to, so when they told me they weren't allowed to buy anything for the four days and were carrying all their rations with them, I decided that I'd give them the bag of sweets from my backpack when we parted as a little morale boost for when times get tough.

On reaching the road where I'd go right and they left, one boy asked if he could give me a donation as he'd still got his wallet as well as their emergency coins. As he handed me £25, I was about to object and give him some back when he became hugely upset and said something about a grandparent dying from Alzheimer's a few weeks ago that I couldn't fully make out. I didn't have the heart to ask him to repeat it and just comforted him, reminding him that the great outdoors is the best place for thinking time and he had a great group of friends for support. I think that donating so much helped him, just as fundraising is helping me. After telling his group to look out for him, we all parted with good luck wishes. I'd been reminded that dementia affects so many people and how hard it is when events are so raw, and my drive to continue putting one foot in front of the other had been boosted to new heights. However, ten minutes later, I was hit by a huge surge of guilt. I'd been so taken aback by the donation and openness of earlier, that I'd totally forgotten to give the group my bag of sweets! The guilt was probably irrational as they never knew I'd been planning to give them anything, but with the raw feeling of earlier and the heightened emotions from pushing yourself to the limit day in, day out, I spent the next hour beating myself up for being so selfish. My bag felt a little heavier all afternoon with the knowledge that the sweets were still in there.

The remainder of the path was nothing special. More evidence of World War II defences were visible at Tonfanau, but the path didn't go close enough to have a proper explore. It wasn't until I was approaching Tywyn that my interest was grabbed again. The mountainous views inland now had a foreground of salt marsh, and the evening light was giving the whole scene a beautiful glow. On turning around to see why the light was so lovely, my eyes found a perfect Jacob's ladder effect streaking through the clouds. The sunset only got prettier and as I walked along the seafront to end my day, I looked back on a route that had surprised me many times. Sometimes with scenes of beauty, sometimes with community spirit and once with a brilliant group of young adults challenging themselves to survive four days in the wilderness, one of whom who will hopefully find some comfort in the beauty of Mother Nature.

Nos da, all. I'll see you tomorrow when I've spent an entire day walking away from the sea!

Day 29
Tywyn to Machynlleth

I had a late start again today as I needed a lie-in and wanted to leave Clare and Carl's cottage perfectly clean and tidy. Eventually setting off from Tywyn at about midday, I spent the first hour and a half walking along the beach. A lifeguard gave me a donation after reading Menai's sign on my bag, and shortly afterwards, a group of three walkers stopped to ask how far I was going. After hearing about my challenge, they gave a very generous donation and then the elder of the two ladies told me that she is taking on the Camino de Santiago in two weeks' time. The Camino is a very famous pilgrimage that follows the way of St James over the mountains and flatlands of France and Spain. It is perhaps even more famous thanks to one of my all-time favourite films, *The Way*. It was that very film that made me want to attempt a long-distance walk in the first place, and I watched it on the night before I started my Wander for inspiration. The lady told me that a year ago, she'd barely been able to walk due to an issue with her feet, but after an operation she'd recovered well. She then developed breast cancer and after winning the battle with that, decided to do something to claim back her active life. She is such an inspirational person, taking on the 500-mile trek after all of those recent health scares, and after parting, I considered how lucky I am that my biggest health issues have been Crohn's Disease and the occasional ear problem.

Deserted pebbles turned to deserted sand and I could see Ynyslas getting closer across the sea. Although I would get as close as 800 m away today, it would take me a day and a half to reach it due to the 30 inland miles I'd have to walk in search of a bridge. The beach in Aberdyfi was heaving due to the hot and sunny weather and after negotiating tents, windbreaks and soft, energy-sapping sand, I decided a break was in order. Popping into a pub on the seafront, a regular noticed the sign on my bag and after quizzing me about my route, kindly donated £5 to my fundraising.

Half an hour later, I was on my way again to tackle the 12 miles walking inland over the hills to Machynlleth. The steep climb from Aberdyfi made me feel quite ill, but once I hit the road at the top, all that was forgotten. The hills and mountains were laid out in front of me like a scene from Lord of the Rings – I admit that I was humming various parts of the soundtrack to myself as the miles tumbled. I also felt closer to home than I have in a long time. From some hills near our house on a clear day, I'm sure you can probably see the other side of some of the hills that I was looking at today. It was nice to think that somebody back in Presteigne might be looking at the very same hill I was in that moment, and I was suddenly filled with a mix of warmth and homesickness. The sights, smells and general day-to-day life of home hit my memory in a sudden jolt and for a brief while, I wished I was there. However, the view around the next corner of the ridge soon blew away thoughts of wanting to be anywhere other than this beautiful spot.

After dropping down to Pennal, the path climbs into the hills once more, now following forestry tracks. I'd been dreading this part all afternoon after finding the first climb so hard, but my legs surprised me. I felt like the Chris Froome of that hotly-contested sport, 'hiking with an 18 kg rucksack on your back'! The path wasn't too steep, but around every bend it continued to climb. There was no break from it. Had I been in a different frame of mind, I could have found this torturous, but my legs were propelling me up the gradient so quickly that I was actually pleased when each corner revealed more uphill! I maintained the fast pace for the entirety of the 3-mile climb and completed it in under an hour from bottom to top. The scenery had been remarkably similar to my training walks around a forest in Presteigne called The Folley, and I felt proud of the difference in my stamina. Back then, I'd been struggling to walk for any great length of time without having to put my bag down, and my legs were usually aching after only a few miles or any short uphill. Today, I'd done 13 hilly miles before this continuous climb and my legs were carrying me up as if it were flat ground.

Arriving in Machynlleth after a short, steep descent, I met Margaret by the clock tower. Margaret is a good friend of Gareth and Menai, who I stayed with in Llanbedrog, and her sister Valmai is friends with my Mum, having worked together at John Beddoes School in Presteigne. Wales feels very small when there are personal links stretching right across the country! Margaret cooked a wonderful dinner of duck while I was soaking in a bath and when I came down, her friend Mair was at the table too. Mair has been following my blog recently and it was lovely to chat to her and Margaret about the local area and walks that they have been on. The Blue Lake, which I passed yesterday without going to see it, sounds amazing and has been added to the list of places I want to come back to visit when I have the use of my car again. I feel a Welsh road trip coming on! Mair also gave me a kind donation with a lovely letter, which was a really thoughtful touch.

I'm now sitting on a comfortable sofa with a full belly, good company and a cosy bed waiting for me upstairs. It's interesting hearing Margaret's stories of teaching college-age children and how the workload got so much that now she has retired, she is filling each day with productivity and is amazed at how much she gets done!

Nos da, pawb! I'll see you tomorrow when I've walked back to the sea and along to Aberystwyth to meet my good friend Matt. I'll also be celebrating a big milestone too.

PS Today, I managed not to fall over. First time in three days! Long may that continue.

Postscript

That night, a comment on my blog made me wonder whether family has a mysterious connection that we still don't fully understand. Mum told me that in the exact moment I was gazing at the hills towards home, feeling a little homesick and wondering if anyone there was looking at the same peak, she was standing atop the hill on our farm, looking towards the very same hills wondering the very same thing about me. While in that brief moment, I could feel everything that my home is so clearly in my mind. It's strange to think that one of the people I love most in the world actually was looking back at me.

Ceredigion Coast Path

Day 30
Machynlleth to Aberystwyth

Waking up today, I knew that once I'd walked my 21 planned miles, I'd have reached my halfway point for the whole journey. It was a doubly-exciting prospect, because I'd be meeting my great pal Matt in Aberystwyth ready for a rest day tomorrow. As an added bonus, I'd be having a cup of tea with one of my two Offa's Dyke walking friends, Sharon, in Borth. There was a lot to look forward to, but first there were the 15 isolated miles to take me back to the sea.

When I finally managed to drag myself out of the amazingly comfy bed at Margaret's, I came downstairs to find fruit salad and beans on toast all ready for breakfast. While eating, Margaret rushed out to grab a mysterious item of food that I had to try before leaving Dolgellau. Five minutes later, I was tucking into my first honey bun – it was delicious!

Well-fed and well-rested, Margaret drove me back to Machynlleth ready to start my longest day in the past week. I can't thank her enough for everything that she did for me yesterday evening and this morning. It's been lovely to meet her and her friend Mair, and a real bonus to be treated to amazing food, a warm bed and a packed lunch for today on top of an evening of good company. I couldn't have had a better set-up for a day's walking.

Machynlleth is the ancient capital of Wales. Owain Glyndŵr set up his parliament in a building near the town centre, and it was interesting having a little look around before I got going. The town is very proud of its history, so there are numerous Glyndŵr references and monuments to be spotted while walking around. The WCP follows Glyndŵr's Way up into the lowland hills and then veers off to continue heading towards the coast. It's an attractive section of path and as I rose and fell through woodland and fields, I felt that I was making good time. The occasional views over the estuary and Ynyslas were beautiful, and despite the fact that I only saw one group of people during 11 miles of walking, the promise of meeting two friends near the end of the day meant that I never felt lonely.

By five o'clock, I'd reached Borth and met up with Sharon and her partner Ray. It was lovely to catch up and reminisce about Offa's Dyke, which now feels a very long time ago! Today had actually felt very like the last few days of walking on the ODP. The landscape of rolling hills and wooded vales had been similar, and I'd known I'd be seeing Sharon (although this time without Leigh) near the end. I still had six coastal miles to go though, so after a cup of tea, some banana loaf, and meeting Sharon's friend Janet, it was all too soon time to leave.

The start of the Ceredigion Coast Path was as stunning as it was hilly. It rises and falls steeply over dramatic black cliffs, and despite the rain, the views back over to Borth and Aberdyfi were pretty. As I reached a stretch of coast that has become very special to me, the horizon started to light up in a bright orange colour and silhouetted the hills of the Llŷn Peninsula and Bardsey Island. It was showing me how far I've come in the last eight days of walking, which was a perfect moment for the bit of path I was on. It was while I was walking this stretch of coast over a year ago that the idea for this challenge first came to me. I was waiting for Matt to finish work, and decided that I'd walk along the path to see how far I could get. Enjoying walking on my own, I imagined how good it would be to do the whole Pembrokeshire Path, camping along the way. As I continued walking and enjoying the thinking time, the idea grew to the whole coast path and then to linking in Offa's Dyke to encircle Wales. I didn't know if I'd ever get the opportunity to do this amazing trek, but the thought stayed smouldering at the back of my mind until it became what it is today. As I remembered this moment of inspiration, the orange horizon started to stretch south from the Llŷn and eventually reached the end of Cardigan Bay at the start of the Pembrokeshire Coast Path. My completed sections were handing on the baton to my future sections as I stopped and gazed out to sea in amazement.

The moment was perfect, and I felt quite emotional at being so close to halfway through my challenge in the spot where it had all begun.

A short while later, I spotted a familiar figure ambling along in the other direction not too far away. Matt was also transfixed by the bright horizon, but he eventually saw the weird, bearded man heading towards him. It was amazing to see him again and the sunset turned truly radiant while we walked towards Aber. As we reached the top of Constitution Hill to look down over the town, a rainbow glowed over my halfway point. It felt as if Mother Nature was congratulating me on the 550-mile mark. The pot of gold at the end of the rainbow was a great meal in the Glengower followed by a couple of celebratory pints and cocktails and a few close games of pool! I'm looking forward to the rest day with my good friend tomorrow, before seeing what the rest of the Ceredigion Coast Path has to offer.

Reaching halfway is a brilliant feeling. My body still feels strong and I'm still loving my nomadic life, trekking around my home country. I'm learning new things every day, meeting amazing people and finding lots of hidden gems that I want to revisit with friends and family in the future. I know that the remaining 550 miles will be just as interesting, varied and beautiful.

Nos da, pawb! I'll see you in two days once I've had a good rest, walked to Aberaeron, and am only six miles away from seeing my parents and grandparents again in New Quay.

Day 31
Aberystwyth to Aberaeron

This morning was the earliest start I've had in at least a week, with Matt having to get to work before half eight. We'd stayed up quite late watching a film and chatting, so it wasn't easy to drag myself off my roll mat and pack my bag. It had been a great couple of days with a good friend and the rest had been much needed, but now it was time to tackle the second half of my Welsh Wander.

I had a leisurely start, ambling along the seafront of Aberystwyth before stopping to sit for a while and take in the views on the first cliff section. I had 18 miles to cover, but I was in no rush as there was plenty of time to complete them within the day. Besides, the panorama before my eyes was too beautiful to rush past. Aberystwyth is set in the perfect place for expansive views of the entirety of Cardigan Bay. As I looked out to sea, my gaze wandered from the mountains and islands of the Llŷn in the north to the cliffs and small towns of the south. I could see New Quay perched on its rocky outcrop and thought ahead to tomorrow when I'll be meeting my grandparents and parents there. I'm really looking forward to seeing them, and New Quay has long been a place that we've visited for a spot of dolphin watching, so I'm also looking forward to a slice of normality again while potentially getting to see some more marine life.

The path continued to provide pretty views as it rose and fell over crumbling cliffs. The beautiful weather was bringing a new problem though: flies. There were swarms of them every time I reached a high point in the path, and at times it was hard to see where I was going through the haze of bugs. The first swarm took great pleasure in landing all over me, to the point where I couldn't possibly knock them all off, so I just gave up and accepted my hitch-hikers' company. After escaping rapidly down into a valley, I plastered myself in insect repellent, which solved the landing problem, if not the swarming!

A little further along the path, I bumped into a couple of women walking the other way. After sharing fly stories, we talked about my challenge and they asked where I lived. I went through my usual spiel of 'It's a small town near the border that nobody has ever really heard of. It's called Presteigne and it's near...' At this point, I was stopped mid-flow by a shout of 'Get out!' from the ladies. They explained that one was from Presteigne and the other from Knighton. Unbelievable! We didn't recognise each other, despite having lived in the same town for 20 years, and the Presteigne resident had even worked in our old farmhouse, which has now been taken over and converted into a guesthouse. To see two people from home was a real boost, and wishing each other luck in avoiding the flies, we set off again in opposite directions.

The remaining miles to Aberaeron passed without major interest, but the sea was always pretty and my mood stayed good with the help of some film soundtracks to match the scenery. I met a nice family in a bar on a campsite, and chatted while my phone and my legs recharged. I also met Geoff and Dai Morgan and had a brief but pleasant chat about hiking and potential campsites, then had a nice conversation with a lady on the beach near Aberarth. A sense of calm was in the air as the sun dipped below the clouds, and I felt completely relaxed. I'm on the second half of my challenge. I've proved that I can handle the strain, both physically and mentally, so all that is left to do is to enjoy the remaining time on the path.

Aberaeron is a busy town this weekend. As a result of the bank holiday, mackerel run, a rugby sevens tournament and the carnival, every campsite was full. I was considering pitching on a cliff somewhere quiet, but was craving a shower with the scent of sweat and insect repellent strong on my skin. Thankfully, one campsite allowed me to pitch in a corner spot that they usually keep free and as I was erecting my tent, my camping neighbour came over to give me a cup of tea. This was just the way to end a relaxed day and after my much-needed shower, I walked into the Royal Oak in town for some food to find my two walkers from Presteigne and Knighton at the bar! Two amazingly coincidental meetings in one day! We ate together, swapping stories of home and travels before they treated me to my meal. It was a lovely gesture, as an evening with good company was more than enough to end my day on a high already.

Now I'm enjoying the internet in the pub with a full belly,

knowing that I have a nice dry tent to go back to. Seeing my parents and Grandma and Grandpa in New Quay tomorrow will be fantastic, and hopefully I'll have some dolphin sightings to talk about too!

Nos da, pawb. I'll see you tomorrow when I've had another relaxed day, and stopped in one of my favourite places in Wales with some of my favourite people in the world!

Day 32
Aberaeron to Llangrannog

The rain of the night quickly eased off this morning and I was able to pack up everything while keeping it all dry. I also had a nice chat with Marianne and her husband, who had shared my pitch on the campsite last night, and they gave me a very kind donation before they left. This sent me off on the first six miles of today's walk happy and I knew that at some point along the way, I'd be met by my parents and Grandma and Grandpa too. Today was going to be a great one!

Despite a hint of drizzle, the sun soon shone through the clouds and after five fast-paced miles, I stepped down onto Cei Bach beach to see four familiar figures walking towards me. It was amazing to hug Grandma and Grandpa again, and Mum and Dad too of course, and set about walking the final mile into New Quay. After a steep climb, we got chatting to a local man about my walk and were later joined by a nice couple. A kind donation sent us on our way again and we were soon arriving on the harbour wall. I've spent many a happy day with family on this wall, watching the dolphins frolicking in the harbour, so it felt really good to be back here, even if the dolphins had disappeared after putting on a spectacular show for my family on their arrival. Grandma and Grandpa treated us to a lovely meal in a restaurant overlooking the sea before we spent a chilled-out hour or so chatting and

117

spending quality time together on the end of the wall. It was fantastic!

All too soon, it was time to say goodbye and we parted as we had met earlier; hugs all round! I set off along the coast path again and kept at least one eye on the sea at all times hoping for a dolphin sighting. I didn't get lucky and at one point when I had both eyes on the sea, I missed a coast path marker. I realised after only 20 m but before I could return to the trail, I got chatting to a group of people. They kindly donated, as did a passer-by who read my bag and a man who came out of his house after hearing our conversation. My 20 m mistake had raised £20 in donations!

The coast path between New Quay and Cwmtydu passes a couple of stunning sections. There's an old Iron Age fort with a little island in the sea in front, and some sheer cliffs which tower over the turquoise sea. I met a lot more friendly people while strolling along and nice chats ended in more donations! On arrival in Cwmtydu, I sat down for a rest and the sign on my bag got plenty of attention. A nice couple gave me £5 and I had a good talk with a family who apologised for not having any cash on them. As I was striding out of the village, I heard a shout of 'Wait!' The family, including a daughter who hadn't been with them at the beach the first time we met, were running out of the front door of their holiday cottage to give me yet another donation! I was touched by the thought and effort, as they had intended to walk all the way back to the beach to give it to me, and we stood and chatted for a little while again. I could have stayed much longer as they were all genuinely lovely people, but the remaining five miles beckoned and the sun was already growing low in the darkening blue sky.

A short while later, a sign warned me of the isolation and steep terrain of the section to come. It was with a little trepidation that I set off up the first climb, wondering what lay in store for my already tiring legs. In actual fact, I found the going quite easy. Yes, there were ups and downs and the path ran close to big drops at some points, but it was always wide and I'd expected far more challenging walking after the warning signs. A nice couple I met donated yet more money, and I strode past the Urdd Centre onto ground that I was familiar with, having walked this small section with the year five group that I brought to the centre from Presteigne. Looking over the hillock and island at Lochtyn, the sun was growing a pale orange colour as it dropped closer to the sea and its light was reflecting in a bright bar across the waters. As Llangrannog came into sight, the scenery grew as stunning as the sunset was and I ambled along completely entranced by the beauty of my surroundings. The calmness of everything around sent me into a deeply peaceful mood, and my mind emptied of all thoughts apart from those of the views in front of me.

I was snapped out of my daydreaming state by a shout of my name. I looked ahead and there, with their dog Bisto, stood Valmai and Jen, who will be my hosts for the next three nights. We took some photos and discussed how the walk was going as we dropped into the picturesque little village of Llangrannog. The sun was nearly touching the sea as we reached the sandy cove, and when we were getting into the car, a passer-by gave me all of the change in his pocket. It took today's sponsorship up to £69! I can't believe how many people have been generous and kind enough to delve into their pockets and hand over money to support a slightly smelly, bearded, tired-looking man with his fundraising. My total is now about £3000 and it continues to rise. I'm humbled by everyone's giving nature, and am now hopeful of tripling my original target!

This evening, Valmai cooked me a delicious dinner of spaghetti bolognaise and the four of us (Valmai, Jen, Bisto and I) spent a pleasant evening talking about anything and everything that came to mind! I'm now writing my blog in the comfort of a warm bed, knowing that I'll be returning here for the next two nights. Shower, hot food, a proper bed and perhaps most importantly, great company. Heaven! I'm having a hard job deciding which photograph to set as my featured photo today, as the scenery has been so spectacular and I've met up with loved ones and new friends. I have about 30 candidates!

Nos da, pawb! I'll see you tomorrow once I've finished walking the Ceredigion section of the coast path!

Day 33
Llangrannog to Cardigan

When I came downstairs this morning, Valmai had gone to a huge effort, cooking a full English (or Welsh!) breakfast to give me the energy for what would be a difficult section of walking. Llangrannog to Tresaith is widely regarded as the hardest part of the Ceredigion Coast Path, but at least the sky was blue on arrival at yesterday's finishing point.

Walking out of the village of Llangrannog, the path climbs steeply to a black statue. I was familiar with this statue following the residential trip to the Urdd Centre with the year fives from Presteigne. A legend has been passed down from year group to year group about the terrifying 'Black Nun' who will come and get you while you sleep. She passes notes around rooms, moves objects and even knocks on doors and runs away. She made an appearance in this year's visit too, but when Mr Davies (me!) had a loud rant about note-passing and knocking on doors, and threatened to remove the culprits from all of the activities, he became much scarier than any statue and we heard no more from her for the remaining two days. In reality, the statue is of a man – Saint Carannog (Carantoc in English) – who is said to have founded Llangrannog in 510 AD. He looks out over a scene that could have been lifted straight from a postcard, with the hill fort and headland of Lochtyn joined to the beach and quaint village by a dramatic set of cliffs with interesting rock formations. I stood next to him and admired the scene for a few minutes before heading on up the path.

The natural beauty continues as you head towards Penbryn. Beautiful little coves are protected by steep cliffs, and tiny islets stand in the sea attached by the narrowest strips of golden sand. On the way down to the cove, I came across a family who were blackberry picking. I chatted to Huw, Eleri and Owen as we ambled along slowly and swapped stories of adventures and teaching (both Huw and Eleri are teachers). It was strange to think that they're in the last week of their holiday and I'm only halfway through mine! It was lovely to meet them, but at Penbryn it was time to go our separate ways before I tackled the next steep climb.

At the top of this climb, I came across Jeannie, who was walking in the opposite direction. She lives in Ludlow, which is only half an hour from my home in Presteigne. We got chatting at length about the beauty of nature and how even the smallest thing, such as an unfurling fern, can be so fascinating and yet most people would pass it by without a second glance. It was lovely to meet somebody who was as passionate about experiencing the great outdoors as I am and before we knew it, over half an hour had passed! Neither of us was in a hurry though. During my three hours of morning walking, I covered five miles. I could have walked faster and done ten, but I'd have missed the incredible scenery and lovely people that made the path as enjoyable as it was. They say life is meant to be taken in at a steady walking pace, and this morning had certainly called for that to be put into practice.

While walking into Aberporth, I got chatting to a couple of ladies about my challenge. We ambled along nicely and a pleasant discussion ended with three donations from the ladies and their husbands, which sent me on my way even happier still! The town itself was extremely busy, but I stopped to enjoy a quiet drink in the coolness of a small pub while everybody else was on the beach. The rest was needed as the path climbs steeply out of the town and has to take a detour around a Ministry of Defence site. Apparently there is low level radiation in the air here, which gave me a slight sense of anxiety as I passed the base, imagining lots of different potential uses for it. On returning to the coast, the cliffs grow dramatic and rugged again as you head towards Mwnt. This is a special place for me, as it was from the top of Foel Y Mwnt (the little hill next to the beach) that I saw my first ever wild dolphins. I hoped that today would bring the same good luck. I was so thrilled that my parents and grandparents had seen dolphins yesterday, but I'd be lying if I said that I wasn't a little disappointed that I hadn't seen them too. My fingers were crossed as I approached the conical hill along the cliffs.

At the base I met a couple, Lewis and Sarah, who were holidaying nearby. They had heard that no dolphins had been sighted here for two weeks, so my hopes of a sighting began to fade. Nevertheless, we climbed the steep slope to the summit together and stood talking for a little while. Whist looking out to sea, I suddenly spotted a seal swimming right below us, which dived shortly afterwards. As we looked for its reappearance, Lewis and Sarah spotted a fin. Two dolphins were swimming by directly beneath us! Mwnt had delivered for me again, and I felt privileged to stand and watch these graceful creatures going about their day-to-day life. Walking down to the edge of the cliff to get a closer look, I pointed them out to a guy that was standing next to me. We spoke about wildlife for a good ten minutes with occasional pointing and shouts of 'THERE!', and when I started to tell him about my challenge, the man turned around and enlightened me to the fact that we had met yesterday! We'd been so transfixed by the dolphins that we'd not looked at each other once in the ten minutes of talking, and spoke with renewed enthusiasm after the comic moment of realisation!

As the dolphins swam away, I tore myself away from the spot that had twice gifted me a special dolphin sighting and tackled the remaining miles to Cardigan, which was the site of the very first Eisteddfod back in the twelfth century. I'm looking forward to exploring the town a little more at the start of tomorrow's walk. I'd originally planned to get to St Dogmaels today, but my leisurely morning pace had cut me short by two miles. I thought to myself that days like today are the very reason I didn't set myself a time target. I was able to stop and admire the views, to chat with many genuinely lovely people and to spend half an hour watching my favourite animal from a special place on the coast. I'd enjoyed every minute and as the sun set, I arrived in Cardigan to see Valmai and Jen waving from the bridge. They'd met a man who has 12 children, and after an interesting chat, he kindly donated £10, taking my total for today up to £57! People's generosity continues to astound me – every person who I spent any sort of time chatting to today had donated!

Nos da, pawb! I'll see you tomorrow once I've started the 187 miles of Pembrokeshire Coast Path. I've been excited about this section since the beginning, so hopefully I'll have lots to write about in the blogs to come.

Postscript

I was a little naughty during Day 33. For years, my family has visited the Cardigan Island Coastal Farm Park on the way home from holidays in Pembrokeshire and enjoyed the clifftop views with almost guaranteed seal sightings. I'd heard in the news some years ago that the owners were going to great lengths to block the coastal path going through, which had disappointed me. So when I arrived at the point where the path goes miles inland to skirt around the park, I decided that I wasn't going to miss out on one of my favourite stretches of coast in all of Wales. Climbing a gate that said 'Private', I was in a very torn state of mind. The farmer in me despises trespassing and would never normally do something like that, but at the same time, there was no reason that the path couldn't go through the farm park, other than the owners being awkward about it. I wasn't going to affect any crops or livestock and would be walking a well-trodden path that sticks to the perimeter of Wales more thoroughly than the WCP was able to.

My stubbornness won the internal struggle and I hopped over the gate, dropping down to an old family favourite spot on the cliffs to eat my packed lunch in the company of the Cardigan Island seals just offshore. After following the path around the cliffs, I came to a junction. I could climb another private gate and walk 200 m to a footpath just a little further along the coast without being noticed, or turn left and go up to the Farm Park reception to pay my way (despite not seeing any of the animals). Being a generally honest person, I decided to go and explain and pay whatever the cost of entering the park would be.

However, on reaching the building, the gate and doors were locked. My only way to the carpark was to hop a fence, which I did easily after years of practice on the farm! Unfortunately, this was the exact moment that the owner of the park looked out of the front door. He came charging out to question me on where I had been, while his wife shouted through the door that I was a trespasser. Explaining my challenge and why I had done what I'd done, I offered to pay the entry price and was cut off by the angry man. He ranted for a good while about the fact that he'd paid £250,000 to stop the WCP coming through his land because if somebody fell and hurt themselves he would have to pay twice that amount in court. It occurred to me that for a fraction of that money, he could have put in some signs saying 'Keep away from the cliffs' and he would have been covered. The path is already well-maintained and the cliffs fenced off because of the Farm Park. This was not the time to challenge him though, as he was clearly very riled, so I just let him say his piece, apologised, offered to pay the entry fee once more (which was rejected due to the fact that he didn't want to take money from a charity walker) and then got on my way.

I was left reeling by the encounter and it was all I could think about for the next few miles, which was a shame at the end of such a great day. I understood his anger as I have felt the same way seeing people walk off the footpaths on our farm, but the difference is that we do actually have footpaths that are open to the public and we encourage people to come and enjoy the pretty scenery that we are blessed to live in. I couldn't understand why he would go to such lengths to stop people enjoying his beautiful stretch of coastline. It angered me that I hadn't been able to put across my point of view to him and while walking, I actually drafted an email to the Farm

Park apologising for my actions but challenging their motives for blocking the WCP. I didn't send it though. Writing my thoughts down had helped me shed my anger, so I didn't see any point in poking the hornet's nest again. I was still disappointed nonetheless. I'd loved Cardigan Island Coastal Farm Park as a child, but that evening, I wished I'd just ignored my stubborn streak and bypassed it on the path. I know I was in the wrong for trespassing and honestly regret doing it, even if I do still strongly disagree with the Farm Park being so anti-walkers. I guess two wrongs don't make a right.

Pembrokeshire Coast Path

Day 34
Cardigan to Newport

After another tasty breakfast cooked by Valmai and a lift back to Cardigan, I set off over the bridge towards a day of walking that I was very excited about. Pausing for a look back at the recently refurbished castle, I began to climb out of the town. I had told myself that I would walk a little more quickly this morning so that I could spend more time on the apparently stunning cliff path between St Dogmaels and Newport. However, within ten minutes of leaving Cardigan I'd found my first distraction. The hedges alongside the path were laden with ripe blackberries, their dark skin glistening in the morning sun. I ate my way along the side of the path through three fields, enjoying the beautifully sweet fruit and ending up with very purple fingers. I was reminded of the days when I would arrive home from school with hands looking much the same, although a lot smaller, and try to convince mum that I hadn't eaten enough blackberries to put me off my dinner, which was usually a lie. Today at least, I would have plenty time to burn off the blackberries and would undoubtedly eat all of the packed lunch that Valmai had made for me.

My thoughts of St Dogmaels in the past have always centred on the fact that it's the start (or end, if you're walking north) of the Wales Coast Path. I hadn't given the town itself much consideration at all, so I was surprised and delighted when I walked into the town centre and found a bustling local market next to a picturesque pond, and a pretty church on the grounds of a large ruined abbey. The abbey was built in the twelfth century for the Monks of Tiron, and is one of very few Tironian houses in southern Britain. It spanned four centuries of monastic life, but was closed in 1536 during the Dissolution of the Monasteries under Henry VIII. I spent a nice half hour looking around the cathedral and learning about St Dogmaels' history, before I tore myself away from the attractive little town, passed the display signalling the start of the Pembrokeshire Coast Path and headed for Poppit.

The beach at Poppit Sands has attractive views across to Cardigan Island, but I couldn't stay long as thanks to blackberry and abbey distractions and the need for a cup of tea in the café, I'd managed to spend another whole morning getting not very far. I knew that the remaining 13 miles are viewed as the toughest section of the 186-mile Pembrokeshire Coast Path, with steep ascents and descents and vast distances of isolation, so I was slightly concerned about reaching Newport before it got dark. I tackled the hill out of Poppit at good pace, and walked well until a nice couple pointed out a seal colony on the beach far below the cliffs of Cemaes Head. I could spot over 20 of them sitting on rocks or lazing about in the protected cove, and spent a while standing watching them from my towering observation point. After pointing them out to a couple of other people, I marched onwards, enjoying the stunning cliffs and rock formations that had been promised. The folds of the rock were formed millions of years ago when the old seabed was crunched and lifted due to tectonic plate activity and the result today is a set of huge swirls running through each giant rock face. When the sun was out, the sea that gently lapped at the base of these domineering cliffs turned a beautiful turquoise-blue and the odd seal would pop their head up to keep me company. I was loving the path as much as I'd hoped to, and reached Ceibwr Bay in good spirits.

Things were set to change though. I was using the only bit of mobile signal that I'd found all day to update Valmai on my progress, and must have missed a waymarker. Following a path past a cottage above Ceibwr Bay, I ended up in an overgrown mix of briars, nettles and thistles. Seeing an acorn signpost and being fed up of wandering around getting stung, I made a beeline for the path through a very dense briar thicket which tore my legs to shreds. Mopping up blood from my shins and knees, I cursed my decisions of the last ten minutes and dropped down to the beach. Being in a less than happy mood, I didn't fully appreciate the beauty of the bay until I was standing above it on the south side. There are numerous caves and rock formations in the dark cliffs and the beach sits nestled back into a steep-sided cove. It was a very beautiful scene and momentarily distracted me from beating myself up over my earlier stupidity.

A short while later, I met Franziska and Henrik, who are from Germany and on holiday in the UK. I stopped to chat to them after noticing their large rucksacks and they explained that after some time hiking and wild swimming in the Brecon Beacons, they were hiking the whole Pembrokeshire Coast Path. On finishing tomorrow, they'll take the bus to Holyhead and a ferry over to Ireland. They were having quite some holiday and after discussing our walks so far, we set about planning new adventures both at home and abroad. Before we knew it, 45 minutes had passed and we had to get cracking if we were to reach our destinations by sunset. It had been a pleasure to meet them, even if their parting words about an overgrown section of path worried my already stinging legs.

If I'm being honest, I was disappointed with the path from Ceibwr to Newport. There were some impressively high cliffs, but the view didn't change around every corner like it had this morning. The path was overgrown in many places, which I'd not expected on the Pembrokeshire Coast until the earlier warning, and the seals had long since vanished. My mood was as flat as the terrain was hilly, and I struggled to enjoy anything. My only saving grace was that my legs were strong on the undulating ground and so I completed the nine isolated miles quickly, feeling a sense of achievement on arrival at Newport Sands.

After a nice detour along the beach and foraging for some wild damsons, I rounded a corner to see Valmai, Jen and Bisto walking towards me. I was an hour earlier than I'd told Valmai I would be, so we took in some of the beautiful countryside on the way home. I can see why both Valmai and Jen love staying in the cottage as it really is situated in a great location! Following a cup of tea and a shower, I wolfed down Valmai's tasty chilli dinner and was presented with a Welsh flag wallet for donations and a pin badge for my bag. It was such a lovely gift from Valmai and Jen as they had satisfied my urge to have the Welsh flag somewhere in my kit. I'll be truly sorry to leave the cottage tomorrow morning, knowing that I won't be returning in the evening. Valmai and Jen have been so welcoming and kind during my three days of walking nearby, and their care and company have made this section of walking so much more enjoyable. Words cannot begin to describe how thankful I am. I know that we'll keep in touch regularly for the remainder of my walk.

Over the next three or four days, I'll be walking paths that I've trodden before on family holidays. I know the scenery is spectacular, but I'm interested to see what effect the familiarity of the walking will have on my state of mind. I may feel homesick because I'm walking these paths without Mum, Dad and Em, or I may feel closer to them because of all the happy memories we've shared in this area. It may be a mixture of both depending on my mood. I guess only time will tell, but I do know that I'm looking forward to the beauty that lies ahead.

Nos da, pawb! I'll see you all tomorrow after a 24-mile hike along paths that I know and love.

Day 35
Newport to Pwll Deri

It was strange packing my bag to its full weight again this morning, knowing that I wouldn't be returning to Valmai and Jen's cottage tonight. Thanks to their warmth, kindness and generosity, the place has grown to feel like home, even after such a short space of time. After driving back to Newport, the four of us (including Bisto the dog) walked along the tidal inlet and out the other side of the town. Too soon, it was time to part and hit the coast path for my longest day of walking since my last day on Anglesey. Valmai and Jen have been incredible over the last three days, and have made my challenge so much more enjoyable. As I looked at the new pin badge on my bag with the flags of Wales and St David, I knew for sure that we would meet again in the near future.

The path to Dinas Head is undulating and winding as it navigates around coves and cliffs. The views are beautiful, and were made even more so by the bright sunshine. Reaching Cwm-Yr-Eglwys after an hour and a half, I hit ground that I had walked with my family last year. It felt good to be back here and as I sat on the bench next to the one remaining wall of the old church, I could almost see Mum, Dad and Em wandering around exploring and trying to find the start of the path to Dinas Head. I had a little smile to myself, and set about the climb to 170 m above sea level.

I talked to a few friendly groups of people on the way up to the summit and even more by the trig point itself. This was by far the busiest stretch of path I've been on since leaving home, probably due to Dinas Head's reputation as a stunning part of a beautiful national trail. I think I'm going to have to get used to my peaceful coast paths being a little more congested for the next week. The views from the summit were gorgeous, despite a little haze, and I watched with interest as the ferry from Ireland docked in Fishguard Harbour.

After returning to sea level, I stopped in a little restaurant to have lunch, and got talking to a group I'd met in Cwm-Yr-Eglwys. Half were Canadian and half were their Welsh relatives, and all were very kind; leaving me with three different donations. My bag kept receiving attention as I ate and I left with a total of £35 in sponsorship! Spurred on once again by the generosity of strangers, I tackled the tricky six miles to Fishguard. The scenery on this section was spectacular, with jagged outcrops of rock reaching towards large stacks that stand proudly in the sea. The water itself was a million different shades of blue, and I walked along transfixed by the new vistas that were being revealed around each bend or over each rise on the path.

Eventually, I reached Fishguard after some very tiring walking. Having a look around the ruined little fort with its four cannons, I wondered what it had been used for – it turns out that in 1779 *The Black Prince*, an American privateer, appeared off the coast and demanded a ransom from the townspeople. When this was refused, the ship began a bombardment of the upper town. A surviving cannonball was recently found embedded in a thick hotel wall during renovations! A local smuggler took the defence of his hometown into his own hands and, using his one cannon, kept up such an accurate attack on the privateer that they were forced to flee. The local authority built the fort to defend themselves against the possibility of similar future attacks.

Arriving in Goodwick shortly afterwards, I bought some breakfast biscuits and headed for another part of the path that I had walked with family during our holiday in the town last year. It was nearly five o'clock, and I knew that the eight miles from here to the youth hostel that I was booked into were tough ones. All day, I'd been dropping steeply down into coves and immediately climbing equally steeply to get back out of them. My legs were aching and I wanted to take the remaining miles slowly, but I was faced with an issue that wasn't there at the start of my challenge, and will be getting worse as I get closer to the end. Daylight hours. Every day after the summer solstice, we lose roughly two minutes of daylight in the evening. That may not seem a lot, but having left home on 26th July, walked for 35 days and had two rest days, I now have an hour and a quarter less daylight in the evenings than I did on Offa's Dyke. Sunset tonight was at 8.10 p.m., and I did not have any desire to walk the cliff path by torchlight. So despite my sore legs and the 14 draining miles already covered today, the last eight were going to have to be the quickest.

After a brief snack on a bench and a chat with a nice local photographer, I ignored the stiffness in my legs and hiked quickly for three miles until I was stopped in my tracks by an incredibly loud moan from a cave far below. I looked down to see five seals settling in for the night. Two were jostling for position, hence the loud calls, and a scuffle broke out as I watched. It didn't take long to decide a winner, and the defeated warrior slunk back to her inferior spot on the pebbles. Telling myself that I had to get shifting, I made great time for the next 200 m, where my attention was grabbed again by more seals! This time there were nine of them on a beach: seven adults and two pups. One pup looked fairly old, but the other was still covered in its white baby fluff and was thoroughly uncoordinated as it rolled left and right, trying to move along the beach towards the crowd. I stood and watched for at least ten minutes before dragging myself away again, only to bump into Jasmine around the next corner. Jasmine is a writer and has just got back from walking the Camino de Santiago in Spain. We spent a really lovely 20 minutes discussing hiking and the beauty of the local area that we were in, and that she was lucky enough to grow up in. Eventually parting to continue in opposite directions, Jasmine took a card with the address of my blog on. I hope my amateur writing is up to standard!

The sun was getting low in the sky and I knew that I now had to walk hard for two hours to reach the hostel by sundown. I didn't once regret stopping for the seals or for Jasmine, as I had wanted to do so and had enjoyed each occasion greatly. If worst came to worst and cliff walking got too dangerous in the dark, I would just find a spot to pitch my tent and call in at the hostel to explain in the morning. After passing a set of tiny 'fairy swings' in a magical little wooded valley, I dropped down to a cove that Mum, Dad and Em had had a close seal encounter in last year. I had been ill at the time, and so had missed out on being so close to 'Scooby' – as they had affectionately named their wild marine friend. You can imagine my delight and amazement when I dropped into the same cove to find 'Scooby' very close to shore with a friend! We stared inquisitively at each other for a wonderful few minutes until they dived under, and I took the chance to leave. I knew that if they resurfaced, I'd sit and watch them all night!

I soon started listening to some film soundtracks (without earphones) to distract me from my tiredness and what happened next actually made me gasp out loud. As a particularly happy and moving soundtrack was playing, a seal started singing along! The calls were very different to the aggressive moans and grunts of earlier, sounding much happier and more tuneful. I could see the seal bobbing in the water and every time she called in response to the music, the hairs on the back of my neck stood up instantly. When a new track started, she stopped her calls, obviously not as keen on *Braveheart* as she was on *We Bought A Zoo*, so I flicked back to the previous song and she started singing again. It was a magical moment that I know will be a highlight of this trip and something that I will remember for years to come. A moment when I truly connected with a wild animal through enjoyment of music, and felt totally at one with nature.

Strumble Head emerged over the next crest, and I snapped a few photos of the picturesque lighthouse on its rugged outcrop of rock before walking away from the bright warning beam towards Pwll Deri. I had a little over 40 minutes before sunset, and two miles to travel. This was doable, despite the previous 22 punishing miles, and I was on target until the sun dipped below the clouds in its last moments before disappearing beyond the horizon. My first indication that this sunset was going to be extra special was the sudden deep orange light that bathed the hill above the bay. I half walked, half ran to a higher point to get a view of it, and was treated to a sky full of deep oranges and pale purples and the sun dipping its toes in the sea. Silhouetting the jagged headland that I'd just walked over, the sun slipped below the horizon and the temperature plummeted. I looked to my left and could thankfully see the hostel with its lights on.

Ten minutes and a final steep climb later, I checked in and was taken to a room to choose my comfortable bed. The Pwll

Deri hostel is kept so nicely by its volunteer staff, and I felt at home as soon as I walked in. The hosts are lovely and the windows look out over a beautiful bay. I could see the lights of all the little settlements that I know so well, having stayed in many of them on family holidays. Tomorrow, I'll walk through each one on my way to Whitesands Bay, where we've spent countless happy days relaxing on the beach, bodyboarding in the waves, exploring caves and coves that are only accessible at low tide and of course, playing many different competitive sports! It'll be my second 24-mile day in a row, but with beautiful clifftop scenery and a thousand happy memories to be stirred around each corner, I know my legs can go the distance.

Nos da, pawb. I'll see you all at sunset on Whitesands Bay tomorrow evening.

Day 36
Pwll Deri to Whitesands

I managed to sleep through another alarm this morning. As a result, my eight o'clock start became nine o'clock after I'd hurriedly packed my bag, wolfed down some breakfast and thanked my hosts for a comfortable night in the hostel and for their donation. My aim for the day was to walk 24 miles at good pace to get to Whitesands Bay before sunset. On family holidays, we'd often drive down to the beach to watch the sun dip into the sea behind St David's Head, once even swimming as it happened. As I started my first mile of the day in bright sunshine, I knew that that was how I wanted it to end.

I completed the four miles to Abermawr in such good time that I allowed myself half an hour to sit on the pebble beach and relax. The waves were gently rippling on the rocks and I knew that within two miles, I'd be hitting the 40-mile stretch of coast that I've trodden before, albeit a couple of miles at a time, with my family. Each step along the familiar ground would bring back memories of happy afternoons walking in the sun with those I love the most. I knew it was beautiful, I knew I was likely to see seals, and I knew it would feel like arriving home.

The coastline from Abermawr onwards is stunning. The sun was lighting up the crystal-clear water as it swirled around the base of numerous rocky outcrops. A group of kayakers were paddling in and out of each little nook and cranny and they stayed alongside me all the way into Abercastle. I sat on the bench here to have a quick snack, having completed eight and a half miles in very good time to get here. The bench overlooked the pretty little harbour and also the car park. It was the latter that put a big grin on my face. One holiday, when we were staying in Porthgain, we'd visited Abercastle in the evening. On arriving back at the cottage in darkness, Dad realised he didn't have the key. After searching all over and turning the car inside out, we started to retrace the day's steps in reverse order. Suspecting they'd fallen out of his bag in Abercastle, we positioned the car to light up as much ground as possible and set about scouring the gravel. Em was the hero of the night, announcing with a shout that she'd found them. We've never let Dad live it down since!

My next stop was Trefin. We've stayed here on holiday, and love sitting and watching the sunset from the picturesque pebble bay. My stomach was grumbling, so I decided to stop for lunch in the Ship Inn. The family owners were so friendly, donating £10 to my fundraising and offering to sell some novelty straws that they had been given for the charity as well! The food was amazing too, and I met a nice couple as I was finishing up. After chatting for a while, I had to get shifting. I'd made excellent time in the morning, covering 12 miles before lunch, and so could afford to take it a little easier during the afternoon's 12 provided I started them early enough.

Porthgain was just a short walk along the coast, and I could almost see my family walking along the harbour wall as we've done on many evenings. The village is very pretty, and the

137

coastline that lies either side is incredible too. The short walk to Abereiddy brought me to the Blue Lagoon, which is going to be the site of an international cliff diving championships this month. The 28 m and 20 m platforms were being secured into the rockface, and to stand at the bottom looking up gave a true impression of how high they are. The divers are either brave or mad. Probably a good mixture of both!

On the way out of Abereiddy, I met Fiona and we walked and chatted together for a good distance. She's on holiday in the area and has been walking as much of the coastal path as she can, averaging about 25 miles a day! When Fiona stopped for a break, I forged ahead and soon spotted a very young seal pup rolling around a beach far below. Stopping to watch the newborn's laboured attempts at moving on land, I stayed ten minutes before deciding that it was time to move on. As I walked away, I hoped that Fiona would spot the cute pup too.

More dramatic cliff views and stunning scenery later, I heard a noise that I'm growing to know well now. More seals! I looked over into a very sheltered cove, and saw a mother seal fending off an intruder to her family home. The pup was sitting ashore playing with a plastic bottle. It was banging it on rocks, chewing it and whenever a wave came and drew its toy away, the pup would give chase and retrieve it from whichever rock it had got wedged under. I didn't know how to feel, with two strong but conflicting emotions hitting me at once. On the one hand, what I was seeing was incredibly cute and the pup was obviously very happy. On the other hand though, this plastic bottle was pollution and should never be found where it was. It could be dangerous to wildlife and it certainly wasn't a natural toy for the pup to have selected, however much it was enjoying playing. As I sat entranced, Fiona caught me up and we watched the show for a while before cracking on.

Just as Fiona was about to turn inland, we came across another bay of seals. Four became six, and after bidding goodbye to my walking companion, six became ten! They were riding the waves into shore, rolling back down the pebbles to the water and lying out in the afternoon sun; a picture of happiness. Tearing myself away, I rounded St David's Head – the most westerly point of my walk – and practically ran the last mile into Whitesands Bay. Banks of cloud were rolling in from the sea, so my romantic idea of a sunset swim had gone out of the window. I was just praying that the café was still open, as although I had enough food to sustain me overnight, I'd be using nearly all of my emergency rations to do so.

As I arrived in the car park, the owner locked the front door of the café and I ran over to tap on the window. Thankfully, seeing my desperate look, she let me in and cooked me a meat and potato pasty and a sausage bap. It was such a lovely thing to do and I was so grateful after three hungry miles at the end my day. I pitched in a small spot at the already full campsite and was given a shower token by a group of regulars who told me to join them once I was done.

After filling up and freshening up, I felt human again, and went to join Ted, Cat, Joe, Callan and Matthew in their gazebo-style area. Sharing a few drinks (or one, in my very disciplined case – which I was given free and promised some sponsorship if I drank it – win win!) we talked and laughed the evening away until nearly 11 p.m. The time had flown by, and it felt amazing to be in such a great, sociable group for a while. I've missed that type of social interaction, and it was really hard to leave to go back to my tent!

I'm now curled up in my sleeping bag, listening to the wind and rain outside. My tent has so far proved to be infallible in keeping the elements at bay, so I feel confident that the night will be a dry one, even if I am packing away a wet outer layer in the morning. Tomorrow will be an easier day, spending a relaxed morning at Whitesands before heading along the path towards Newgale – about 17 miles away.

Nos da, pawb. I'll see you all tomorrow when I've walked the section of coast that I've walked more often than any other.

Day 37
Whitesands to Caerfai

I decided that I was going to have an easier day today. Having covered near enough 50 miles in the previous two days, my legs were in need of a shorter one. I slept a full nine hours in my tent through wind and rain, and woke up feeling refreshed. Matthew gave me a generous donation on my way to the café for breakfast, and the owners of the site refused to take any money for my pitch. Thank you both! I enjoyed a leisurely breakfast in the café, chatting to the staff about my challenge, and then Ted walked in. We hung out for a while before I had to shoot off, but not before Callan popped in to say goodbye. I thoroughly enjoyed spending time with these Whitesands Bay Campsite regulars last night and this morning, and they made the place feel really special. Part of me just wanted to stay put and join them as a summer site resident. However, the lure of revisiting some of my favourite childhood holiday spots was too great, and I eventually got going at about 11 a.m.

A short way along the coast path, I looked down onto the far side of Whitesands and saw the spot that my family claims whenever we visit the beach. It's far away from the car park and the crowds, and is nestled into a pretty little cove that isn't accessible at high tide. I saw a little track leading to the cliff, and couldn't resist scrambling down to spend half an hour in a place where so many happy family memories have been made. It was strange being there alone, but visions of us playing tennis on the empty sand and hammering pyrite crystals out of the rocks played before my eyes like a movie and I felt closer to home than I have in a long time.

I dragged myself away at about midday and after rejoining the coast path, I bumped into a lovely elderly couple who were admiring the views across the beach. Both well into their eighties, we spoke of favourite Pembrokeshire spots and they told me that they used to live in the little green house above the beach. Mum has often looked at those few small houses and longed to own one, so to meet someone who actually had lived there was amazing! We set off in separate directions and as I walked away, I thought to myself that if I was still able to hike so far uphill to my favourite coastal spot at the age of 88, I would be very proud of myself!

The two miles to St Justinian were pretty and on arrival in the small bay, I was surprised to see a brand new lifeboat station next to the old one that I'm so familiar with. It looked very impressive and towers over the old one, which is just a few metres away. Beyond this point is a stretch of coast that I've walked with my family nearly every time we've been in Pembrokeshire. It has a perfect mix of beautiful scenery, interesting wildlife and fantastically fast-flowing waters. At the bay where we always saw seals, I saw a seal! After pointing it out to some fellow walkers, I continued my trip along memory lane and saw many more, all bobbing about lazily in the turquoise water and enjoying the sudden emergence of the hot sun. Ramsey Island was a beautiful mix of greens, browns, purples and dramatic black cliffs, which contrasted perfectly with the bright blues of the dangerous waters of Ramsey Sound. The currents around the rocks known as The Bitches are treacherous to navigate, and as I stood on the point watching the swirling torrents of water racing past in all manner of different directions, it was easy to see why.

The path continues to be beautiful all the way around the headland and I was soon arriving in St Non's Bay. St Non was the mother of St David, and there is a ruin of a small chapel where the famous patron saint of Wales is said to have been born. Nearby is a well which apparently sprang up during the stormy night that St Non gave birth, and a white statue of her stands opposite a modest arch. A few hundred metres away stands the current St Non's Chapel, which is tiny. I stepped inside the little church, totally alone, and felt the urge to light a candle for my late grandma and for my grandfather, who's currently in hospital following a fall that broke his hip. It's not been easy this week, being so far from home and feeling totally useless. I've had times where I've wanted to hop on a bus and go home to help out. So as I stood in the chapel lighting my candle, I said a little prayer for them both. I am not, nor have I ever been, a strong believer in religion, but this small moment made me feel like I was doing something to help, and I truly hoped that there was someone out there to listen.

A short while later, I arrived at the campsite in Caerfai. I'd walked about ten miles, but my legs were telling me it was time to stop as I've covered an awful lot of miles since my last rest day in Aberystwyth. The campsite is amazing and they've let me stay free, which is a real bonus! I think if last night's site was one of the best because of its people, tonight's is one of the best because of its facilities and location. I've washed all my clothes in the laundrette, have access to Wi-Fi from my tent and there is even a kitchen with free tea and coffee. Just what I needed!

I'm now in a pub in St David's, having amazingly bumped into my old secondary school German teacher, Mrs Victor, and had a nice chat. Another reminder of how small Wales really is! I'm sitting with a lovely German couple who let me share their table, and we've chatted the night away in between eating good food and my blog writing! If you make the effort to start a conversation with a stranger, it's amazing how many interesting things you'll discuss and learn. It's not something that's done very often in today's society, but it's something that makes each day of my trek special.

Today hasn't been great in terms of mileage, but it has been great in terms of people, scenery and memories. Tomorrow will be an easier day too, spending the morning exploring St David's Cathedral before walking eight miles to Newgale. I didn't want to take a rest day in Pembrokeshire because the interesting spots are mainly along the coast, but I hope that two short days will have the same effect for my body and mind.

Nos da, pawb. I'll see you tomorrow after walking through some more favourite spots from years past.

Day 38
Caerfai to Broad Haven

I'll start today's blog with yesterday. I woke up to the sound of my tent being battered by wind and rain. It was holding strong and I had no desire to poke my head out, so I went back to sleep! An hour and a half later, Mother Nature's bombardment was not letting up. My initial plan for the day had been to see St David's Cathedral in the morning and then walk to Newgale in the afternoon. However, after nearly getting blown off my feet just walking to the toilet block, I decided that walking along the slippery coast path with a bag that's much wider than I am and covered in a waterproof cover would be rather dangerous. It's felt like a sail on my back in far calmer conditions than that morning, so I made the sensible decision to take an enforced rest day and explore St David's a little more.

My first stop was the cathedral. It's so impressive from the outside, but I was actually a little disappointed with the interior. I guess that having recently been into St Paul's Cathedral in London, I was expecting something a little more ornate. This was much more functional. The tombs of various medieval bishops were interesting, and the treasury had some nice artefacts, but the centrepiece of the shrine of St David left me a little cold. It holds a great religious significance though, as two pilgrimages to St David's Shrine used to be the equivalent of one to Rome. Personally, I had felt a much stronger spiritual feeling the day before when I stood alone in the tiny chapel at St Non's. I did enjoy looking around and the building is very impressive, but maybe the mood I was in that morning was a little off due to being forced to change my day's plans.

Afterwards, I went to have a look around the Bishop's Palace, which is right next door. Despite receiving only a fraction of the money that cathedrals such as Winchester used to, Bishop Henry de Gower had made this palace the grandest in all medieval Britain. Despite its ruinous state today, the

143

upper-storey rooms certainly had a sense of grandeur about them. Intricate stone carvings can still be seen on the walls and the sheer size of the great hall and chapel were enough to impress. The contrast between the upper rooms and lower rooms was huge, and it was clear to see where the bishop and his important guests had lived. The lower rooms were much darker and more basic. With barely any windows, they gave a feeling of being underground and at one point, I was genuinely surprised to walk out into the grounds without going up any steps. The lower rooms were used to serve those in the upper rooms, and I could almost hear the hustle and bustle around the palace as I walked around.

After these two trips back in time, I went to the information centre and gallery following a tip from a man at the campsite. He'd told me that one of John Constable's six-foot masterpieces was on display until next week, and that it was worth a look. I've never been one to take an interest in art, as many who know me can confirm, but I had enjoyed seeing famous paintings in the National Gallery in London last year so thought I'd give this one a go. Standing in front of the painting, *Salisbury Cathedral From The Meadows*, I could see why Constable called it his greatest work. I was transfixed by the detail in the turbulent sky and even after looking for ten minutes or more, I was still spotting more little features in the foreground. It was quite something to behold, and I was glad I'd listened to the campsite receptionist and put aside my usual indifference towards art.

In the afternoon, I made full use of the campsite Wi-Fi and enjoyed a couple of films in the cosiness of my little tent and the lounge area. I enjoyed myself so much that packing away my canvas home this morning was quite upsetting. We'd ridden out the storm together and my tent had kept me completely dry for the duration. I liked it before, but I fell in love with it yesterday and combined with the excellence of the campsite's facilities, I didn't really want to leave. I think that when you're walking almost every day, to stay in one place for two nights makes it begin to feel like home. Everything stays as you left it for a whole day and you form a bond with the place. As I walked away this morning, despite the fact that my canvas home was on my back, I felt genuinely sad to be leaving our base at Caerfai behind.

This is a feeling that stayed with me for a lot of the day. The scenery was pretty, and I bumped into an old university mountain walking club friend, Matt, but after each little high point my spirits began to sink again. It was lovely walking through Solva harbour and remembering all of the happy times I've had with family while crab fishing from the harbour wall. The town is picture-postcard perfect too, and I enjoyed a hot meal in the pub right on the seafront. Walking away, the sadness hit me again and I began to understand why. Once I'd passed Newgale, I would be leaving the area that my family have frequented on holiday. The last four and a half days have felt so familiar, with happy memories around every corner, that I've felt as if I were on a holiday and would be going home soon. Coupled with the fact that I have now walked over 700 miles, home has felt very close indeed. But as I was walking towards Broad Haven, I thought about the nearly 400 unknown miles still to go, and how far away home really was.

There is a lot of beautiful scenery to be taken in between Newgale and Broad Haven. Newgale beach itself is a vast expanse of sand that stretches for miles. The centre is backed by pebbles and a road, but at either end the cliffs rise dramatically with many folds and layers to catch the eye. Beyond Newgale, the cliffs rise and fall with the occasional towering stack in the sea, and the headland that leads out towards Dale begins to come into focus. There are many tankers anchored off the coast here, which when coupled with the huge funnels I could see in the distance gave a hint about the type of walking that lies ahead. Before I reach the attractive southern section of the Pembrokeshire Coast Path, I'll have to walk through a lot of industry. Hopefully it'll be interesting, so I won't miss North Pembrokeshire as much as I fear I might.

Tonight, I'm staying at the youth hostel in Broad Haven to

give my tent a rest from the elements. I arrived with two guys who are doing five days of coastal walking here, and who I'd met a few times today on our identical routes. After an interesting shower that wavered in a constant scale between scorching hot and freezing cold (with me jumping in for the middle, warm sections), I met up with Matt again and we went to The Swan in Little Haven for a couple of drinks. It was great to catch up, as we haven't seen each other since university, and we chatted the evening away until well after ten. To spend some time with a friend was just what I needed at the end of a day where I've felt pretty flat. Hopefully the good end to today can carry on tomorrow and I'll enjoy exploring new coastline once more.

Nos da, pawb! I'll see you all in Dale tomorrow after my day's mileage has once again climbed above 20.

Day 39
Broad Haven to Dale

After taking full advantage of the youth hostel breakfast buffet, I set off just after nine for a day that would see me walking in many different directions around two peninsulas. Although I'd be covering a lot of miles on the ground, I wouldn't be getting much closer to home. In fact if anything, I'd be further away. This is something I'll have to get used to as there are two big peninsulas to come along the south Wales coast that will take me directly away from where I need to be going. I was interested to see how my mind would cope with walking the wrong way after yesterday's general slump.

The weather was dull this morning, with fog settled over the coast so that the pretty scenery that I knew was there might as well have been behind a three-foot-thick wall. I could only see things within a 20 m radius of myself, and occasionally a tantalising little glimpse of what I could be seeing would emerge, only to be erased by greyness again a moment later. I wasn't as down as I was yesterday, but I wouldn't say I was enjoying myself either. I was just getting on with the job in hand and walking at as good a pace as my legs could manage. There was the occasional distraction of blackberries and my fingers took on a purple hue for a couple of hours, but other than that there was nothing and nobody else in sight. It wasn't until mile six that I saw other people. I had a nice chat with Colin and his wife about the different trails we've walked and about North Wales. They live in Anglesey and have completed that section of the coast path, so we had an interesting chat about the changes that have occurred on the path in the intervening years between our circuits.

I stopped for lunch in Martin's Haven and while eating, my bag sign received attention from no less than four separate groups of people! One group comprised of five ladies who are walking the Pembrokeshire Coast Path in three sections over three years. They were going in the opposite direction to me so we shared information about our future routes, and then between them, the ladies left me with £20 in donations. Thank you! This raised my spirits a little and the mention of seal pups just over the headland gave me something to look forward to. I think that is part of the reason why I've felt low recently. Until last week, I've always had a visit from family or an arrival at a friend's house to aim for. A date had been set so I knew how long it would be until I saw a familiar face. I had something to look forward to in the not too distant future. I haven't got a set plan to meet up with anyone at the moment, so instead of walking towards a meeting, I'm just walking along as far as I can. The lack of a short term goal was making the last 400 miles seem colossal. On recognising this issue, I stopped dwelling on how far there was to go and made a big effort just to focus on reaching the end of the day. This restored some positivity into my thinking, but it was nothing compared to the effect that the wildlife of Martin's Haven was about to have!

On arrival at the cliff edge above a little bay, I quickly spotted the snow-white fur of six seal pups. Three of them still had distinct necks, which meant they could be no more than ten days old and possibly much less. As I stood and watched, I scanned the beach and eventually spotted a total of ten adult seals. One pup was suckling from mum and when full, it went off in search of adventure. Smelling and nudging every little rock that it came across, the pup moved clumsily while trying to propel itself forward with front and rear flippers. It was struggling to change direction and mum was turning around on the spot, occasionally nudging her pup and seemingly trying to teach it to manoeuvre on land with equipment that is ill designed for the job. I felt privileged to be allowed to witness this intimate moment between mother and child, and watched for a good half hour before forcing myself to walk on. A hundred metres later, I happened upon a second similar bay that contained three pups and seven adults. Absorbed by the scene in front of me once more, it took a further ten minutes for me to tear myself away.

Mother Nature wasn't going to let me escape that easily though. I spotted a bird with very straight wings circling in the distance and wondered if it might be a fulmar. I've only ever seen one before, and as I tried to figure out if I was correct in thinking that this was my second, a very definite third shot past my face no more than a metre away. I watched as the pair danced on the turbulent winds above the clifftops, and the avian display was added to piece by piece in front of my eyes. A gannet flew past low over the water, two kestrels were hovering over the path nearby, choughs performed aerial acrobatics, gulls of every sort were soaring overhead and oystercatchers were sitting on the cliffs providing a soundtrack to the awe-inspiring performance. The cliffs were sharp and jagged and the fast-flowing waters being forced between the mainland and Gateholm Island completed the scene with a dramatic backdrop. I could have stopped and watched all day, but time was marching on and I wasn't! There were still ten miles to go, and I didn't want to lose daylight on a day as misty as this.

I met two nice couples in the next ten minutes and chatted to both for a short while, before upping my pace greatly. The fog thickened to the point where I could barely see the beautiful Marloes Sands that was little more than 20 m below me. We spent a day here once on a family holiday, and the jagged outcrops of rock that litter the beach were something I was looking forward to seeing again. I was a little disappointed not to be seeing the incredible views that I knew were there to be seen, but I genuinely think that if the weather had been as beautiful as the scenery, I would still be walking now – four hours after I actually finished!

The fog had thickened to a point where I had no idea whereabouts on the coast path I was, but on rounding St Ann's Head I finally started walking towards Dale. I'd been less than half a mile away an hour ago, but the shape of the peninsula meant that I still had five miles of walking to do from that spot. A heartbreaking realisation when you've already done 18 miles of walking that day. There was interest at Mill Bay, where a plaque informed me that this tiny inlet had a big claim to fame. It was here that Henry Tudor landed his 4,000 man army before marching east to the Battle of Bosworth, picking up support along the way. After his victory, Henry became King Henry VII and the Tudor era of British history began. An era that took its first steps on this misty, windswept peninsula in south-west Wales.

I arrived on the campsite at half seven, hurriedly putting my tent up with the aim of getting to the pub in Dale before it stopped serving food. A kind man from a camper van opposite my pitch gave me a £20 donation, and while eating a tasty burger in the Griffin Inn 20 minutes later, I got chatting to a family who ended up giving me £15 – thank you to you all for your generosity!

I'm now back in my tent with the prospect of a later start tomorrow. There are two sections that cannot be crossed until a couple of hours after high tide, so I'll be forced to have a lie in. I'm sure I'll cope.

Nos da, pawb. I'll see you tomorrow when I've ventured into some very industrialised coastline.

Day 40
Dale to Milford Haven

I was able to have a big lie-in this morning. There are two little estuaries that meet the sea between Dale and Milford Haven and the coast path goes across a low footbridge at each one. However, the footbridges are submerged for two and half hours either side of high tide, resulting in a potential four-mile inland diversion at each one. Knowing that high tide was at half nine this morning, I decided to sleep in and relax in my tent until midday, before packing up to go back to the Griffin Inn for food. I'd then walk 12 and a half miles to a campsite just the other side of Milford Haven.

After loosely planning my next week of walking, I enjoyed fish and chips and set off along the path once more. I could still feel yesterday's 24 miles in my legs and the humid air made the going quite tough, but the sweet blackberries that lined much of today's route kept me well fuelled. There wasn't an overly large amount to enjoy in terms of scenery. Some bays were quite pretty but compared to northern Pembrokeshire, this section was dull. In between my tidal river crossings, I met two hikers who looked like they were carrying even more than I was. Intrigued, I asked where they were headed to (St David's) and we got chatting. Melanie and Bradley are brother and sister. She lives in Australia and he lives in Canada and their four days of walking a beautiful section of the coast path was something of a reunion. I loved their idea as there is no greater way to spend time with somebody than on a long walk. You have hours to talk, see each other's high and low points and help each other to reach the end of the day. My mind sprang back to Emily and me hiking in Snowdonia together, and what a brilliant thing it had been to do with the person who has been my best friend since she was born. I'm sure that Bradley and Melanie must have a close bond too and that it will be even stronger after these four days, even if they are on opposite sides of the planet. They were such lovely people, and we agreed that we must stay in contact.

After my second river crossing, I had a chat on the phone with Dad. Whilst we were chatting, a lady read my bag and mouthed that she'd see me before I left. When the phone call was cut short by poor signal, I went to find the lady and was invited to sit on her rock on the beach. Janet was litter picking – she does so most days – and had built up quite a pile in the ten minutes since reading my bag. It's sad to think that so much washes up on our coastline, and it made me wonder how much litter pollution is floating around in the seas around us if that much can be found on one tiny section of beach in ten minutes. Janet and I spoke for a while – she knows people in Kington, six miles from my home – and I helped a tiny bit by finding a small handful of litter under the cliff as we talked. Nothing compared to the work Janet has done, but as Tesco say, 'Every little helps!' It was lovely talking to Janet, but the time soon came to move on again and tackle the remaining four miles to Milford Haven.

These miles took me into true industrial country. Oil refineries dominate views all around, with towering chimneys and huge jetties that reach out to the deep water channel in the middle of the estuary. After walking under one of these jetties and climbing the next headland, the largest refinery came into sight. It sits on the southern shores of the inlet, almost directly opposite Milford Haven and although it is known locally as the Texaco refinery (having been owned by Texaco since 1964), it has recently been bought by Valero. Five colossal tankers were docked at the vast jetty and what must have been millions of gallons of oil were being pumped off. Although the sight was interesting, I couldn't help thinking about how beautiful this area could be without the interference of humans. Milford Haven itself is a town that was founded in 1790 as a centre of the whaling industry and was developed into a naval dockyard in 1800. It gradually became a commercial port and then in the 1960s it grew into the hive of petrochemical activity that it is today. The days of natural beauty are long forgotten, but hopefully one day of putting my head down and walking a good distance will bring me back into Mother Nature's territory by the end of tomorrow.

I'm now blog writing in the comfort of my tent (though this won't be posted until lunchtime tomorrow when I find Wi-Fi) on a lovely campsite just the other side of Milford Haven. The owner of Eco Escape has very kindly let me stay for free, and I feel totally relaxed in my tiny tent next to the large glamping tents! However wonderful they look, I'm happier in my little canvas home, having fallen in love with her during last week's storms. I did enjoy the hot shower though! I had two nice phone calls tonight, one with dad while mum was cycling, and one with mum while dad wasn't cycling! It was nice to touch base and hear news from Presteigne, and to share stories from my past week of Welsh wandering. We've arranged to meet near Llanelli on Tuesday next week when Em flies back to Cardiff from the US open in New York. I can't wait to see my little sister again, as it's been a long time since we've even been in the same country and I know we'll both have some very interesting tales to tell. It's also given me another short term goal to work towards, which I know will help me stay more positive over the next six days.

Nos da, pawb. I'll see you tomorrow when I've spent an entire day walking in almost exactly the opposite direction to where I need to be going. It could be an interesting one mentally and emotionally.

PS I've now more than tripled my original fundraising target! I cannot begin to express my gratitude to everyone who has been kind enough to donate whatever they can to Alzheimer's Society on my behalf.

Postscript

In an adventure full of new experiences, I had an unusual one on the campsite that night. As the name may suggest, Eco Escape campsite is a place that tries to impact on nature as little as possible. Rather than having a toilet that would need plumbing and would waste an awful lot of water, they have a composting toilet. I'd never heard of these before, so I will enlighten you to the details in case you, like me, have only experienced toilets that have water in them! Lifting the lid, you are met with a toilet seat that opens up to a hole in the ground filled by a large container. There is a white chute at the front for liquid waste, meaning men too have to sit down and aim when having a 'number one'. For 'number twos', you aim for the hole and try not to hit the liquid chute. You don't realise how accustomed to a splash you are, until it isn't there! Once the deed is done, you simply sprinkle sawdust down the hole. I was expecting this to be a rather unpleasant experience, but in reality, it was rather nice! There was no smell the following morning and the knowledge that you're saving water makes you feel quite good about yourself! Still, I wouldn't like to be the person that empties the container, so I don't think I'll be making the switch at home just yet.

Day 41
Milford Haven to Angle

I'm going to start today a little differently – by telling you about the end first. Standing by Pembroke Castle at 4.30 p.m., I was left with just over 11 miles of walking to do in the remaining three hours of daylight. I was going to have to walk at a faster pace than I have done in my whole Welsh Wander to date, and I already had 12 fast-paced miles in my legs from earlier in the day. There were three reasons for my delay: my amazing ability to convince myself that I can have an extra half hour of sleep in the morning, finding Wi-Fi, and Fiona Bruce.

So back to the beginning of Day 41. I slept in a little later than I'd originally intended to and then spent a long time packing my bag. The result was a near ten o'clock start instead of the nine o'clock one that I'd hoped for. My planned 23 miles had just become a little more challenging. I soon made up for the late start though, as I set a good pace for the first two hours of walking. The gigantic wind turbines that I walked under provided a little interest and I had to restrain myself from picking too many blackberries, but other than that I was able to put my head down and crack on.

Reaching Neyland in good time, I climbed the hill to the two bridges that carry a road and pavement high above two estuaries. The views were interesting, if not pretty, and I was growing accustomed to the sight of towering chimneys and oil refineries dotted along the inlet. The largest bridge delivers you into Pembroke Dock, where I stopped for lunch in the Shipwright Inn. After an elderly gentleman helped me through the narrow door with my large bag, I got chatting to him and his wife about my challenge before repeating the story to the lady behind the bar. While tucking into a tasty hunter's chicken, the elderly couple took the addresses of my blog and Just Giving page and the landlady gave me a donation of £10. The kindness of strangers had once again amazed me. I then spent far too long using the Wi-Fi to catch up with various social media notifications before heading to the bar to pay, where the landlord refused to take any money! This final kind gesture sent me on my way with a huge smile on my face, and I made short work of the two miles to Pembroke.

Having been unimpressed with the scenery and the look of the towns in the inlet so far, I was completely taken aback by Pembroke. The impressive castle stands proudly on a crag of rock overlooking a quaint town centre and pretty river. The path around the castle's base gave a true impression of the brilliance of the eleventh-century architects who'd first built it and the thirteenth-century architects who'd adapted it. I'd been warned about the crowds that would be around the castle due to the fact that the *Antiques Roadshow* was being filmed there today, but on this path there were few other people. Leaving Pembroke, I looked back at the castle and then at my watch. When would I get the chance to go and see the *Antiques Roadshow* being filmed again? I wanted to come back to go around the castle anyway, so why not pop in for half an hour today? I'd still have plenty time to get to the campsite in Angle if I left by half three.

Returning to the castle, I had a chat with the stewards and then made for the biggest crowd. There sat Fiona Bruce filming an interview about an interesting piece of crystal. I watched for a while before wandering around the castle to get a taste for everything else there was to see. When I got back, Fiona was moving to a different table to see a man with a strange-looking hat. I thought that maybe after this interview, I could get her attention and maybe prompt a donation or a share on Twitter to boost my fundraising. I couldn't see any harm in trying, anyway! I ended up standing right behind her while the interview was filmed, and so am almost guaranteed to be on television when the episode airs... keep an eye out for the scruffy, bearded man in amongst the crowds of people dressed in their Sunday best!

The strange hat turned out to be a cap worn by the Pope during the Second World War, and the man's stories about it were fascinating. After shooting the interview from one angle, the camera was positioned differently and Frank was asked to repeat the interview in a similar way to his first effort. I couldn't help but laugh when he changed a rather big detail of his story the second time around. Fiona had asked Frank if he'd ever worn the cap, to which he'd replied 'No!' However, in interview two, he surprised everyone by saying 'Once!' The look of shock on the cameraman's face was brilliant, but Fiona handled it very professionally, asking for more details. Frank revealed that he had donned the very precious historical artefact during a visit from his grandchildren, where he'd put it on his head for the first and only time and danced around the living room saying 'Look kids! I'm the pope!' I'll leave it to final cut to see which version of Frank's story gets in.

After standing watching the interview twice, it was after four o'clock and I was hoping Fiona would get up soon so that I could get her attention, hopefully get her support and then rapidly get on my way. However, the interview started a third time with close-up camera angles on the cap itself. At this point, I knew it was a lost cause and I had to move on. I'd already phoned to campsite in Angle to book my spot, and would have a huge day tomorrow if I didn't get there tonight. I left feeling a little dejected and was beating myself up for spending so long in Pembroke. I had received some interest from other people in the castle though, and so had had some kind donations already which stopped me feeling completely down. I was also glad that I'd seen some amazing antiques and Fiona Bruce, but I now had a huge challenge ahead of me.

I walked like I was on an army route march for eight miles to get to Angle Bay. The trip around the Valero refinery was fairly interesting, with tankers docked at the jetty and the occasional jet of flame from a tower, but there was a very oily smell in the air too. I couldn't decide if I liked the area or not. After stopping for a much-needed and very rushed bite to eat, I had a brief but pleasant chat to a policeman who was letting the police dog out for a run. We enjoyed the beauty of the sinking sun and discussed the peacefulness of the spot, despite the power station. His love of the area was infectious and I began to share it. Although industry has clearly dominated any natural beauty that was once here, there is a certain charm to it that grows on you after a while. The policeman offered me a lift, which I was sorely tempted to take, but I turned it down and accepted that I'd probably be arriving in Angle by torchlight.

During the last three miles, my legs found a new lease of life. The occasional sharp pain in my feet disappeared when I ignored it, and I arrived in Angle with enough light left to have a chat to two nice walkers in a tent next to my spot before I pitched. They're walking the whole Pembrokeshire Coast Path in the opposite direction, so we were able to share campsite tips for our routes ahead.

I'm now sitting in a pub that looks over the bright lights of the refinery – it's a rather pretty sight. Today has been a challenging one, but it's had many high points to keep me positive. I'm glad that I stopped in Pembroke, and I'm proud of the following 11 miles that I walked in three hours. Tomorrow will see me rounding the peninsula and heading in the right direction again. I'll also be returning to the natural beauty that Pembrokeshire is famous for, which is something I'm looking forward to despite my slightly growing affection for the industrial landscape.

Nos da, pawb. I'll see you all tomorrow after I've enjoyed cliffs again, before detouring inland to avoid the flying bullets of a military firing range.

Day 42
Angle to Bosherston

Last night in the Old Point House Inn on Angle Point, I enjoyed an hour indoors writing my blog and was engaged in conversation afterwards by two regulars and the landlord. We spoke at length about Alzheimer's, the Welsh Coast and about my challenge. As I went to leave, one of the regulars donated £5 and the landlord ran to the till to fetch a £20 note, explaining that his mother had died of Alzheimer's. Again, I was reminded just how many people dementia has touched. I'd been grateful just to sit in the pub with a drink and use the Wi-Fi, and I was leaving with £25 in sponsorship. Feeling incredibly grateful, I took a moment to enjoy the bright, colourful lights of the refinery reflecting in the water and then went back to my tent in the campsite, where I was staying free of charge. It had been a tiring day, and I soon sank into a sleep that was deep enough for the heavy rain we had overnight not to wake me up.

This morning started with another nice chat to the walkers who are doing the Pembrokeshire Path in the other direction, and they pointed me in the direction of a shop that did hot breakfast rolls. On the way there, a lady who was driving by slammed the brakes on and asked if I was the fundraiser. I answered yes, she explained that she had seen me at the *Antiques Roadshow* and she then kindly donated £3. In the shop, I stocked up on food for the day and a breakfast roll, and left with another £11 in donations from customers and the owner. My total is climbing rapidly!

As I left Angle, I rounded the point looking out over the Valero power station with mixed feelings. Yes, it's ugly by daylight, but it serves a purpose. We all use the products it produces and it needs to go somewhere coastal, so why not in an inlet where it's fairly hidden away? I then rounded the corner, saw two huge tankers at the nearer jetties and gasped audibly. This told me all I needed to know. Despite expecting to hate this industrial area of the coast, I couldn't help but be impressed and appreciate its awesome scale.

I was soon back to beautiful cliffs and coastline, with stunning views over the fort on Thorn Island and St Ann's Head – where I'd been standing two and a half days ago. As I looked out to sea in wonder, I realised that I hadn't fully appreciated the magic and mystery that comes with not being able to see the other side of the water until I'd been without it for a few days. Since rounding St Ann's Head, the 'sea' has never been more than a couple of miles wide, so to see it stretching out beyond the horizon was like seeing an old friend after a long time apart.

It wasn't long before I met a couple of couples and stopped to have a nice chat each time. The second couple kindly donated £5 and shortly afterwards, I was joined in admiring the view by a group of eight. They proceeded to quiz me about my challenge, take photos and thrust donations into my hand. I felt a little like a celebrity! The group were so nice, and we shared an admiration for the stunning scenery that surrounded us. Before I could move a step, I was chatting to another couple. A pleasant discussion ended with a very generous £20 donation, and I left feeling on top of the world. In the last 20 hours, I'd received no less than £83 in donations and met lots of lovely people to talk to.

The path between Angle and Freshwater West is rather challenging. I was thrilled to be back enjoying dramatic cliff scenery and jagged rock formations, but the steep ascents and descents that go with such terrain were a shock to legs that had grown used to fairly flat walking. They coped pretty well though, and I was soon sitting on a beach that I'd been looking forward to seeing since leaving home. This is the place where Dobby died. For those who aren't huge Harry Potter fans, Dobby was a heroic house elf and the filming of his very emotional death scene took place on Freshwater West. I found a spot in the dunes that looked like the place where the fictional character had been buried by Harry Potter, and scribbled in the sand the words that had been written in the film; 'Here lies Dobby. A free elf.' Chuckling at how much of a nerd I was, I sat down for lunch and enjoyed the views along the golden sand.

After bumping into some of the people I had met earlier again, I walked to the other end of the beach and saw a plaque commemorating a very real tragedy that had taken place there. 79 Royal Navy and Royal Marines personnel drowned when two landing craft guns and a rescue boat were swamped by giant waves off the coast in 1943. Only three men survived, and many bodies were lost to the deep forever – 29 were never found. It was hard to imagine such a devastating tragedy happening in such a beautiful and serene place, and all of a sudden I felt very guilty for jokingly mourning a fictional character half an hour earlier.

The afternoon of walking was one that I was prepared to be disappointed by. Because both Castlemartin military firing ranges were in use, I wasn't able to go down to an apparently spectacular section of coast, and was expecting to walk nine miles along roads all the way to Bosherston, where I planned to camp. However, shortly after setting off from Freshwater West, I came across a permissive path (one whose use is allowed by the landowner, and so can be closed at any time for any reason) that ran alongside the firing range for the entire nine miles I planned to walk. After checking that it was safe to walk the path even when live firing was taking place, I gratefully stepped off the tarmac onto the grass and started feeling slightly happier.

Immediately, I could hear a large gun being fired and the pops moments later as the bullets hit metal. It was quite unnerving being so close, but it was also fascinating to listen to. Further along the path, I could hear a large artillery gun bring fired. Suspecting that it was from a tank, I kept an eye on the range to my right and sure enough, soon saw three tanks trundling along a track in the distance. The eight-year-old version of myself who still lives inside me got excited at being so close to live tank fire, and I stood and watched until they disappeared behind a crest. My eight-year-old self was also excited when I heard the firing of fully-automatic weapons in the distance, and even more so when I reached the entrance to the range and saw two tanks on display. The inland diversion hadn't been as delightful as the coast would have been, but it had certainly had more interesting moments than I had expected it to have, so my overall feeling was a happy one. I will, however, be driving back to walk that section of coast on a day when there's no live fire!

Arriving in Bosherston before the rain, I pitched my tent and made for the local pub. After I'd eaten, a couple came to sit next to me and the lady asked if she'd seen me hiking at

Freshwater West earlier. After only driving past and seeing me for a second, we were all impressed at her memory and got talking. Rachel and Joe are on holiday down here from Stoke, and we chatted the evening away for a lovely couple of hours. With Joe being a big sport and film fan and Rachel liking history, we had plenty of common interests to keep us occupied. It was fantastic to sit and chat in a pub for an evening with new friends. It felt like a slice of normality in this thoroughly abnormal, nomadic lifestyle that I am currently living. After kindly buying me a drink and giving me a donation, they returned to their comfy cottage and I returned to my tent.

The moon was hanging low in the sky and the stars overhead were shining like diamonds. The Milky Way joined one horizon to another with a star superhighway and to my north, I could see the bright orange glow of the refineries around Milford Haven. I've always been fascinated by the night sky and when I jumped out of my tent to clean my teeth wearing only my boxers, I couldn't help but stop and stare upwards again. I thought it unlikely that anyone else would be around the nearly empty campsite at half past ten, but as I remained transfixed by the heavens, a car's headlights swept across where I was standing as the owner of the site came to check the field. They must have decided against approaching the strange man wearing only his underpants and a beard, so I think I'll be leaving my £3 fee for camping in the box by the gate! I may make my sleeping bag smell a little tonight, as the campsite doesn't have a shower. I have at least managed to wash my feet under the drinking water tap, so things could be worse.

Nos da, pawb. I'll see you all tomorrow when I'll have walked my last full day on the stunning Pembrokeshire Coast Path.

Day 43
Bosherston to Tenby

This morning, I packed my wet tent away and went on a little wander to the end of the campsite. Discovering a shower in a portable toilet container, I felt a little foolish for not checking all of those last night. It was pointless showering before a long day of hiking though, so I headed towards the coast once more. I was excited to reach the sea again for two reasons. I'd spent all afternoon yesterday being so far away that I couldn't even see it, and at the end of the road I was walking down was St Govan's Chapel. This is a rather interesting little place as it's built into the side of the cliff.

Legend has it that St Govan was being pursued by pirates when a cleft in the rock opened up for him to hide in. The cleft closed until the pirates had moved on, and St Govan stayed in the place that had saved his life, worshipping and teaching there until his death in 586 AD. The altar in the chapel is said to hold his remains and a doorway next to it leads to the cleft in which he is meant to have hidden. Rib-shaped markings in the rock are said to be the imprint he left behind while encased and protected. The building has a mysterious feel inside, but it's when you step out of the third door and walk down past the holy well to the base of the cliff that its true magic is revealed. Building a chapel here today would have its challenges, so looking at the work done by thirteenth-century architects makes you wonder how on earth they managed it back then. The walls seem to blend into the rock, as if the chapel is part of the cliff itself. It really is a special place, and I was glad I'd made the detour down (and back up) the 52 steps to see it.

I detoured out to St Govan's Head too and it was here that two things struck me. Firstly, I hadn't really considered how beautiful the cliffs in southern Pembrokeshire could be until the moment I was standing admiring them. The coastline is very different to northern Pembrokeshire – everything down here seems to be in straighter, more ordered lines, but it is very dramatic and just as stunning in its own way. Secondly, it really was quite windy! Today's walking was not going to be easy.

I spent the first two hours of walking being pleasantly surprised and violently buffeted in equal measure. Around each little headland, I was met with more towering cliffs and tall stacks or rock formations in the sea, and also a renewed gale-force wind. With my wide bag on my back, each strong gust would send me staggering two or three steps sideways, and after leaning far into the wind to compensate, I would be sent staggering back the other way when I suddenly hit a sheltered spot. The effect of the rugged coastline meant that the sudden gusts were often coming from different directions too, and each time I would be knocked about for a moment until I adjusted my balance. It was extremely hard work and incredibly good fun! I've always loved being out in rough winds, and the addition of a churned-up sea hitting me with an occasional faceful of foam or spray had me grinning from ear to ear as I staggered from side to side. I must have looked quite mad to anybody watching from afar – like I was frantically looking for the proverbial marbles that I'd lost – but in my own world, it was a one-on-one battle with the elements. And I do love a good competition.

I passed the pretty beaches of Broad Haven and Barafundle, enjoying the golden sand and interesting cliffs at both, and arrived at a café in Stackpole Quay in time for lunch. While enjoying a bacon and sausage bap, my bag and Alzheimer's Society shirt must have grabbed people's attention because as I went to leave, everyone jumped for their wallets and purses. I had many nice chats with the people at various tables and left with £25 in donations. I couldn't believe people's kindness again and I was positively bouncing as I set off on the remaining 13 miles to Tenby.

The wind only grew stronger through the afternoon and after getting sandblasted at Freshwater East and Manorbier, the latter of which has an impressive-looking castle very close to the beach, I passed my original planned stop at a youth hostel and was pleased I'd decided to do the extra seven miles. There were some stunning natural arches to enjoy and I was still having great fun fighting the wind. I also saw my first adder of the walk. It was lucky that I looked down at that exact moment as I was a fraction of a second from stepping straight onto it! At the last minute, I clumsily lengthened my stride by half a metre to avoid an accident that could have really hurt the snake and seen me bitten and in a hospital bed. I got over the brief shock quickly enough to admire the beauty of the snake's intricate markings as it slithered off into the safety of a gorse bush.

I'd been warned by many people that heavy rain was forecast from five o'clock onwards and so had booked into a hotel in Tenby as a treat. My competitive streak reared its head again as I passed Lydstep 45 minutes before the storm was due and still five miles from my destination. How far could I get before I got wet? My battle with the elements had taken on a new edge, and with renewed vigour I flew up the climb to Giltar Point. The gales were stronger than ever and it was a combination of powering on with my legs and some skilled counter-steering with my walking poles that kept me on a fairly straight course. Feeling a real bond with my bag (affectionately named Wilson after the volleyball in *Castaway*) for the first time, I shouted lines from the film back to it, urging him to just hang on and let me do the work. It was half tongue in cheek, but I did genuinely feel like the two of us were taking on the storm together as a team.

I soon hit Tenby's South Beach and strode out towards the colourful buildings in the distance. The storm was now overdue and I started to believe I could make it to the hotel before a drop of rain fell. And that's exactly what I did. At 5.25 p.m., I walked into the reception of the Clarence House Hotel in utter disbelief. I'd beaten the elements hands down today, walking seven miles further than my original plan and doing it without falling over once or getting even a little damp. I enjoyed a hot shower for the first time since Milford Haven, and after a nice meal out, the man behind the hotel desk kindly washed my clothes in the hotel machines to save me a rainy trip to the laundrette down the road.

I'm now sitting with my feet up enjoying a film on the television while listening to the rain outside. My tent is laid out drying instead of getting soaked again, and I'll be heading deep into Carmarthenshire tomorrow after a more productive day than expected today. I'll have the final few Pembrokeshire miles to enjoy first though.

Nos da, pawb. I'll see you all after a night in a clean room and a day of walking in clean clothes. I'd forgotten what smelling nice felt like – it really is rather pleasant!

Day 44
Tenby to Laugharne

Emotionally, today's walk was like trekking across one of our famous Welsh valleys. I started on a high, but gradually dipped down to a low point in the middle. However, as surely as my spirits sank to the bottom of the valley, they rose to the top of the hill on the other side by the end of the day.

Waking up in a bed with my tent dry and my clothes nice and clean was wonderful. I had a full breakfast in the rather posh hotel restaurant and set off feeling refreshed. I hadn't fully remembered how beautiful Tenby was in the sunshine, so as I rounded the corner to North Beach past St Catherine's Island and saw the colours of the buildings and the boats in the harbour, I had to stop a minute to take it all in. The scene looked like it had been painted on canvas, using only the brightest paints.

The next seven miles weren't spectacular, but there was the occasional pretty view back to Tenby. I soon arrived in Amroth and after walking along the seafront, I reached a sign pointing in the direction I'd just come from. It said 'St Dogmaels 186 miles'. I'd reached the end of the Pembrokeshire Coast Path. Looking back down the seafront towards Tenby, I thought back on the last ten and a half days of walking with warmth in my heart. I'd made so many happy memories in Pembrokeshire before, and I knew I'd added a lorryload of fresh ones. From mass sightings of seals and pups, to an evening of 'beery banter' at Whitesands Bay. Reliving old childhood memories on the spectacular cliffs in the north and discovering new and amazing places like St Govan's Chapel and Martin's Haven in the south. I'd battled wind, enjoyed beautiful sunshine and weathered storms in the comfort of my tent in Caerfai Campsite. It had also been ten days in which I'd met many wonderful people. Pembrokeshire has always held a special place in my heart, and now that I know how incredible all 186 miles of her coastal path is, she always will. Diolch am bopeth, Sir Benfro. Thank you for everything, Pembrokeshire.

A mile further on is where my mood started to dip. I'd been looking forward to every day on the Pembrokeshire Path, but the Carmarthenshire section would take me far inland and I'd been warned that it wasn't particularly nice, and was a pain to navigate. I'm going to be staying with two of Valmai's sisters for three nights starting from tomorrow, so I have nice evenings to look forward to, but I didn't hold out much hope for the days of walking. My fears were confirmed during the first three miles of this afternoon. The path needed to get to the other end of a ridge before dropping into Pendine. The two sensible options would be to either climb and walk along the top all the way enjoying views across to Tenby and the Gower, or to stay low and hug the sea shore. What the path did, however, was meander from near the top to near the bottom repeatedly. Instead of climbing the ridge once, I climbed it about five times and in the roasting hot and humid weather, I was getting more and more irritated with every new ascent. It felt like the path planners had given the pen to a toddler, let them scribble across the map, looked at it and said, 'That'll do'. Thankfully, I had a couple of nice chats with groups of walkers at the end of the penultimate climb to cheer me up a little.

Finally arriving in Pendine, I was feeling rather ill. The heat was getting to me and I'd been having to work very hard to keep a good pace going over the undulating ground. After admiring the vastness of Pendine Sands, the scene of many land-speed record attempts throughout the modern age, I ordered two cold drinks in the nearest pub and sat to enjoy the shade for a bit. I was feeling sick, and was debating whether finding a campsite nearby would be more sensible than pushing on with another ten miles to Laugharne. I decided to press on despite my urge to pack it in for the day, and began to stress about how far I had to go. It seemed unlikely that I'd finish before sunset.

The path heads inland after Pendine to avoid a large firing range and as I trudged along the road, I very quickly reached the village of Llanmiloe. This surprised me as it looked about a third of the way to Laugharne and I could only have been walking for half an hour from Pendine. Checking the distance table, I was overjoyed to realise my mistake. Laugharne is ten miles from the Pembrokeshire border, and only six miles from Pendine. I could be there within an hour and a half! The walking remained dull for these miles, but the reduction in my expected walking time had started my climb out of the emotional valley of misery.

The rising spirits continued when I reached the end (or start for me) of Dylan Thomas' Birthday Walk. The views across the estuary of the River Taf were spectacular. Emerald-green salt marshes met the turquoise-blue estuary with its glistening tributary rivers at golden strips of sand, and it was easy to see why the famous Welsh poet had found inspiration for such beautiful pieces of writing when surrounded by this scenery. I'm looking forward to seeing his writing shed tomorrow.

Passing through Laugharne, I eventually arrived at the Ants Hill Caravan Park and they were kind enough to squeeze me onto a little patch of grass despite being completely full. I was then helped to find the showers by a group of women dressed as the Pink Ladies from *Grease*. Once clean and tidy, I accepted their invite to join them in the clubhouse and realised that the reason for dressing up was a 70th birthday party for a fellow Pink Lady. The celebrations were in full flow and I was welcomed with open arms by everybody inside. The bar staff and residents were also kind enough to donate a total of £30! We played bingo and then the Pink Ladies and T Birds treated the birthday girl to a lap dance and musical performances from *Grease*. Once the professional singer was allowed to have the microphone back, I was loaned a T Birds leather jacket and dragged to the dance floor by the Pink Ladies. Much dancing and laughter later, I had to be the lightweight and return to my tent to sleep. I am after all, walking 20 miles tomorrow and need my legs to recover, however much I would love to still be on the dance floor! My climb out of the emotional valley had ended on the highest summit, and I can't thank everybody at the park enough for making sure a difficult day ended so brilliantly.

I'm now sitting in my tent listening to Robbie Williams' 'Rock DJ' blaring out from the party. Despite my temptation to go back and join the dancing again, I know that once I switch off my makeshift light (a tiny torch hung from the hook in my tent) even the T Birds' version of 'Greased Lightnin'' couldn't keep me from falling straight into a deep sleep! Today has been extremely tough physically and mentally, but thanks to some wonderfully bonkers people, I'm beaming from ear to ear at the end of it.

Nos da all. I'll see you all tomorrow when I've tackled more of Carmarthenshire's not-so-coastal coast path.

Carmarthenshire Coast Path

Day 45
Laugharne to Llangain

As I set off from the campsite this morning, sadly leaving my new friends behind, I looked forward to passing some more places associated with Dylan Thomas in the first couple of miles of my day. The rest I was uncertain about, as it would be mostly inland walking around tidal estuaries with potentially unclear waymarking. Still, I approached it with an open mind, and was hoping to enjoy the path more than I expected.

My first sight to see was Dylan Thomas' grave. The modest white cross had very elaborate, decorative writing and people had left coins and stones on top. I thought about the Welsh genius beneath me and added my own small token to the collection. A short walk through Laugharne brings you to the Dylan Thomas Boathouse. His writing shed is next to the coast path, so I was able to look inside at the space where his greatest works were created. The room has been recreated as he would have left it and the glass in the door acted as a window to the past, with every detail inside being accurate. I looked at the desk where *Under Milk Wood* was written and thought of the generations of Welsh schoolchildren who've struggled to scrape any shred of meaning from the nonsense. Ten years ago, I was one of those children and didn't understand why Dylan Thomas was held in such high regard. But standing here, ten years on, I could appreciate the majesty in his words. Reading 'A Poem In October' yesterday in the spot where it was written had helped me tap into the beautiful descriptions and deeper meanings behind every line. He had a true gift with words and I felt privileged to be standing so close to the place where he'd written his most famous ones.

After some culture, I was ready to tackle the 19 remaining miles to Llangain. There, I would be meeting Valmai's twin sister Jan, who would drive me to her house in Carmarthen to spend a night in a comfy bed again. I just had the small task of finding my way along the coast path first. This was not as easy as it sounds. Having grown used to the excellent way-marking on the Pembrokeshire Coast Path, I had to tune back into the sometimes unclear Wales Coast Path signs. About halfway to St Clears, a WCP arrow pointed me up a muddy climb to a ladder stile. After negotiating the slippery slope, I was left to guess which way to go next. I wandered directionless through fields and couldn't help but notice various other sets of footprints doing exactly the same. Knowing that at some point I had to hit a main road to take me towards St Clears, I made for the sound of cars and spent the next 40 minutes feeling very vulnerable, hiking angrily on the side of a busy road. Still, it got me back to the WCP on two occasions and I was pleased to eventually arrive at a bridge over the first of three Carmarthenshire estuaries.

Deciding to get some hot food in St Clears, I headed away from the path and into town, but found only closed-down pubs and out-of-business shops. The place didn't feel very alive, and so I did a 180° turn and continued along the path. A phone call with my good friend Matt helped to bring me out of my emotional slump, despite finding more obstacles in my way such as electric fences across the path, and I stopped to enjoy my packed lunch on a log with a view that reminded me very much of home. The fields were green and divided up by a network of dark hedges. Hills and woodland were dotted across the landscape and a small town lay in the valley below. At a glance, it could have been Presteigne and I felt a warmth coming over me like a wave of positivity.

With renewed energy and enjoyment for the task in hand, I set off again and was soon munching my way along hedgerows of blackberries. The waymarking was still almost non-existent in places, but the combination of a descriptive guidebook and my improved instincts kept me on the correct path. The sea eventually came back into sight after 13 miles away from it, and I marvelled at the views over the Tywi (or Towy) Estuary to the Gower and Worm's Head. Curving around the headland,

I arrived in Llansteffan and stopped for a bite to eat. Finally getting yesterday's blog posted felt good, and the food fuelled me nicely for the fastest five miles of my day. I shot up the hill to the church at Llangain and it wasn't long before Jan showed up to take me home. It was lovely to meet her, and later Steve and Celt, and the hot tea and food, warm bath and warm company were a nice way to end my day. It's always good to chat with new friends!

I'm now in a cosy bed struggling to keep my eyes open to reach the end of this blog. I apologise if you are feeling the same while reading it! Tomorrow will take me around the top of the largest Carmarthenshire estuary, before returning to seaside walking once more.

Nos da, pawb! I'll see you all in the morning when I post this blog!

Postscript It was hard to find words to sum up what an enjoyable ten days I'd had in Pembrokeshire. To be honest, it still is! You have to see it to believe it. I had had such high expectations that I feared the reality might not be able to live up to them. In fact, it surpassed everything I could have imagined. The variety of scenery peppered with such an array of wildlife makes the full 186 miles a national trail that is a must-walk. If you have a spare fortnight, and enjoy being outside, take the drive down to St Dogmaels and discover the wonder for yourself. I promise you won't regret it.

Day 46
Llangain to Kidwelly

I was treated to an excellent fry-up cooked by Steve this morning. Jan made me a packed lunch and after far too short a time, I was bidding farewell to my wonderful hosts ready to head to Jan's sister Ann's house for the next two nights. When Valmai got in touch about my challenge, I had no idea quite how much she and her three siblings would contribute to it! Yesterday evening had brightened my mood after a dreary day of walking, and Jan and Steve's kindness is worth so much more than they know.

I set off from Llangain with an open mind again. I was determined to enjoy some of my Carmarthenshire walking and bounced along through woodland, quite happily enjoying the sights and sounds of nature in the morning. Soon however, I was walking along a busy road as the path made its way towards Carmarthen. There was no pavement, which made it incredibly difficult to find any sort of rhythm while having to step aside for cars every 30 seconds. The road was a fast one too, which made walking around corners feel a bit suicidal.

After safely returning to footpath walking, the path crossed the River Tywi in Carmarthen and set off along pavements and country roads towards the sea again. Mile after mile of tarmac followed through heavy rainstorms and humid greyness, and boredom began to set in. There was nothing really to look at, no interesting features or historic landmarks, and the biggest source of entertainment came from trying to spot the next waymarker, which was often easier said than done. One had even been bent out of shape to point in the wrong direction. I followed this wrong route until I reached a main road and realised that I shouldn't be where I was. A brief check of the guidebook told me where my error had been and on returning to the sign, I realised where it should be pointing. I briefly tried to return it to the correct direction, but there was no shifting the metal. The hammer marks left by whoever had forced it out of shape in the first place were a telling sign that it had been deliberate. I couldn't understand why somebody would want to tamper with a coast path sign, and was irritated at the 15 minutes it had cost me.

Soon after, I walked past another waymarker which was completely covered by a hedge. Thankfully, I realised I'd missed a turn almost immediately and once again returned to where the guidebook showed I should be. The route went through a tiny gap in a hedge that was far too narrow for a big bag, and then down overgrown tracks to boggy fields. I was still trying to enjoy myself, but was struggling to find anything positive to help me succeed.

The final straw came when I tried to walk past a house at the side of the road and was charged at by two angry-looking dogs. Turning away and leaning on the wall at the front of the garden to show no threat, I spent five minutes with the dogs barking and growling less than a foot from my heels, waiting for their owner to come out and help. When nobody showed, I edged my way past the dogs hoping to avoid a bite and was followed closely as I started to walk away. Turning around to look back at the house, I saw a figure in the frosted glass window of the front door. The owner had been watching the whole thing and when I raised my arms in a questioning manner to ask why they hadn't come to help, they turned away and disappeared. I was gobsmacked at the lack of care for a fellow human being and it took all my restraint to walk away without saying anything. They hadn't made any attempts to stop their dogs frightening a harmless passer-by, and I was starting to get the feeling that a few Carmarthenshire locals weren't just ambivalent to hikers, they actively disliked us. This feeling was only strengthened when I had similar experiences with dogs at the next two farms.

Walking on, a lady in Ferryside asked if I was having a nice walk. This was a very small thing, but the fact that somebody had shown a little bit of care boosted my morale hugely. I realised that in the last two days of walking, I'd only seen one other hiker. I'd greeted everybody else that I'd passed, but a fairly large proportion of people hadn't replied. To be acknowledged, even in such a simple way, felt so nice and I walked on with a smile on my face once more. My mood was further improved by a phone call home to arrange meeting times and places for tomorrow. It'll be great to see my family and I can't wait for the four of us to be together again for the first time since mid-July!

During the remaining five miles of walking, the sea views gradually began to emerge again and I could see light at the end of the tunnel. Tomorrow I'll return to the coast and head towards the Gower, which is a lot more geared up for walkers. Before then, I have two nights with Valmai, Margaret and Jan's eldest sister, Ann, and her husband Alun. It was lovely to meet the fourth of four sisters and complete the set! Ann and Alun are so lovely and after a tasty chicken dinner, we sat down to chat in front of the Paralympics. We have lots in common with our love of sport and the outdoors, so I know we'll have a very enjoyable evening tomorrow too!

I'm now in bed looking forward to finishing my Carmarthenshire walking tomorrow. I'd been warned about how uninspiring the path was here and that is proving to be very true, but thanks to the evenings spent with lovely people, I'm at least ending each day happily.

Nos da, pawb. I'll see you all tomorrow after I've had a wonderful few hours with family, and completed the not-so-wonderful Carmarthenshire section of the Coast Path.

Postscript When people today ask if Carmarthenshire was really as bad as I made out in the blog, I say yes. More so! I would rather walk through a week of rain and wind than repeat those two days again. Gareth and Menai had shown me a route-tracker map of how many times they got lost in Carmarthenshire while walking there for a few days, and I think my own map would have looked very similar. Because Carmarthen isn't coastal, I believe that some people don't want the coast path to be there. At one point, even my guidebook said, 'Cross the field, hoping that waymarkers have been left in place to guide you!' I also think that because there is very little in the way of spectacular scenery, the path is very rarely walked. People are drawn a few miles further down the coast to the beauty of Pembrokeshire. Perhaps because of this, the county council don't worry too much about its maintenance. There are pretty sights, of course, and nice little towns (I don't think I walked far enough into St Clears to do it justice), but having just walked 186 miles of well-established national trail, the next section of WCP was always going to have a lot to live up to.

Day 46 was the worst all-round day of my entire hike. There was nothing to stimulate me mentally as I trudged along back roads, the sea wasn't within sight so it didn't feel like I was making any ground, a few people were downright unfriendly and the weather was hot and humid with enough rain showers to make sure I had to keep my waterproofs on. So as I slowly cooked inside my outer layers and inside my own head, I desperately longed to be back at the coast.

The promise of the next day's walking being by the seaside again cheered me up slightly as I neared the end, but Carmarthenshire wasn't done with raining on my parade just yet.

Day 47
Kidwelly to Llanelli

Today's blog may say Day 47 in the title, but to my body and mind this morning, it felt more like Day 1. I've not even been outside in the last two days, after suffering from a nasty sickness bug from the early hours of Tuesday right through to the evening. I was unable to keep even water down and was worried about how much this would take out of a body which is already being pushed to the limit. I was so thankful to be in Ann and Alun's house, as I don't know how I would have coped alone in a tent. They have been so kind and caring and made things so much easier than they could have been otherwise. For that, I will be forever grateful. Yesterday, I gradually started reintroducing food and began to feel a little stronger, so I decided last night that I would have an easy day today; either doing nine miles to

Day 31: My little canvas home on a busy campsite in Aberaeron

Day 32: Mum, my grandparents and me, New Quay

Day 32: Iron Age hillfort and tidal island near Cwmtydu

Day 32: Sunset on arrival in Llangrannog

Day 33: St Carannog (or the Black Nun!) above Llangrannog

Day 33: Mwnt

Day 35: Valmai, Jen and Bisto in Newport

Day 35: Cwm-yr-Eglwys

Day 35: Looking back towards Dinas Head

Day 35: Sunset at Pwll Deri

Day 36: Cliffs between Abercastle and Porthgain

Day 36: Seal pup with controversial bottle toy near Abereiddy

Day 37: Whitesands Bay

Day 37: Ramsey Island

Day 38: Solva Harbour

Day 39: Seal and pup at Martin's Haven

Day 41: Pembroke Castle

Day 42: Freshwater West

Day 42: St Govan's Chapel

Day 42: Barafundle Bay

Day 44: Pendine Sands

Day 44: Taf estuary

Day 45: Nearing
Llansteffan

Day 49: Rhossili and
Worm's Head

Day 49: Family photo at Rhossili

Day 50: Beth and me at Rhossili

Day 51: Three Cliffs Bay

Day 54: Glamorganshire
sheer cliffs

Day 54: Derek and me at
Rhoose Point

Day 55: Cardiff Bay

Day 57: Newport Transporter Bridge

Day 58: Graham and me in front of the Severn Bridge

Day 58: The Old Wye Bridge in Chepstow – end of the WCP

Day 58: My final dragon shell sign, in Chepstow

Day 59: Tintern Abbey

Day 60: Crossing farmland similar to home near Llanvetherine

Day 61: Walking with Auntie Denise on Hay Bluff

Day 62: Descending into Newchurch

Day 62: Rob Dingle – ODP trail officer

Day 63: A very special final 14 miles

Arrival at the golf club

The first and final waymarker

Arriving home to family and friends

Reflecting on the best experience of my life

Burry Port or thirteen to Llanelli. I'd just listen to my body and see what it told me.

After a tasty cooked breakfast, Ann and Alun dropped me off back in Kidwelly where I'd finished two and a half days ago. I was concerned about how much muscle tone I may have lost, and as I started walking with legs like jelly, I knew that today was not going to be easy. Thankfully, I'd been able to shed most of the weight from my bag because I was returning to Ann and Alun's tonight courtesy of a kind lift from Jan. Still, as I wobbled along leaning heavily on my sticks, I thought that a slow nine miles to Burry Port with plenty of stops would be the most likely outcome of the day.

I soon reached the estuary and had nice views across the water once more. I'd forgotten over the last two house-bound days just how much I enjoy walking. The sounds of wading birds filled my ears and a deep happiness filled my heart. I was back on track. Over the next two miles, my legs began to remember how to walk normally and I was feeling stronger than I've felt since leaving Carmarthen. I was motoring along and not getting weary in the slightest. I reached Cefn Sidan Sands and grinned like a manic Cheshire cat. I was back at the open coast after two dull days of inland walking, and the mackerel sky reflecting off the wet sand at low tide was so clear that you could almost have flipped the image upside down without knowing the difference. There were multiple remnants of shipwrecks half buried along the beach and the backdrop of a Jacob's ladder over the Gower completed the breathtaking scene with a promise of more beauty to come in the next few days. The cherry on top of this glorious moment was that after five miles of walking, my legs still didn't need a rest!

I hit the sand and weaved between the barnacle-covered wooden wrecks, taking the time to investigate each one. I could see bolts and metal joints that would have held the helms together and began to wonder when they would have been built and why there were four in such a relatively small area. Had they all sunk or been abandoned? The mystery of it all fascinated me and I once again smiled. It was good to be back exploring new parts of my beloved home country.

After three miles of beach walking, the coast path turns inland and winds through the beautiful Pembrey Country Park. On passing the ski lodge, I dropped in for a cup of tea and the four guys working there noticed the sign on my bag. We chatted for a long while about the challenge, the centre and teaching and they kindly paid for my tea and cake as well as donating to my fundraising. After feeling very unwelcome on the inland sections of the Carmarthenshire Coast Path, it was lovely to feel so totally welcome here. After a very enjoyable half hour in the lodge, I had to crack on, so I was pleased that my body still felt strong.

The remaining mile and a bit to Burry Port flew by in a flash and I arrived at the harbour four hours earlier than I'd thought I would during the first mile this morning. It was just offshore here that a seaplane, *Friendship*, carrying Amelia Earhart touched down on Monday 18th June 1928, making her the first woman to be flown from America to the UK. The buoy that *Friendship* was tied to has been placed at the point where she came ashore, to pay homage to this and Earhart's subsequent achievements. As I stood in that spot while in the closing weeks of my own comparatively small adventure, I imagined the joy that she must have felt in that moment. On landing, Earhart reportedly pondered, 'Maybe someday I'll try it alone.' She would return to the USA four years later and do just that, flying to Ireland and in doing so, becoming the first woman to fly solo across the Atlantic. After living a life of exploration and adventure, Earhart mysteriously disappeared over the Pacific in 1937 aged just 39, never to be seen again.

Still not feeling the need to have a break, I pushed on into the Millennium Coast Park between Burry Port and Llanelli. The area has been transformed from the days when a power station used to dominate the landscape, and is now filled with a much more natural beauty. Lakes and wooded areas are dotted throughout the linear four miles and the Wales

Coast Path follows a wide tarmac cycle path. The walking was easy and in the end, it was hunger that stopped my legs from carrying me for the entire 13 miles without once sitting down. Finding a comfortable bench with a lovely view across the bay to Llanelli, I wolfed down the packed lunch that Ann had made me before merrily hiking on. Everyone I had passed today had either returned my greeting or been keen to chat, which made a nice change from the strange looks and deliberate avoidance that I'd grown used to in the previous two days of walking.

I walked a short way whilst chatting to a couple who regularly walk on the Millennium Coast Path, before arriving at a rugby memorial. The old posts are from Stradey Park, the previous home of the Scarlets, which before being demolished in 2010 had seen 4,605 rugby matches, been home to 192 international players and hosted some famous games involving the likes of Australia and New Zealand. A silhouette of Phil Bennett sidestepping a New Zealand flanker stands beneath the posts and the uprights are topped with two small saucepans – a tribute to Llanelli's once-thriving tin plate industry. I thought ahead to the Wales vs. Australia match that Em and I are going to see in November, and hoped for a match as legendary as some of those that these posts have seen.

Arriving at a café in Llanelli at three o'clock, I was thrilled at my retained strength. I felt like I'd started today on Day 1 and finished on Day 47, right back where I should be. I sat with a cup of tea and through conversations with kind staff and other customers, ended up with a further £15 in donations. The last lady that spoke to me had completed the whole coast path in ten weeks two summers ago. It was amazing sharing stories and seeing her memories of the life-changing adventure come flooding back. She is completing Offa's Dyke this year to finish the loop, which I hope she enjoys as much as I know I will in a couple of weeks' time. Her mum was kind enough to donate £5 too, saying that she was grateful for every little bit of kindness her daughter had received on her travels so it was nice to pass some on. My brilliant day's walk had finished off on such a lovely note, and I was in the best spirits I've been in for ages while chatting to Jan and her daughter Sara as they gave me a lift back to Ann and Alun's house.

Carmarthenshire hasn't been the best county to walk though by far, but it has ended with a day that has not only restored my muscle strength, but also my love for this challenge. I'll walk on with a renewed spring in my step tomorrow, especially with the promise of a slightly-belated meeting with Mum, Dad and Em on Saturday – I told them to stay away while I was ill on Tuesday.

Nos da, pawb. I'll see you all tomorrow when I'm back up to full pack weight and starting the Gower section of walking that promises so much. I can't wait!

The Gower Coast Path

Day 48
Llanelli to Llanmadoc

It was hard leaving Ann and Alun's this morning. I've spent four nights with them through illness and recovery and they've been amazing every step of the way. The house felt very much like home and Ann and Alun like a second family. I can't put into words how thankful I am for everything they've done since picking me up from Kidwelly on Monday night. Without them, I know my challenge would have been ten times more difficult and ten times less enjoyable. As I walked away, Ann chased after me with a £10 donation from their grandchildren as a final hugely-generous gesture. She and Alun are such genuinely lovely people and I know we'll keep in touch.

I was slightly nervous about today's walk. Yesterday, I'd been proud of my 13 miles, but they had been with a pack weighing less than half what it usually does. Today, my pack was back up to its full 18 kg and I was tackling a route that is just over 20 miles. Nevertheless, I put a lot of effort into the first seven miles and due to the scenery being unchanging – salt marshes and trees – I was able to get to the Carmarthenshire/Swansea border before midday.

Pleased with my morning's progress, I motored on towards Penclawdd and allowed myself a slower mile while I was on the phone to my good friend Chad. It was great to catch up and the chat boosted my morale enough to up my pace again. I wasn't really feeling down, but there was nothing overly interesting to look at and the terrain was as flat as my mood. Admittedly, the views across the estuary from Penclawdd were expansive. I could see over the salt marshes to Burry Port, Llanelli and right around to Loughor, but this view didn't change for mile after mile and as we all seem to do when we get used to something, I began to take it for granted.

A phone call from Matt gave me an excuse for a pause when I was a few miles from the end of the day. As we spoke, a young horse took an interest in my bag and then in me. I was sitting on a redundant stile in the middle of a field and so was well below the eye level of my equine friend, but he was so calm and tentative that I didn't feel the need to get up. He stood no more than a foot away from my face for the entirety of the phone call, appreciating nose strokes and pushing games and when the time came to leave, he walked by my side until I left the field. I'd made a new friend while enjoying talking to one of my oldest ones!

The last three miles have passed quickly and I am now sitting in a pub in Llanmadoc. I've received £35 in donations from generous people who've read the sign on my bag, and enjoyed a hot meal at the end of a long, but fast day. I'm about a mile and a half from the campsite still and will be making a move soon to pitch my tent before it gets dark.

Tomorrow, I'll be walking 12 miles before meeting Mum, Dad and Em on the beach at Rhossili (if all goes to plan this time!). I can't wait to see them all and spend a few hours together on the sand to celebrate Em's 22nd. It'll be just like our family holidays in Pembrokeshire!

Nos da, pawb. I'll see you all on my sister's birthday!

Day 49
Llanmadoc to Rhossili

I'll start today's blog with last night. On arrival at Llanmadoc Campsite, I began to pitch my tent and was soon offered a cup of tea by a lady in a camper van across the field. We got chatting and I discovered that Isabelle's mum had died of Alzheimer's the day after I started my Welsh Wander. She'd fallen and broken her hip in a nursing home and sadly never made it back from the hospital. I felt awful for her, and was startled by the similarities between her story and that of both of my maternal grandparents. As we shared stories of dementia, we were joined by Isabelle's husband, Guy, and the sunset grew ever more beautiful. A deep orange and yellow glow stretched across the horizon in front of us, silhouetting everything except for the lights of Tenby, Saundersfoot, Pendine and Burry Port. It was such a beautiful moment to share with two lovely people; well worth finishing pitching my tent in the dark for.

This morning, I rose bright and early. My family were driving down to meet me at some point on Rhossili Beach and I had 12 miles of walking to get there. Following a lengthy diversion around a newly-flooded bit of marsh, I began to worry that Mum, Dad and Em would have to walk the entire three miles of beach before bumping into me. I hiked as fast as I could to reach the end of Whiteford Point and after admiring the last remaining iron lighthouse in Europe, I set an equally quick pace along the beach on the other side. The views were pretty and I was enjoying walking on firm sand again, but my main focus was still on getting to the beach in time to save my family a huge trek.

Rounding the point at Burry Holms, I was astounded by the beautiful scene laid out before me. The vast expanse of golden Rhossili sand was backed by a bracken-covered hill. At the far end, Worm's Head stretched out into the sea as if trying to escape the mainland and the deep blue waters framing the perfect picture made for a truly breathtaking panorama. What's more, I'd reached the beach in less than three hours and was definitely going to save Mum the walk on her still relatively-new knee.

After half an hour striding out towards the far end of the bay, I finally came within sight of the path to the car park. There, just joining the sand, were Mum and Em with Dad following closely behind. Being able to hug my sister again for the first time since the start of July was fantastic, as was being able to hug Mum and Dad again too. Emily has been travelling the world with the ATP tennis tour over the last 15 months while on a placement year with Hawkeye. Her latest stint away from home had been a long one as she worked at the Toronto,

Cincinnati and US opens. It was great to hear stories from her travels – I'm a very proud big brother! For the four of us to be together again was amazing and after enjoying a hot meal and a long catch-up in a café, we were soon throwing frisbees and balls around the beach as we always do on family holidays. For a few hours, that's exactly where we could have been and I nearly forgot that although Em's big adventure had come to an end, mine still has a couple of weeks to go.

The time we spent together was so special, even more so because it was on Em's 22nd birthday, and five o'clock came far too quickly. Today has been the most enjoyable day of my Welsh Wander so far. It's felt like a day off as I've had a wonderful time with my wonderful family, but I was also 12 miles further along the trail. As an added bonus, my good friend Beth, who has been like a second sister since we shared a house for three years at university, has come to walk with me tomorrow, so I got to ride to the hotel in Swansea with my family to meet her. Saying goodbye wasn't as hard as it has been previously because there was the amazing thought that the next time I see them all, I'll be walking back down the Slough Road and arriving home. The time seems to have flown by and I now only have a little over 200 miles left.

Beth was soon out to meet me and we had a long and enjoyable catch-up before going out to eat. Eventually finding somewhere still serving food, we chatted the hours and food away until well after ten. Although it's been over a year since we saw each other, it instantly felt like we'd been housemates for that whole year. It was such a lovely end to an amazing day, and the combination of being together with my family again in a truly beautiful spot and seeing one of my best friends in the evening has sent me to bed with a truly happy heart. No matter how much amazing scenery or wildlife you see along the way, I'm learning that it is having people to share it all with that makes life truly special.

Nos da, pawb. I'll see you all tomorrow after a great day walking with Beth!

Day 50
Rhossili to Oxwich

Waking up in a hotel bed was lovely this morning and I realised that I've only spent one night in my tent in the last week. I'm living a life of luxury during the latter stages of this little amble! I was excited as a whole day of walking with my awesome friend Beth lay ahead of me and after a grab-and-go breakfast, a drive to Port Eynon and then a bus ride to Rhossili, we were ready to set off. The weather was as stunning as it had been yesterday and Rhossili Beach was shining in the sunlight as I remembered the amazing time I'd had there yesterday with my family. Beth and I had soon walked to the end of the headland to enjoy spectacular views over the now unreachable Worm's Head, which is cut off from the mainland apart from during a couple of hours either side of low tide. A young Dylan Thomas found himself marooned there for a day decades ago after falling asleep on the grass, and he wrote a wonderful description of his time as a castaway on his return to safety. The origin of the name 'Worm's Head' surprised me too. Although the mile-long, twisted and rugged islet looks a little like a worm, the Vikings likened it much more to a *wurm*. This was their word for dragon and if you look closely, it's possible to see the shape of a curled-up serpent sleeping with its wings folded above its back in the shape of the rocks. After taking many photos, Beth and I set off along a section of path that promised to be equally as scenic as its starting point.

I'd forgotten how nice it was walking with a friend. Although people had joined me for the odd mile here and there, I hadn't spent a whole day walking with somebody else since Siân walked from Menai Bridge to Caernarfon with me. It's strange to think I'd been walking alone for so long, and to suddenly have conversation all day was going to be a real treat. The scenery was beautiful from the off, as pale limestone cliffs dropped almost vertically into the calm blue waters below. Around each point was a new sheltered cove to enjoy while our conversation flowed as freely as it does whenever we meet up. The miles and minutes tumbled and we were soon only half a mile from Port Eynon, feeling like we'd only left Rhossili a few moments ago.

Stopping for lunch on a comfy patch of grass overlooking huge, flat areas of rock reaching out into the sea, we were totally relaxed and feeling no pressures or stresses of daily life at all. I've always found that one of the beauties of walking long distances is how much it puts life into perspective. You look back and see a point in the distance that you were standing on a few hours ago, and realise how much you can achieve when you put your mind, and sometimes legs, to it. It gives a sense of overriding calm, and I know we both felt it in that picturesque lunchtime spot.

Shortly after lunch, we arrived at Port Eynon Point and touched the granite monument to mark the achievement. Looking around, the views were stunning for 360°. Our lunchtime bay was behind us, while the white sands of Port Eynon beach dominated the other side of the headland. Following the coast past Oxwich Point, we could see Port Talbot Steelworks in the distance, with white clouds billowing out of one of the chimneys. The coast of South Wales stretched beyond the horizon and then to its right, we could see more land. Knowing it was too far around to be Wales, I assumed it must be south-west England and a quick check of a map confirmed this. Despite the rivalry between Wales and England, I was excited to be able to see our neighbouring country, and realised that this is the first time I've seen it since I left Chester 42 days ago. We could see the island of Lundy and the North Devon coast which gave visible proof that the border, and therefore the Offa's Dyke Path, was getting a lot closer than it has been for a long time. It was a special moment, made even more special because I got to see it with a great friend.

On reaching Port Eynon, we quickly decided that the five extra miles to Oxwich were easily manageable and pushed on along the sand of the bay. Looking behind and seeing two sets of footprints instead of just mine made me smile, and as we started climbing the cliffs again, the views across the bay continued to impress. The final climb up and drop down to Oxwich through pretty woodland got our heart rates up and legs aching, but we arrived in excellent time and had an hour to kill before Beth had to get the bus back to her car. While I was looking out to sea, a man read my bag and kindly gave me a £10 donation, which was added to by a hugely-generous £30 donation that Beth gave me from her grandma. Thank you both so much for taking my total close to £3,900!

We then set off in search of a campsite for me to stay in tonight. Finding that the one I was aiming for was closed until Easter – a little longer than I was prepared to wait – I tried a phone call to the leisure park across the road to see if they would have a patch of grass that I could pitch on. After hearing about my challenge, the lady on the other end of the line said that she couldn't accept tents, but could let me stay in a chalet free of charge! Ten minutes later, Paddy was showing us into a charming home that was to be my replacement for a night under canvas. There was a lounge with a TV and sofa, kitchen, bathroom and two bedrooms, and I wasn't even having to pay a penny to have the whole place to myself for a night. I couldn't believe how kind Paddy had been, and when she returned with tea, biscuits, a bowl of sugar and some shower gel, I just about fell over. The acts of kindness that I've received on this walk will be a huge part of why I remember it so fondly, and here was another one to add to that already huge pile.

After sending Beth off with a big hug and a promise to meet up soon, I ended up in a rather posh restaurant for dinner. As people walked past me wearing their evening best, I felt rather under-dressed in my three-day-old walking shirt, stained shorts and sandy boots. Still, I was sure none of the other guests had walked 900 miles to reach the restaurant either, so when I received a questioning look from a very posh old lady dressed in fur, I replied with my cheesiest smile and carried on tucking into my burger. I'm now back in my chalet reflecting on a second amazing day on the trot. I'd enjoyed every second of today because of the excellent company of a friend who I call my second sister. No matter how long it is in between our visits, we always pick up exactly where we left off and enjoy our time together immensely. I can't thank Beth enough for today, or Paddy enough for giving me such a treat this evening. I know that as I walk on alone tomorrow, my heart will be full due to the last two days and I'll have a spring in my step that will last for many miles to come.

Nos da, pawb. I'll see you all tomorrow when I've reached Swansea and completed my penultimate section of the Wales Coast Path.

Postscript Days 49 and 50 were two of my favourite walking days. Although I'm glad that I took on this challenge alone, being joined by those closest to me for a day here and there are some of the memories that still shine brightest from my Welsh Wander. I think that walking with somebody all the time could present its own challenges, a theory I'll put to the test when I walk Wainwright's Coast to Coast route with friends this summer, but having company every now and again during the two months I was away from home was critical in keeping my emotions in check. In the two weeks I had left, I would be joined my no fewer than five more people! Three of these I didn't know about yet, and one of the other two would be a moment that proved just how big my Welsh Wander had become.

Day 51
Oxwich to Swansea

On handing back the key to my chalet this morning, I couldn't find words to thank Paddy enough for letting me stay at Oxwich Leisure Park for free. It had rained in the night and instead of packing away a wet tent, I'd been able to wake up in a warm bed and make a cup of tea. I felt completely relaxed and happy and while eating breakfast in front of the BBC news, I considered what today would bring. I knew that Three Cliffs Bay was spectacular and that shortly after that, I would arrive at Caswell Bay, a regular family day-trip destination throughout my and Em's childhood. Next, I'd walk into Mumbles, where we've also spent many a happy hour as a family and then finish the day in Swansea. This route would also take me past my 900-mile mark and signal the end of my time walking around huge peninsulas, estuaries and inlets. From tomorrow onwards, the coast takes a fairly direct route to Chepstow, where I'll turn inland and head back up Offa's Dyke to home. All in all, it was shaping up to be a pretty good day.

The white sands of Oxwich Bay were my first 'wow' moment. I reached the beach after following a path through the dunes to find a coastal river forded by a wooden bridge. It was a beautiful foreground to the sandy backdrop. Marram grass was swaying gently in the breeze and I enjoyed the changing view as I walked further around the bay. The soft sand was energy sapping, but my spirits could not be brought down after two fantastic days at the weekend. When I saw a rope swing dangling from a big old oak, the child inside me took over and I jumped on with my bag still strapped to my back. With the wind rushing through my hair (and beard!) and the ground flying past beneath me, I felt an enormous sense of freedom. Nobody else was near and I could do whatever I wanted. Whether that meant meandering off the path to be nearer the cliff edge to admire the view, or flying through the air on a plank of wood tied to a rope like an eight year old!

The adult inside me eventually took over again and I made tracks for Three Cliffs Bay. Taking huge, sliding strides down the soft, sandy path, I soon arrived at the stepping stones that would lead me to the bay and marvelled at the scenery in front of me. The cliffs that give the beach its name jut out from the eastern side of the bay and look like a miniature mountain range stretching across the face of the sand. The beach grew more golden as I looked over to the western side, with dunes and the river reaching around to a limestone outcrop. It was such a beautiful spot, so I sat down for an early lunch to give myself the time to fully appreciate what was in front of me.

The path out of the bay was a draining slog up soft sand that slipped back down the hill whenever your foot dug in. Panting for breath near the top, I met a nice couple from London who are on the Gower for four days. A pleasant chat resulted in a generous £10 donation, and my legs used this kindness to propel me up the remainder of the climb. From the top, the views back over Three Cliffs and Oxwich were so incredible that I could have sat and stared all day, but I had to turn my back and push on to Caswell Bay. After a nice chat and a kind donation from a group of people walking in the opposite direction, I arrived at our old family haunt and memories of playing tennis and catch on the beach came flooding back. It was strange to see the bay so deserted, but also nice because it allowed my imagination to fill the sand with images of days spent here with those I love most.

I stopped for a burger in the café, received a couple of donations and then got on the move again. For some reason I spent the next mile feeling very lightheaded. I'm not sure what caused it, but I self-prescribed a cure of some sugar and stopped in another café in Langland Bay 20 minutes later. After some sugary tea, I was feeling much better and went to leave. The door was a mere 10 m away, but it took me quarter of an hour to reach it! The neighbouring table engaged me in conversation about my challenge and very kindly donated £15 between them as we had a lovely conversation about walking, Wales and travel. The table behind me donated as they walked past too and as I bid farewell to my three conversation partners, the table next to them donated as well! I was overwhelmed by the fact that every customer in the café had sponsored me, and left with a renewed spring in my step.

The walk to Mumbles didn't take long and I was soon back in territory that I know very well. We'd spent many a happy childhood day on the 2p machines in the arcade and along the pier and seafront, and memories came flooding back to fill my mind once more. After a wander out onto the pier, I was snapped out of my trance by a large group of walkers who'd recognised me from earlier. We had a photo, then walked and talked for 20 minutes to find a bus stop for them to get back to their base at Three Cliffs. I can't think of many better places to be based and I hope they enjoy the last day of their minibreak. It was lovely to meet them all!

Setting off around Swansea Bay on my own, I realised just how big it is. From Mumbles to Swansea is six miles, so I hit the gas pedal and pounded the pavement relentlessly. My legs responded well and I was soon passing Singleton Park. It was here, at the age of 12, that I ate some chicken nuggets that made me very ill for our entire Gower holiday. I never seemed to fully recover from it and two years later after multiple tests, I was diagnosed with Crohn's Disease. It was a life-changing moment for me and I could have reacted in either of two ways: been the ill child and used it as an excuse not to do things, or accepted it as a small part of me and never let it stop me doing anything. My family were a huge part in giving me the positivity and strength to take the latter option and as I looked back at that moment today, I realised that my Welsh Wander is proof that I never have let it get in the way of anything in my life. If you don't allow life's obstacles to stop you, you can do anything you set your mind to.

I'm now off to my hotel in Swansea for the night. Tomorrow will see me heading through some industrial towns and towards sections of coast that I know absolutely nothing about, but which I have been informed are beautiful. I hope they live up to the promise.

Nos da, pawb. I'll see you tomorrow when I've started the last section of the Wales Coast Path!

South Wales Coast Path

Day 52
Swansea to Porthcawl

As I wandered through Swansea this morning, I was in a very reflective mood. Dad came to university here, hence why we've visited so often since, and I could almost see his younger self walking through the streets. Slightly more recently, I was looking back on how far I've come in the last eight weeks and how little I have to go. Even more recently again, I was bidding farewell to the Gower section of my challenge. It had only taken four days, but they'd each been amazing and had contained some of my happiest memories of the entire walk. From proving my full recovery after illness by walking over 20 miles on day one, to arriving in Swansea under a sky of a thousand colours on day four, with visits from some of the people I love most in the world to fill days two and three, I knew that I'd look back on this section fondly. Aside from my personal experiences, once you reach Llanmadoc, the scenery becomes spectacular. Rhossili Beach, Worm's Head and Three Cliffs Bay rival anything I've seen on the rest of the Welsh Coast for breathtaking beauty and although the rest of the path doesn't quite match Pembrokeshire, it is charming and pretty in its own way. Diolch, Gower. I know I'll return soon!

Once I followed the path out of Swansea, it spent the next 15 or so miles finding ways around obstacles. Having strolled peacefully alongside a canal, I was very surprised to hit the main dual carriageway out of Swansea and walk inland alongside it for over a mile, travelling under the M4 motorway to a huge road junction. The reason for such a detour was revealed moments later as I crossed a bridge over a river and headed back towards the coast. After scaling the dunes, I was surprised again, though this time in a positive way. Aberavon Beach is vast. It seemed to stretch from the domineering chimneys of Port Talbot Steelworks all the way around the bay to Swansea, although I knew there was a river in the way somewhere! Happy to be back by the sea, I headed along the sand all the way to Aberavon, where I bumped into Pete and his friend. They are walking the same 1,100-mile route that I am, but are doing so in short bursts over ten years. We shared experiences of what was to come and our blog addresses, then set off again in opposite directions.

The next umpteen miles of path were rather unpleasant. There's no way past the huge Tata steelworks site, so I had to walk inland through Port Talbot and Margam. The coast path was again following busy roads and when it found quieter ones, they were through rundown areas that didn't feel overly safe. Margam itself felt tired and I was pleased when I came out the other side, crossed the railway Knuckle Yard outside the steelworks and walked into the dunes approaching Kenfig Sands. The landscape was a total contrast to what I'd been travelling through for most of the day. There was only green and yellow for as far as the eye could see. No chimneys or steel frameworks. No cars or run-down buildings. Just empty dunes with only the occasional sound of a herring gull overhead. Had I not been so relieved to reach a natural area again, I could have felt very lonely and isolated here, but in that moment I was happier than I'd been all day. I cut through the dunes to reach the beach and for miles of golden sand under a pretty dusk light, there was not another person in sight. The wet sand was so reflective that it could have been made of glass and as the sun lowered behind the clouds, an orange glow began to stretch across the sea from the North Devon coast all the way to Mumbles.

Eventually, I reached the far side of the bay and headed on past Sker Point towards Porthcawl. It was on my way along the boardwalk leading to the town that I walked past a couple who were quietly ambling along. On reading my bag sign, the lady called me back and after a brief conversation about why I'd chosen Alzheimer's Society, she told me that she too, like my mum, had lost a parent to the disease, but that for her it had only happened last night. I was so taken aback by her honesty and openness, and felt so emotional for her that a tear nearly left my eye as well as hers. I've been shocked for my whole trip by how many people are affected by dementia, but to find someone who had lost a parent to it less than 24 hours ago illustrated this fact in a way that was clearer than any before. After offering condolences, I left the couple to their important moment of reflection surrounded by the beauty of nature, hoping that the peace and solitude would help a tiny bit towards coming to terms with their loss.

I'm now in my tent reflecting on a long, 23-mile day that made me feel quite flat for large periods of time, but finished by reminding me why I am doing this challenge. There are so many people going through the confusion of dementia or the pain of losing someone they love to it, so I know I'll walk on tomorrow with even more determination in every step.

Nos da, pawb. I'll see you all tomorrow when I'm another day closer to home.

Postscript

Day 52 was a real let-down after the Gower sections. This is certainly not a section of coast that I would recommend walking unless, like I was, you are linking up the whole WCP. Had it not been for the two large beaches, I could have been quite down. I understand why the path had to follow the dual carriageways and busy roads – it's not like it can go anywhere else – but the vast quantity of road miles that I had to walk that day made for a bored and slightly on-edge walker. It wouldn't have taken much to tip me over the edge into an awful mood that evening, but instead, Kenfig Sands gave me something to enjoy, and the openness of that recently-bereaved couple instilled in me an inner drive that would spur me on for the remainder of my Wander. A couple of weeks after I finished, the couple made a very generous donation and told me how much the natural beauty of the coastline and our chance encounter had helped them that day. In truth, they helped me far more than they could know, and I was very grateful to have met them.

Day 53
Porthcawl to Marcross

I had a lazy start this morning, lying in my sleeping bag while using the campsite's Wi-Fi and reading ahead in my guidebooks. While doing this, I worked out for the first time in my whole challenge when I'll be arriving home. The evening of Saturday 1st October will be the big day, and it was a strange feeling knowing that the end was a mere ten days away. I've deliberately not set a time target until now, so having a concrete end to the hike made this morning feel quite different. I was relaxed in knowing when the end will be and I've got to the stage where I think of an 18-mile day as being easy, so when the clock struck 11, I was still chilled out in my tent. Realising that I really did need to get a move on, I packed up quickly and got on the road.

Porthcawl, Coney Beach Pleasure Park and its neighbouring caravan sites and small towns provided the backdrop to my first few miles of walking. In summer, these are full to the brim with tourists, but today they were rather quiet and sleepy. My mood wasn't too dissimilar, but I was able to walk through at pace and after a couple of miles on soft sand, I arrived at the mouth of the River Ogmore. Ogmore-By-Sea was quite literally a stone's throw away, but it would take me another two hours to reach it. There are stepping stones that could be crossed at low tide, but as the Wales Coast Path diverts inland for nearly four miles to find a bridge, I felt that it was only right to follow it.

It was hard to pin down exactly how I was feeling walking around that estuary. I wasn't irritated or miserable, but I equally wasn't happy or particularly interested in anything. I was just getting on with the job and hiking as far and as fast as I could manage. There was a brief flash of excitement though, when I saw a streak of brilliant blue flying over the river and realised that I'd just seen my first ever kingfisher. Sadly it didn't stick around long enough for me to take a photo, but just seeing it had been fantastic.

After crossing the river at the quaint little village of Merthyr Mawr, I enjoyed the salt-marsh scenery outside Ogmore-By-Sea and was then back to coastal walking once more. I'd now entered the Glamorgan section of the South Wales Coast Path, and the promised spectacular scenery soon began to live up to the reviews I've heard from fellow walkers on my travels. The cliffs tower dramatically over the attractive beaches below and seemed to contrast with the gentle lapping of the waves on the shore. The limestone layers in the cliffs are interspersed with layers of softer mudstone. These soft layers erode more quickly and eventually the overhanging limestone gets too heavy to support its own weight and collapses. This leaves the cliffs looking mightily impressive, with sheer faces and overhanging ledges. The layers of mudstone and limestone are clearly visible and are almost as perfectly horizontal as when they were laid down at the bottom of a shallow sea floor near the equator millions of years ago. At their base, the beaches are often adorned with a feature that I've never seen before – a wave-cut platform. These large expanses of rock are revealed at the base of the cliff as it recedes due to erosion. The sea polishes them over thousands of years and as they continue to form, the resulting landscape looks like a series of shallow steps linking cliff to sea. The overall effect was staggeringly pretty, and unlike anything I've seen on the coast path so far. The addition of a flock of about 20 choughs performing aerial acrobatics was the cherry on top of an already delicious cake.

Enjoying the tuneful, rhythmic tolling of the buoy bell near Marcross, I finished the day with rain clouds starting to fill the horizon and was picked up by Christine in her car. I met Christine and her husband, Phillip, in The Ship Inn in Trefin a few weeks ago. After following my blog, they very kindly offered me a bed for the night, which I have been only too happy to take them up on. This evening, we've enjoyed a wonderful meal in the pub next door and have spent a good few hours chatting about the challenge and future adventures. Christine has kindly gone to a lot of effort fundraising for my cause too and when we returned from the pub, there was an envelope on the floor with a kind donation from her neighbours. I'm staggered by the generosity of Christine and Phillip, who I'd only spoken to for a few minutes prior to tonight, and of people they know who have donated to somebody they've never met. The fact that I am in a warm bed on a rainy night is wonderful, and I know that I will sleep soundly until morning, having had a lovely evening with lovely people.

Nos da, pawb. I'll see you all tomorrow when I've had a day that will be unlike any other on my hike, due to an afternoon of walking that I still can't quite believe is happening! All will be revealed in the next blog.

Day 54
Marcross to Barry

Shwmae!

I woke up this morning to a delicious fry-up courtesy of Christine. We had a wonderful relaxed breakfast while chatting about the day ahead and before we left to return to the coast, Christine gave me a very generous donation from Phillip (who was already at work). I was so touched as they'd already given me so much, treating me to a hot meal and cosy bed for the night as well as fundraising around the village and at work for my cause. They really have gone above and beyond for somebody they had only met for a few minutes in a bar, and I can't thank them enough for their care and kindness.

Christine walked a little of the way along the coast with me, and as we were chatting, we noticed a man walking in the other direction. He didn't look too dissimilar from myself: slightly scruffy beard, similar build, height and hair colour and a bag larger than his torso. We asked how far he was going and his response of 'Bridgend', which was only 12 or so miles away, had us nonplussed as to why he was carrying so much. He then explained that he'd done the full loop of Wales and that today was his last day! I've walked 950 miles without meeting anybody doing the same challenge that I've taken on and he had nearly completed the whole loop, also without meeting anyone doing the same thing. To share stories for a few minutes was amazing, but I stopped short of asking how it felt to be on the last leg. Part of me wanted to know, but a larger part thought that it wasn't something I could be told; I would have to wait to feel it myself in just over a week's time. I wish we could have chatted longer, and I hope that Mark gets in touch so we can share more stories from the trail. We are in a select group of fewer than 40 people who are known to have completed this circuit, and it's a bond that will bind us all together in shared trials and triumphs – once I've finished, of course! I had a rather exciting meeting to look forward to today though, so bidding farewell to Christine with a huge thank you, I turned and headed off at pace towards Rhoose.

The next ten miles needed to be quick. A few weeks ago, Mum had emailed BBC Wales to tell them about my challenge and wondered if it could be forwarded on to our most famous Welsh weatherman, Derek Brockway, who is very fond of walking and beloved throughout Wales! His show *Weatherman Walking* has been a favourite of ours for a long time, and we always enjoy seeing his routes to give us ideas of places that we'd like to explore ourselves. After getting in contact, much to my surprise and elation, Derek and I had arranged to meet at Rhoose station today and walk eight miles to Barry together. To say I was excited would be an understatement! I've watched Derek on the TV for years, so to be able to walk with him through the areas he grew up in would be a real treat. My slight concern was that I now had ten miles to cover in a little over three hours before his train was due in. I didn't want to keep a true Welsh legend waiting on the platform! The scenery was still as pretty as yesterday, with more steep limestone cliffs and sheltered, rocky coves, so I did allow myself the odd brief stop to enjoy it in amongst the speed walking! St Donat's Castle, an old party location for the rich and famous including the likes of Charlie Chaplin, came and went quickly and I sped across the clifftops as fast as my legs could carry me.

I arrived at the station with just enough time to empty multiple stones out of my boots before the train pulled in. Off hopped Derek and we greeted each other happily, looking forward to an afternoon of sunny walking – if it can't be sunny when you are walking with a weatherman, when can it be? Our first stop was Rhoose Point. This is the most southerly point in mainland Wales, and as we took a photo with the giant slab of North Walean slate to mark the occasion, I considered the fact that every step I took from that moment on really would be taking me closer to home.

We walked and talked all the way to an interesting viaduct at Porthkerry. Here, we asked a lady to take a photo of us with the view and her recognition of Derek was instant! He very humbly moved the conversation on to my challenge straight away and after a nice chat, we got on our way again up 'The Golden Stairs'. Here, there are 126 steps through woodland and Derek told me that legend has it that a gold coin is buried in one of them. Vowing to return one day with metal detectors and a pickaxe, we cracked on up the climb and were soon overlooking Barry Island, or Barrybados as Derek informed me the locals call it. Having grown up in Barry, he was full of fantastic stories and snippets of information about the places we were walking through and it was fascinating to see it all through his eyes. We spoke a lot about my challenge too, with Derek admitting he's rather jealous of it and would love to take it on once he retires. I know the whole of Wales hopes he carries on working for a good few years yet though!

After Derek kindly bought me lunch at The Knap, we walked out onto the headland of Cold Knap Point, which was once cut off from the mainland. A huge storm piled up barriers of stones centuries ago and the land between the mainland and island was able to dry out and become usable. Derek remembered a time when a wonderful outdoor swimming pool filled the naturally reclaimed land – he'd spent many a happy hour between the pool and beach as a child. We walked across the beach to Barry Island and I was pleasantly surprised by the look and feel of the place. I'd passed a 'pleasure park' the day before which had been very run-down, but Barry Island still felt vibrant and current. I suspected that maybe the success of the TV show *Gavin and Stacey* had fuelled a bit of tourism, but the views across the channel to North Devon, Flatholm Island and Sully and the fun feel of the seafront are enough to attract many to the area too, I'm sure. We stopped to enjoy a tea and a cake in a café on the front, and while there, a group of ladies recognised Derek and wanted photos. Again, he humbly moved the conversation onto my challenge and the ladies kindly donated to my fundraising before we posed for a large group picture!

Feeling a little like a celebrity myself now, we headed on to the last mile of the day to Barry Docks, where Derek was parked. He kindly gave me a lift to the hotel that I'm staying in tonight and we bade each other farewell. It has been an absolute honour walking with Derek today and it's a part of my Welsh Wander that I know I'll remember forever. He is such a genuinely lovely guy and for our six hours of hiking together, the conversation never ran dry. I've learned so much about the eight miles we walked and a lot about the weather and TV forecasting too, and sincerely hope that we can catch up again at some point in the future.

Nos da, pawb. I'll see you all tomorrow when I've reached our nation's capital city.

Postscript This is probably the most memorable day of my entire Wander. From start to finish, it was a delight. Seeing Mark while walking with Christine was such an incredible coincidence, and a very poignant reminder of just how close the end of my own adventure was. When I arrived home, Mark got in contact and told me that he knew I was on the same journey as him as soon as he saw me. It has been wonderful sharing memories and stories with somebody who knows exactly what it feels like to walk those very same footsteps.

Walking with Derek is something that I'll never forget. I couldn't believe how something that had started as little old me walking alone around my home country had grown large enough to earn his attention. Derek was so down-to-earth, so easy to get along with and so open too about his father's battle with dementia that by the end of the day, I had almost forgotten that he was a Welsh TV legend. It was like walking with somebody I had known for years, and we have remained in contact ever since. It's amazing how my little Wander has connected me with such a wide variety of fantastic people, who I am now lucky enough to call my friends.

Day 55
Barry to Cardiff

I started today where Derek parked his car yesterday so as not to miss any of the path. Admittedly, I wanted to take a shortcut straight down to the main road from the hotel as I knew the first miles would be pavement walking, but due to everybody's extreme generosity and sponsorship, I felt I had to do the challenge properly. My pedantic nature probably fuelled that fire a little too!

The pavement miles were as dull as expected. When the guidebook uses the phrase, 'just grit your teeth and keep walking', you know the scenery won't be up to much.

Following roads through Barry and Cadoxton all the way to Sully, I was glad that I was near the end of my Welsh Wander. I'm enjoying myself immensely and so this wasn't because I wanted to stop, but I'm so much calmer now than in my first couple of hundred miles. This strange life of waking up in a different place each morning and walking 20 miles in between has become normality, and so the huge mood swings of the past are long gone. I still feel highs and lows, but they're never all-consuming, so as I walked along the roads past industrial estates and garages, I felt bored, but not too down.

The path returned to the coast eventually and as I passed Sully Island and headed for Penarth, the air got clearer, meaning the views across the channel were beautiful. Flat Holm and Steep Holm Islands were dominating the foreground and as I hit the tarmac path in Penarth, an exciting sight caught my eye in the distance. The grey and white towers of the two Severn Bridges were visible for the first time and an instant wave of happiness washed over me. Only a few miles past those bridges, I'll hit the Offa's Dyke Path again and be 80 miles from home. To be able to see something so close to the end of the Wales Coast Path started a reflective train of thought in my mind and as I was remembering the amazing times I've had during the last seven weeks, I reached a fairly new-looking feature on Penarth Head. Climbing the few steps to investigate, I was delighted to find that it was a huge, raised mosaic-style copy of the dragon shell symbol that has been my guide since I left Chester. The words 'Llwybr Arfordir Cymru – Wales Coast Path' were written along the top of the tiles and I couldn't resist walking around the length of the curved shell to symbolise my nearly complete through-hike of the path.

My next moment of note was crossing the Cardiff Bay Barrage. The views over to our capital city were quite striking, from the corner spikes of the Millennium Stadium, across the bronze front of the Millennium Centre and easily-recognisable red-brick Pierhead Building to the Senedd, where the Welsh Assembly Government now meets. I was reminded of how much I like the bay area of Cardiff, having visited numerous times with family, so as I made my way into Mermaid Quay I was able to reminisce happily as I had done on the Gower and in Pembrokeshire.

I'd arranged to meet an old university friend, Craig, in the Bay. We'd both been keen walkers in Bangor and to share stories of long-distance solo hikes over a meal was fantastic. He completed the South Downs Way for charity a few years ago and so understands the trials and tribulations and sheer brilliance that life on a trail brings. He kindly gave me a lift into the centre of town and helped with my decision making on buying a new roll mat too. I rather foolishly damaged my Vango when I rushed to pack it away in Bosherston before it rained and forgot to open the valve when rolling it up. Ever since, I've woken up to a very flat mat which has only been slightly more comfortable than sleeping on the floor. The new Mountain Equipment one is very nice and I'm sure it will be a fantastic replacement, but as with all of my kit, I have grown very attached to the Vango. It has been part of my canvas home since the start of my challenge and we've ridden out many storms and cold nights together. It is a friend and I simply couldn't bring myself to throw it away! So for my final week of walking, I will carry two roll mats. My Vango will go on the floor of my tent and the new ME mat will lie on top of it, staying nice and clean. Both are essential roles, so I can't possibly ditch my old one in Cardiff! Now I just need to find a way to fit another mat inside my already jam-packed bag. That is a problem for tomorrow morning, though.

Nos da, pawb. I'll see you tomorrow in Newport when I am exactly one week away from arriving back at home.

PS I checked my Just Giving page in the hostel tonight and was staggered by the total raised so far. Considering I originally set out to raise a pound a mile – £1,100 – I have now climbed above £4,100! Thank you to everyone who has donated so far. You've made my Welsh Wander so special, and will have made a real difference to those who, like my grandad, are currently suffering from dementia.

Day 56
Cardiff to Newport

Last night at about nine, I began to lose half of my vision and had pins and needles spreading up from my hands, through my arms to my face. Being all too familiar with these symptoms, I gritted my teeth and prepared myself for the migraine that was to come. Sure enough, by ten my headache was so severe that it was making me feel sick. Thankfully, the best way to deal with a migraine is to lie down in a darkened room and it was nearing bedtime anyway. Three of the four girls in my room in the bunkhouse had gone out and Vicki was tired too and so kindly said that we could turn the light off. I had a wakeful night and when I reluctantly woke up this morning, my vision had returned and the nausea gone, but I still felt like I had the Cadbury gorilla playing his famous drum solo on the inside of my skull.

If I'm being honest, even without the newly-developed severe pain in my head, this was already the section of my walk that I'd been dreading since Day 1. While on a school trip at the age of 16 (though thanks to my Crohn's Disease, my height, build and looks were more befitting of a 12 year old), I foolishly wandered off on my own in Cardiff while stubbornly trying to find the Bay. I managed to find the right road down to it, but it took me right into Butetown, which I learned that day and have been told many times since, is not a place you want to go. I was mugged by two men who were much bigger and older than I was, lost my camera, phone and wallet, was rescued by a guy with a knife as they were dragging me to a cashpoint, and turned up at the bus to go home two hours late after a visit to the police station and two rides in a police car. Ever since,

I've been wary when walking in parts of towns and cities that I don't know, and I was going to have to do a lot of that today: five miles through the back streets of Cardiff, walking past a traveller site that I'd been warned about numerous times, and then finishing the day in Newport, which doesn't have the nicest reputation. The combination of my past experiences and current migraine meant that today's 17 miles were going to be tough both physically and mentally.

I felt slightly on edge as I left the Millennium Centre behind and hit new territory. Ignoring my still pounding head, I focused instead on pounding my feet along the pavement as quickly as possible. I was out of Cardiff quicker than I had expected to be and the traveller site that I'd been warned about so many times was soon upon me. I put my head down and walked purposefully, hoping not to encounter any trouble, but ended up wondering why I'd worried in the first place. Apart from a girl burning something that was kicking out acrid black smoke that made my nostrils tingle, nobody else was around and I had passed the first six miles of my predicted worst day without any hassle.

The next few hours of walking were easy as the path followed a grassy embankment alongside the brown, silty waters that I presumed were a mix of Irish Sea and River Severn. There was never much to look at, apart from three wading birds flying past that I'm almost certain counted as my first avocet sighting. There was also only one person to stop and chat to – Jenny, who is walking the Wales Coast Path in sections and had many interesting stories to share. In the hours of monotony that filled the rest of the afternoon, my mind began to wander. I can't recall the last time that I had the necessary hours with no distractions or stresses to properly daydream, but as I strode out in the cool breeze, I enjoyed many an alternate reality to the rather dull one that I was actually in. I rather enjoyed myself and as a result, arrived on the outskirts of Newport far sooner than I'd originally thought I would.

As I hit pavements once more and started walking down

backstreets and through underpasses, my senses heightened again. The relaxed feel of the afternoon had vanished and I was on my guard once more. Again though, there was no need for this as the only people who approached me were three children on bikes who asked if I was going to the mountains, and didn't believe me when I said I was walking 1,100 miles, until they read my bag. After a few direct questions in a style that only children seem to manage, they rode off into the distance and I was left to reach the famous transporter bridge in solitude. I'll discuss this more in tomorrow's blog as I'm going to be crossing it, high above the River Usk, in my first few minutes of walking! It was looking like I may miss out on this opportunity when I turned up at the bridge too late to cross, with the usual opening time being later than I wanted to set off in the morning. However, after a discussion about my challenge, the three bridge operators (who were just packing up to leave) offered to open the bridge early tomorrow just for me. It was a very generous gesture, and I'm excited to see the contrasting city and coastal views from the top.

Not wanting to wander off the path in an unfamiliar town, especially one with a reputation like Newport, I called a taxi and was dropped off outside the Travelodge that I had booked a few days ago. My shoulders relaxed as I walked in, knowing that I was mere minutes from lying on a comfy double bed in front of a TV. However, the lady at reception thought otherwise, as she had no record of my booking whatsoever. No matter; I'd left my confirmation email unopened so that it would be easy to find if I needed it. And I did find it easily, and instantly regretting not having opened the email as soon as I had received it. It proved that there was a cosy room in a Travelodge waiting for me in Newport. Newport, Oregon, USA, to be precise. Thinking that that was probably a little out of my walking range for the evening and cursing booking. com for putting that hotel in with my Welsh options and for giving me a price in pounds rather than dollars, I felt a surge of worry. Here I was in a town that I didn't feel comfortable in, and now I had nowhere to stay. Despite the correct Newport Travelodge being fully booked, the lady at reception was very helpful. I have no idea how she managed not to openly laugh me, let alone get on the phone to help me find somewhere else to stay.

After a hot meal in a pub across the road and a second short taxi ride, I turned up at the Victoria Hotel, hoping that I hadn't accidentally booked one in Victoria, Canada. Thankfully, the man at reception confirmed the booking that had been made an hour ago and showed interest in my challenge too. Starting to climb out of my dark mood, I lay down on a different bed to the one I'd expected to be on when I arrived in Newport two hours earlier, but a bed nonetheless. This one had effectively cost me double what the American one would have as I was too late to cancel that one, but there are far bigger things in life to worry about. I've also learned a valuable lesson – always read a confirmation email carefully. They are sent for a reason!

As I'm lying on a bed that is very definitely in Wales, I'm reflecting on a day that didn't go at all how I'd expected it to. I made it through Cardiff, a traveller site and Newport without getting shot or stabbed, I'd been so relaxed that I learned to daydream again, I'm lying in a different hotel from the one I booked, and some poor receptionist in Oregon is waiting for a Thomas Davies to arrive, having walked from Cardiff. I'm afraid they may be waiting for some time.

Nos da, pawb. A week from today, I'll be writing about my last day of Welsh wandering. It's both an exciting and a scary thought! For now though, there are still over 100 miles to go, so I will see you tomorrow when I've passed 1,000 miles walked, and reduced the 'to-do miles' to two digits.

Day 57
Newport to Caldicot

Waking up in my hotel bed this morning and watching *Match of the Day* on the TV, I couldn't have felt more different than I did last night. I was relaxed and happily looking forward to the memorable moments that my penultimate day of Wales Coast Path walking may provide. The taxi driver refused to take payment for returning me to the Transporter Bridge and as promised, the guys who I'd met yesterday had kindly arrived early to let me across before the bridge opened. Today was quite literally starting on a high! As I was about to set off up the 278 steps to the top, one of the operators stopped me and said that it would be extremely tiring climbing with my bag. He told me to put it on the gondola and he'd send it over when I reached the other side. A platform used for carrying six cars and many pedestrians would make a special trip over the River Usk just for Wilson!

Thanking the two guys, I set off at pace up the steps to the walkway over the top of the bridge. Cars and buildings soon started looking very small and as I took the 278th step, the views over Newport and the Usk estuary took my breath away. The slightly hazy air over the power stations and industrial buildings seemed to suit the scene perfectly, and Newport was shining like a new penny at the bottom of the famous Welsh Valleys. If the horizontal views were breathtaking, the vertical view was heart-stopping! I was standing on steel mesh 74 m above the River Usk, and as I looked down between my boots, I clutched my phone a little tighter. I didn't want to lose it through the gaps in the floor!

Sure enough, as I began to descend the far side of the bridge, the gondola started to travel towards me. It's basically a suspended ferry that hangs from huge cables attached to a slider underneath the walkway that I'd just crossed. Imagine a swing with its chains sliding sideways along the bar it hangs from, and you'll have a pretty accurate picture of the bridge in your mind. This design was a solution to the problem of creating a route across the river without disrupting the passage of large boats into the busy port. No conventional bridge could be high enough and a normal ferry would cost too much to run. The bridge was revolutionary, and it remains one of only three transporter bridges in Britain today. There are only seven working worldwide! I was allowed into the motor house on the far side too to see how the pulley system worked, and was impressed at the rotational speed of the cable drum as it returned the gondola to the far side of the river, having dropped my Wilson off. I was so grateful that I'd been able to cross the bridge and see its inner workings, and set off on the remaining 18 miles to Caldicot in a very positive frame of mind. The big cities were behind me and had actually been very interesting. Now I was back to quiet estuary walking before returning to the peace and tranquillity of Offa's Dyke.

After a few miles, I arrived at the Newport Wetlands Centre. Following many changes of use in the past, it has now been turned into a haven for bird life and the new centre had a lovely little café where I enjoyed a tea and a sausage bap. I had a nice chat with Dafydd, a keen cyclist who is often found on the trails around Newport, and then got back on my own trail. The birds provided plenty of interest as I walked along inland paths and roads to avoid nesting sites – I saw my second avocets a day after seeing my first – and the occasional heavy shower from invisible rainclouds never came close to dampening my spirits. The path eventually returned to the coast at Goldcliff, and it was here that I celebrated reaching my 1,000th mile. I have totally mixed emotions knowing that I'm now less than a hundred miles from the end of my Welsh Wander. On the one hand, I can't wait to be home and to see my family and friends again, but on the other hand, I have truly fallen in love with this nomadic lifestyle and am slightly nervous about rejoining the real world! For two months, I've seen new and interesting things every day, met new people, learnt new things, discovered brilliant hidden gems and experienced some very special moments. To not have that any more is going to be hard to get used to, I fear.

I was soon snapped out of my thoughts of the end by the brilliance of the here-and-now. On climbing the steps back to the sea defence I was met by a beautiful view and two nice people. John is Welsh, but has lived in Australia for 40 years (never losing his Welsh accent) and was back in the land of valleys and sheep to visit a friend. He was full of questions about my challenge and revealed that he is hoping to walk from London to Dublin next summer, if he can convince his wife that it is good for him! If John's wife gets the chance to read my blog from the land down under, I would tell her to encourage John to take on his dream challenge! I feel so much fitter, stronger and healthier for walking every day and I know that he would be the same. We parted after promising to stay in touch and I hope we remain true to our word so that I can keep up to date with his adventures too.

I turned back towards the estuary and let out an audible gasp at the scene in front of me. The Severn Bridges were shining in the sun and looked so much closer than they had yesterday. I could make out individual buildings in the towns on the English side of the channel and the silty waters of the Severn were lapping gently against the sea wall. The path stayed on the wall for many miles and I enjoyed every twist and turn. I was visibly getting closer to the border and therefore Offa's Dyke, and as another sudden downfall of rain hit, a bright rainbow stretched right over the Severn Bridges from Wales to England. I nearly tripped over a couple of times as I walked along gawking at the stunning display in front of me, but the rain disappeared as suddenly as it had arrived and my eyes returned to the path when the colours faded to sky blue again.

By the last two miles, my legs were struggling. I've done much longer and hillier days, but clearly something in them this evening was on strike! As I dragged my feet over a bridge crossing the M4 motorway, I took a moment to look down on the hundreds of cars queuing to go through the toll gate into Wales. I wondered what parts of this wonderful country they were headed for, and thought enviously of any who would be enjoying the sunset in one of the many beautiful coastal villages I've walked through. Pushing my legs on, I arrived in Caldicot, where I'm meeting my mum's cousin Graham tonight. He's travelling all the way from Leeds to walk with me tomorrow and I'm really looking forward to having his company as I walk my final ten miles of the Wales Coast Path. While killing time in town waiting for Graham's train, I've met some lovely people. The lady who runs the local chippy was very friendly and a few of the customers also showed great interest in my walk. One donated a few pounds and on entering The Cellar Inn, my bag again drew many questions. A rather entertainingly drunk local man kindly donated £5 and bought me a drink while we had a nice, if slightly repetitive conversation! I've now found an empty corner in which to write my blog, though the loud music is making it hard to string a logical sentence together. Hopefully this blog isn't too disjointed as a result.

Nos da, pawb. Today has been fantastic and I'm sure that walking with good company will make tomorrow even more so. I'll see you when I've finished the entire Wales Coast Path and have only five days of walking up Offa's Dyke remaining.

Day 58
Caldicot to Chepstow

Last night, I met Graham from the train and we had a bit of a game trying to find a taxi company in Caldicot that was running on Sunday evenings and wasn't already fully booked. On our fifth time of asking, we succeeded in finding someone that could take us to the B & B, and within a few minutes, we were in the back of a Bumblebee Cab. After a nice chat with the driver, he very kindly told us to donate the £10 fee to my

Just Giving page. It was a lovely gesture and the good times kept on coming as I was shown into the room that Graham had very kindly booked for me. It was rather luxurious and I spent far too long in the shower before relaxing in bed with a film. It was a brilliant end to a brilliant day and I had the prospect of walking with Graham the following morning. I went to sleep feeling very happy.

The happiness continued when I woke up and met Graham for a full cooked breakfast. The forecast rain was starting to fall, but walking ten miles to finish the Wales Coast Path with great company would mean that the day would be a good one despite the soaking we both knew we were about to get. The B & B owner kindly gave us a lift into town and we set off in drizzle that we were sure would soon turn to downpour. I was really pleased to have Graham walking with me today. The first mile along roads and back over the M4 would have been rather dull without him there. As the heavens began to leak a little more persistently, we passed under the Second Severn Bridge which carries the M4 over the estuary to England. This gigantic feat of engineering was completed in 1996 to help the first bridge cope with a huge increase in traffic. At over 5 km long, it dwarfs the original 1966 crossing as it snakes over the tidal mudflats. Although you wouldn't describe either bridge as pretty, they were very interesting to look at. The same could be said for the Severn Tunnel pumping station, which had to be built after the Victorian tunnel workers hit a huge spring in the middle of construction and only narrowly made it out before the tunnel flooded completely. It was the job of one brave individual to walk down into the abyss without light, plug the leak and return safely while wearing a heavy metal helmet with only a bag of oxygen. I certainly don't envy his task!

Walking on, we passed a striking crumbling red sandstone cliff at sea level before crossing the train track and heading upwards and inland. The rain started falling rather heavily, but the miles flowed by as easily as our conversation did and we soon found ourselves arriving in Chepstow through a fantastically-decorated tunnel under the M48. Young graffiti artists had been given free rein and had designed a wonderful tribute to Chepstow itself, highlighting many of its features through a chain of colour stretching from one end of the tunnel to the other. We took a moment to enjoy their work and then pressed on into town.

All too soon, we were approaching the muddy banks of the River Wye at low tide, with the white cliffs of England on the opposite side. I walked in a trance-like state as I felt a draw pulling me towards the end of the Wales Coast Path. It was like my legs were carrying me without any need for my brain's input. I was excited to be nearing such a huge milestone, but there was sadness in my confused mess of emotions too. The WCP has been my life for over eight weeks and now, just like that, it would be over. The end of coastal walking is also my last big milestone before home, which makes the end of my challenge feel very near. I can't wait to arrive back in Presteigne and see my family and friends again, but I love my life on the trail as well and don't want that to come to an end! Amongst all these mixed feelings about my wider challenge, I was also sad that my day of walking with Graham would be over. We'd had such a laugh together that ten miles didn't seem nearly long enough.

On the path along the riverbank, there were lots of ornamental stones bearing the Wales Coast Path dragon shell and the Offa's Dyke acorn. A mosaic-style circle of pictures showing all the counties that both the paths travel through stood in the middle and there was a map of Wales with the coast path highlighted nearby. As I stood and took it all in, a wave of emotion hit me and I had to fight back a tear. Although there have been some tough moments, my 900 miles of coastal walking have been so special and given me many memories that I know will last a lifetime. From Anglesey's wild and rugged coastline to the limestone cliffs of the Gower, the industry of the River Dee and southern cities to the breathtaking beauty of Pembrokeshire, every mile has showed me something magnificent or taught me something new. I've met so many wonderful people every day too – both old friends and friendly strangers, close family and distant relatives – and each individual has made each day a little more special. To be standing at the end of it made me feel elated because I'd achieved a huge goal, but also sad because it was over. I was glad that Graham was there with a pat on the shoulder and congratulatory hug to stop me from getting too lost in my own thoughts and emotions. We walked over the attractive Old Wye Bridge to take some photos of Chepstow Castle, which stands proudly on a low cliff by the river, and I set foot in England for the first time since leaving Chester 51 days ago. We soon beat a hasty retreat back to Wales though, to enjoy a hot meal and a couple of celebratory pints!

By early afternoon, I was bidding farewell to Graham as he set off to the station to start his long journey back to Leeds. I'm so grateful that he travelled all the way down to walk with me as he has made every moment from the minute he arrived brilliant. We had a comfortable night in a fantastic B & B, walked through heavy rain while happily chatting and, together, completed the path that has made up nearly 90% of my challenge. It's been a wonderful day and his company made it even more special.

I'm now lying on a comfortable double bed having closed my Wales Coast Path book for the last time on my challenge. Again, I had to fight back a tear as I look ahead to my final five days of walking. The beautiful scenery of Offa's Dyke will soon return me to home once more, and I intend to enjoy each moment that remains of my Welsh Wander to the fullest. Diolch, Llwybr Arfordir Cymru – thank you, Wales Coast Path – you've given me the experience of a lifetime over the last 51 days. It has been a true privilege to follow your dragon shells from start to finish.

Nos da, pawb. I'll see you tomorrow, when I'm back in my tent and following the acorn signs through beautiful borderlands.

Offa's Dyke:
Chepstow to Presteigne

Day 59
Sedbury Cliffs to Monmouth

When I woke up this morning, I was excited to get back on the Offa's Dyke Path. I picked up my faithful Scarpa boots and slid my feet inside for what feels like the millionth time. This morning, however, for the first time, there was a distinct dampness seeping up from the inner sole to greet my feet. They've been dunked into numerous seas and rivers and fought through many storms, all while not letting a drop of water in, but the mileage has finally begun to take its toll. The other issue that I've been noticing is the slow-but-sure decline in traction on slippery surfaces. The soles have been ground against tarmac, concrete, gravel, rock, sand and all other forms of high-friction terrain, and so have worn down to a rather thin layer. I can feel every stone that I stand on, and have to be more careful than normal when coming downhill. They are my faithful friends, though, and have carried me for over 900 miles of walking, so they will stick with me until the end.

I had a nice chat with a lady on the bus to Sedbury Cliffs at eight in the morning, and was soon standing looking over the River Severn at the start of the Offa's Dyke Path. A simple stone marked the beginning, so I took a photo and then set off along the ancient earthworks once more. As I looked around at the scenery, I instantly felt guilty. When people have asked about my favourite sections of walking to date, I've automatically thought coastal and haven't even considered the ODP. In fact, even while I was walking the northern section in my first week of Welsh wandering, I was thinking mainly about reaching the coast and then Bangor. I hadn't properly stopped to take in the wonderful borderlands scenery. The dyke was lined with oak and ash and I walked along the top with a big smile on my face. I was back in proper walkers' country, and was loving every second. A local lady added to this feeling by tipping me off about a less slippery route down a field as soon as she saw me. People on the dyke are used to long-distance walkers, so the alien looks of south-east Wales were to be no more.

The dyke wound its way through woodland and open fields as I revelled in the natural beauty all around. I was totally in the moment, losing myself in the sounds of the songbirds, the smells of the flowers, the feel of the raindrops trickling off the leaves onto my bare arms and the sight of a million shades of green reaching towards the horizon as far as the eye could see. My merry state continued all the way to Wintour's Leap, where I pushed through some shrubbery to reach the cliff edge. My jaw dropped as I took in the scene before me. The high cliff drops vertically to a huge meander of the River Wye, which then straightens up and heads towards Chepstow. The tree canopy was a deep emerald and beyond the breathtaking valley views, the rolling hills of eastern Wales reminded me oh-so-much of home. Legend has it that the royalist Lord Wintour was on the run from the Roundheads when he was headed off in this spot. Not wanting to be captured, he took a huge leap off the rocks and landed in the deep waters of the Wye, somehow surviving the fall and swimming to safety on the other bank. Whether this happened or not, I don't know, but I wasn't even slightly tempted to put the physics to the test! Much better to just sit and marvel at the beauty.

After more pretty woodland walking along the dyke earthworks, I let out another audible gasp of ecstatic shock. I'd reached the Devil's Pulpit and had an eerily misty view down to the ruins of Tintern Abbey in its bend of the Wye. It is said that the devil stood on the naturally protruding rock and preached to the monks in the abbey, trying to lure them away from their duties. He never succeeded, of course, and his 'pulpit' now serves as a perfect viewpoint down to the picture-postcard village.

I arrived in Tintern 20 minutes later, after a steep descent from the ridgeline, and stood in awe of the Abbey. Although partly ruinous, much of the gigantic gothic-style building is still standing and as I wandered around the outside, I was fascinated by the intricacy in the stonework that was created with only basic hand tools over 800 years ago. The sheer scale of the abbey boggles the mind, and I was snapping some photographs when a familiar car pulled in. Gareth and Menai were on their way to take Guto back to Bath University before heading to Gatwick and then on to Peru! We'd arranged to meet for lunch in Tintern and thankfully, our timings all fitted in nicely. It was so lovely to see them all again, after staying with this wonderful and inspiring family on the Llŷn Peninsula section of my walk, and we spent a happy hour swapping stories of our travels. Gareth, Menai and I have now all completed the Wales Coast Path so we had plenty of notes to compare, and Guto has recently returned from an exciting trip to Thailand. After seeing a video of his holiday, I think a new place has been added to my holiday wish list! Gareth sorted me out some free sandwiches from the Anchor Inn after kindly buying our tasty lunches, and then it was time to part as we continued on our very different travels. I was so pleased to have been able to spend more time with Gareth, Menai and Guto, and hope that they can come to visit us in Presteigne soon. Peru has nothing on Powys!

I spent the next hour and a half in the abbey itself. I'd only intended to stay for half an hour as I still had over ten miles to walk, but I had become totally absorbed by everything around me. The abbey living quarters, though mostly ruined, show remarkably advanced designs and revolutionary drainage and plumbing systems for the thirteenth century. The kitchen still shows a hatch and two areas for washing up and many octagonal column bases show where second floors were supported. The real star of the abbey though, is the church. This outstanding building towers above everything else on the site, with lavishly-carved arches and windows. As I walked around in a trance-like state, each new perspective revealed a new and fascinating feature. There is even some surviving medieval glass in two high windows. The church was very spiritual and I felt totally at peace as I ambled around gazing at the colossal arches and

Great West Window. I met some nice people to chat to as well, but as my watch hit half three, I had to drag myself away and make the steep climb back up to Offa's Dyke. I had known that Tintern Abbey would be nice, but I found it so special and the whole quaint village has become one of my very favourite places in my whole Welsh Wander. I know I'll return to spend a full day there soon.

Climbing back to the ODP, I knew I had to get cracking. I had ten miles to do in a little over three hours before sunset, and my legs were finding the going tough. After a couple of flat weeks along the South Wales coast, they've forgotten what a hill feels like. The scenery was still incredible, but I was beginning to focus more and more on the end point at Monmouth. I was pitching my tent tonight and though I can do it in the dark now, it's a lot easier by daylight. Despite the pain in my legs, I flew up the final hill of the day with three miles ahead and didn't even stop for breath at the top. This changed when I reached the Kymin Estate though. The strange white building with battlements was suddenly lit up in a deep orange glow and as I rounded the corner, I could see why. The sunset had turned beautiful and it silhouetted the hills and valleys behind the town of Monmouth and the winding River Wye. I allowed myself a minute to snap some photos and then began my descent. The vivid orange light from the setting sun was scattering through the trees onto fallen leaves, giving the impression that the whole forest floor was on fire, just as my legs and feet needed to be to get me to Monmouth before darkness descended!

On this walk, I've often run short sections of downhill to save the constant effort of slowing myself down. Today, though, I ran the whole last mile downhill into Monmouth. My slick-gripped boots meant that my walking poles were acting more as ski poles than anything else as I slipped, slid and charged my way down the side of the hill. Crashing into the gate at the bottom to stop, I eventually followed a road into Monmouth and set up camp before going to eat again. Although I've loved the last few nights in real beds, I'm quite pleased to be back in my little canvas home, lying comfortably on both of my roll mats. I know that I will sleep well tonight.

Today has been really special. I've fully appreciated the wonders of the ODP, seen some truly stunning vistas of the Wye Valley, met up with wonderful people, experienced the spirituality and total peacefulness of Tintern Abbey, and ended with a stunning sunset over my final evening destination. I'm hoping for more of the same on Day 60 of my Welsh Wander.

Nos da, pawb. I'll see you tomorrow, when I've got a bit further along my final leg of this beautiful, varied and interesting national trail.

Postscript

By this point of my Wander, I was only too aware how close the end was. Each mile was one nearer to my last and as a result, I was more intensely involved in my surroundings than I had been in my entire 1,020 miles to Chepstow. Each time I saw an interesting building or the sunlight scattering through leaves, a pretty view of a valley below or a buzzard circling overhead, I knew it could be the last time I'd see that on my adventure, and so I would stop and take the time to study every little detail of what was before my eyes. Each would bring a wave of happiness with a tinge of sadness, but one moment in Day 59 still makes me laugh to this day. I didn't include it in the blog for fear of embarrassing the person responsible if they ever read it, but in the book, I feel safe!

While I was wandering in a trance-like state around the kitchen in Tintern Abbey, a lady stepped over the foot-wide, shallow drainage system. Looking to her husband in amazement, she exclaimed in the most excited American accent you can possibly imagine, 'Look Hunny! Do you think that's the moat?' I turned away and leant against a wall in a fit of silent giggles, slightly disbelieving of what I'd just heard, before remembering that the history of North America is very unlike ours. Composing myself, I turned to chat to the couple and explained the purpose of a moat, and that it would therefore be far wider and deeper than this drainage ditch. We chatted a few more times as we looked around, and they kindly donated to my cause as I went to leave. I hope they enjoyed the rest of their UK visit and found a real moat to enjoy somewhere!

Day 60
Monmouth to Pandy

I had a nice chat with my Dutch camping neighbours this morning before walking through the gatehouse on the ancient Monnow Bridge – the last surviving bridge gatehouse in Britain – and treating myself to a Waitrose cooked breakfast. Starting walking at quarter past ten, I feared that I may have underestimated today's 17 miles. Yesterday, my legs had struggled with the return to the hills and I'd only just managed to pitch my tent before it got completely dark. I set off with speed and determination in my stride, telling myself that I would reach Llantilio Crossenny before two o'clock to give myself a slower second half of the walk.

The dramatic cliffs and stunning meanders of the Wye were behind me and the path became gentler as it left Monmouth. The open fields and forest tracks were still pretty, but there were fewer 'wow' moments to halt progress. I had a long conversation with a lady at the top of a fairly easy, but long, climb and then pushed on down the other side towards a more open landscape. As I emerged from the forest, I spotted two roe deer in the field below. They were oblivious to my presence, so I slowly took my camera out of my bag and edged behind a tree. As I looked on, the deer began to skip and suddenly came sprinting up the bank towards me. They chased each other around trees and pronked (leapt with all four feet leaving the ground simultaneously) without a care in the world. I watched avidly as these graceful creatures played, and felt so privileged to be allowed to enter their secret world for a brief minute or two. The moment of realisation that they weren't alone was as comical as it was saddening. One strayed too close to my place of partial-concealment, physically jumped in the air in surprise before landing and waiting stock-still to see if I'd noticed them. Soon working out that I had, the deer broke eye contact and set off at a gallop across the field in the opposite direction, closely followed by its friend. I watched until they were out of sight and then set off again myself. It was one of many special wildlife encounters that I will treasure from this trip.

My return to Offa's Dyke has also brought the return of an old friend. During my first week of walking, there were some very physically- and mentally-demanding moments. My body wasn't yet used to the strains of daily 18-mile hikes with 18 kg on my back and my spreading feet meant that I was wearing boots that were half a size too small. But through all of the physical and emotional struggles, one constant presence kept me happy and focused: feathers. They were sticking out of the majority of waymarkers and the link to my maternal grandparents' surname of Bird didn't take long to make. The thought that the two people who are the reason for me choosing Alzheimer's Society to fundraise for were helping to guide me along my route was a huge comfort, and no matter how bad things got, the feathers were always there to keep me going. I broke into a big smile yesterday when I saw my first feather marker and glanced upwards towards the heavens. It felt very different seeing them now than it did all those weeks ago in my first hundred miles. My body is still tired, but I know that I'll complete my challenge now. I have no doubts about my physical capabilities or mental strength any more, so the reappearance of the feathers felt more like a celebration. They are cheering me home on my last 70 miles, and every one I see puts a little grin on my face and a little warmth in my heart.

While roaming through the fields in my own happy world,

I came across a lovely Canadian couple going in the opposite direction. They're walking the whole ODP and will finish in Sedbury tomorrow. Like me, they have very mixed emotions about the finish. They expected to feel ecstatic, but it's amazing how quickly you adapt to this way of life and how attached you can grow to the freedom of it. Every morning, I wake up and think about where I'm going to sleep and where I'm going to eat. Once that's sorted, I'm free to wander and explore my beautiful home country along the trail, discovering new places, learning new things and meeting new people. To return to the real world is going to be difficult and so although I can't wait to see everyone at home again, a large part of me worries that I'll find it very hard to settle back into 'normal life'. Still, only time will tell, and I'm sure I'll be too distracted by friends and family to miss my nomadic life too much.

After passing Llantilio Crossenny at half one, I was ahead of schedule. I soon caught up a group of walkers from Farnborough and we got talking about my challenge and their hike. As they were following the ODP too, we walked together for a couple of miles to White Castle, where we enjoyed looking around the impressive ruins of what was once a formidable fortress. I'd forgotten how different it is walking with a group. There are always conversations to dip into and people to get to know, questions to ask and answer and beautiful scenery and historic sites to discuss together. It was fantastic! I also met a nice couple from Cwmbran at the castle who'd read the sign on my bag. They, along with the walking group, kindly sponsored me and we chatted for a long while in the shadow of the thick-walled inner castle gatehouse. The man was a professional photographer and as I bid farewell to my short-term walking friends and left the castle, he took a couple of snaps of me with my bag and is going to email them to me in a few days. I dread to think what my scruffy beard will look like in a professional-quality photograph!

Over the next few miles, I enjoyed the familiar scenery of rolling green hills and could see higher ridges ahead that will make up tomorrow's 17 miles. At Llangattock Lingoed, I spent a quiet moment in a whitewashed church that was offering tea and coffee to walkers. As I was about to leave, a nice couple from Sydney walked in. We spoke for a good time before parting warmly, them wishing me luck for my remaining 50 miles and me hoping they enjoy the rest of their week in beautiful Wales. I cracked on with the last two miles of the day and was soon arriving in Pandy, where I'd seen two campsites on the map. Opting for the one nearest the pub, I turned right and was disappointed to find on arrival that it was a Caravan Club-only site. Apparently the guests would complain to the club if they saw a tent, meaning that the site would lose its status and much of its business. I left wondering how some people could be so petty and uncaring. How much offence can a small bit of canvas and two poles cause? The site owner's hands were tied and she was very apologetic, kindly recommending the bunkhouse across the road rather than the half-hour walk to the other site. And that is where I am now! I have the whole place to myself and will enjoy an evening in front of the TV while my tent dries out, instead of getting even wetter in tonight's forecast rain. I guess everything happens for a reason!

Nos da, pawb. Tomorrow, I will have a fantastic day walking with my Auntie Denise along the ridge to Hay Bluff and down into Hay-On-Wye – a mere 24 miles from home. Journey's end is starting to feel very close indeed!

Day 61
Pandy to Hay-On-Wye

Waking up this morning in my own private bunkhouse was a delight. I put the news on as I was packing up my bag and then joined Alan in the Old Pandy Inn, where he cooked me a wonderful breakfast. As we were discussing the day's route, my walking partner for the next 17 miles, Auntie Denise, walked in with my Uncle Dave (who had driven her to our start point and would meet us again at the end). It had been a while since I last saw them, so it was lovely to catch up before we set off on a three-mile climb to the first trig point of an 11-mile ridge high in the Black Mountains. Today was to be a real test for both Auntie Denise and myself!

We hit our stride on the uphill and reached the top, requiring only a couple of minutes' rest on the steepest sections. Ahead of us, the ridge reached beyond the horizon and behind us, the rolling hills of yesterday's walking gently fell to touch the valley floor at Pandy. A brief photo stop is all we needed and we cracked on with 11 miles of walking that would be fairly easy in terms of ascent and descent, but challenging with the exposure to the buffeting winds. There was to be no shelter or respite from it for the next few hours as we travelled across empty bog and heather, but the beautiful views on all sides would be enough to keep us going.

While on the ridge, it didn't take long to notice the stark contrast between Wales and England. To the west, the mountains of the Brecon Beacons dominated the skyline with steep-sided glacial valleys cutting deep into the landscape. Many bluffs were visible where the interlocking spurs of river valleys had been truncated by the sheer weight and force of ancient ice unrelentingly creeping south. To the east, a comparatively flat patchwork of fields of all shades of green was spread out like a carpet, only broken by the occasional darker woodland or tiny settlement. Both sides were equally beautiful, though strikingly different, and as we traced the fine line between the landscapes, a mottled, ever-changing pattern of sunlight highlighted individual features all around. One of these features was the ruin of Llanthony Priory. We could just about make out the stone arches and from afar; it looked like a smaller version of Tintern. It is a sight that I want to see at some point in the near future as I've been told it's a very special and spiritual place, but having worked so hard to climb to 600 m on the ridge line, we decided against dropping over 300 m only to have to climb steeply back up again. I will return with my car so I can conveniently park outside and then drive on to the Old Pandy Inn to eat!

A habit we adopted in the University Mountain Walking Club was having a first lunch and second lunch. It spreads energy through the day more effectively and you don't have that overly full feeling which is horrible to walk through. As today is the most mountainous walk of my whole hike, we enjoyed first lunch in the minimal shelter of a trig point. Auntie Denise had very kindly bought a lot of my favourite foods and snacks and it took a lot of restraint not to eat all 16 Jammie Dodgers in one sitting! After refuelling, we pushed on and noticed a wall of dark clouds gathering to our left. As the wind picked up and the temperature dropped a few degrees, we donned our waterproofs and prepared for a sideways onslaught from Mother Nature. The rain did arrive a minute later, but although it was heavy and the wind threw each drop at us with five times its normal force, we soon walked out the other side of the downpour and were back in glorious sunshine.

We reached the final big milestone of my walk, apart from the actual finish, at about half past two. Above Hay Bluff, we hit a spot that is 703 m above sea level, making it the highest point of my entire Welsh Wander. We took a selfie to mark the moment, and I was once again hit by how close the end now was. In the valley below we could see Hay-On-Wye, which is somewhere we class as being in our local area, and the mountains we were standing on top of are clearly seen from my golf club in Kington. Home was getting very near indeed. After stopping for second lunch in the only sheltered spot we'd seen since first lunch, I got another reminder of how close home was in the form of a visit from my neighbour David, who lives across the field from us. This was no ordinary visit though! David has his own plane and we had arranged last night for him to fly over us on the ridge. Through the day, the prospect of a flypast had got more exciting as David texted updates such as 'got a professional photographer to join me' and 'the MOD are flying low helicopters in the area, but they've given us special clearance to fly over you!' By half past three, Auntie Denise and I were brimming with excitement and approaching the trig point on the summit of Hay Bluff. We'd seen David fly by at altitude a few minutes before, though he obviously hadn't seen us, but his return along the ridge was much lower and with a wing wobble for a wave, he circled us a couple of times before setting off into the distance. Grinning from ear to ear, we marvelled at the perfect timing of our own flypast and felt a little like royalty as we left the summit and started down the hill towards the valley below.

The sun was still shining on the countryside that I know so well and we were soon bearing down on Hay, after Auntie Denise had had a little slip resulting in that *Great British Bake Off* worst fear – a soggy bottom! Arriving in the town, we walked through the quaint streets to the hotel where she and my Uncle Dave are staying. They gave me a lift to a local campsite and picked me up again once I'd put up my canvas home for the last time on my Welsh Wander, and made myself less smelly. We had a very interesting meal in the hotel, with lots of little dishes that were packed full of wonderful flavours, before we parted for the night. I was proud of my auntie for how well she'd coped with a long day of challenging walking, and had thoroughly enjoyed her company throughout. It was a pleasure to walk with her to the highest point of my trek, and to spend the evening together with my uncle enjoying the poshest dinner I'd had in the last two months!

Back in my Coleman tent that I've grown to love so much, I reflected on all of the nights I've spent in here throughout my challenge. We've ridden out violent storms, holding strong without a drop of water reaching the inside, slept under countless clear, starry skies and stayed warm through the recent cold nights. As I drifted off to sleep, there was a tinge of sadness that our adventures around Wales together had come to an end, and I wondered when I would next be closing my eyes under the canvas that has become my home.

Nos da, pawb. I'll see you tomorrow when I'm only a 14-mile day away from arriving home.

Postscript
I actually did return to Llanthony Priory and The Old Pandy Inn with my friend Chad less than a week after finishing my Wander! The Priory was even more magical than I'd hoped it might be. The old building feels very similar to Tintern, if a little smaller, and the row of stone arches frame the ridgeline that the ODP follows. I spent a lot of time leaning against them, gazing up at some of the miles I'd walked a week ago with Auntie Denise. A mixture of happy memories, pride and sorrow that it was all over ran through my mind all at once. Alan in the Inn remembered me too, despite my lack of beard, and it was nice to reminisce for a while over a plate of fish and chips and a diet coke!

The end of Day 61 came with a little sadness too. Shortly after David's flypast, my phone went berserk and the memory card stopped working. I lost all of the photos I'd taken since Caldicot as I hadn't yet uploaded those few days to Facebook. I was hugely upset to lose some of the pictures, because they are memories that cannot be repeated. It does, however, give me an excuse to walk the first three days of Offa's Dyke again. Every cloud has a silver lining – you just need to look hard enough.

Day 62
Hay-On-Wye to Gladestry

Breakfast today was a lovely treat, enjoying a full Welsh at the Swan Hotel in Hay-On-Wye with Auntie Denise and Uncle Dave. I'd felt quite sad half an hour earlier while packing away my little canvas home for the last time, but that was all forgotten as we recalled highlights from yesterday's walk and looked ahead to the next day and a half. Parting with a hug and a handshake, they went to pack, ready to go home via a visit to my grandad, and I set off in search of the nearest café. I had only ten miles ahead today and saw no reason to rush them. I enjoyed a couple of cups of tea and slices of cake before grabbing some snacks for the trail and setting off over the bridge on the River Wye!

The first few miles were pleasant and easy as I walked along the river bank and through fields. The scenery was very similar to home and I felt the need to savour each step as there were now not many of them left in my challenge at all. Red kites were soaring overhead and the sunshine was managing to hold out for large stretches with only the occasional downpour. I followed country lanes and grassy tracks all the way to Newchurch, where the church itself was offering tea and biscuits. It's little touches like this that make the ODP feel special. Feeling a little peckish, I popped in and enjoyed a quick snack while spending a couple of minutes reflecting on my journey to this point. I didn't want to get too bogged down in the past to enjoy the present though, and so soon cracked on towards the next rolling green hill.

On the summit, I was due to meet Rob Dingle, who is the Offa's Dyke Path National Trail Officer. I was excited to find out more about the route that makes up my first and last days of walking, and knew that he would be full of interesting snippets of information. We met near the top of a steep climb and greeted each other warmly, despite my panting! The views all around were stunning and I could pick out a lot of places that I regularly drive through. Rob and I soon turned to the topic of the trail and I asked the question that has been nagging in my mind for a while. Was the dyke built for defence or as a show of power? I'd been leaning towards believing the latter and Rob shared this suspicion. He knows the path well, having walked its length at least eight times, and said that there are many places where it seems strategically placed to be very visible from the west. Strategically, it would make no difference if the dyke was in those spots or 20 m away, but the number of times it's more visible on the western side seems to suggest that its main purpose was King Offa showing the wild Welsh that he had the influence to create such a gigantic feat of engineering, and so wasn't to be messed with. This is all guesswork, of course, as Rob told me that the earliest written record of the dyke's creation is dated some 200 years after its completion.

We walked for a fascinating three miles into Gladestry, discussing my challenge and the dyke along the way. When I put the ODP in my top three sections of walking during the whole challenge because of its variety of scenery, Rob said that 'every day on the dyke has something different to Offa'. It was a perfect summation of the path that I have grown so fond of, and so when Rob presented me with a bottle of Monty's Best Offa beer and some genuine path waymarkers to keep, I was very touched. I'd had a wonderful time walking with him and finding out all about the trail, become very envious of his job and now had my own little piece of the path to keep.

My accommodation for my last night of Welsh wandering was sorted by my colleague and friend Suzanne, who lives in Gladestry. She had offered me a bed at hers a long while ago, but as the decorators are there this week, her parents Viv and Margaret had kindly said they'd let me stay. I bumped into Sue from the local school, who kindly gave me a lift up to the bungalow, and after I'd showered, Suzanne popped round for a catch up. It was lovely to see her again, though it felt strange being back amongst people that I know. I later discovered that I had many links with her parents too. Viv and Margaret often dance with my grandparents at their ballroom dancing classes, and Viv's brother Mike and sister-in-law Gill are members at Kington Golf Club. I've played with them before, and Gill's sister Betty is my regular partner in mixed competitions! All of the familiar faces, names and little connections were adding to the feeling of being nearly home and, for the first time, I began to feel really excited about it. The sad tinge caused by the end of my adventure being around the corner is still there, but I know that an overwhelming happiness and delight at seeing many people who I love and care about before walking through my front door again will dominate the next 24 hours.

I've had a lovely evening chatting with Viv and Margaret and am now in a warm bed looking ahead to a day of many significant moments. Tomorrow, I will walk to Kington with my friend Francis, have a little gathering with fellow members at the golf club, walk six miles to close my loop of Wales alone and then retrace my first steps on the challenge down the Slough Road to see friends and family at my home. I'd had offers from various people to join me for the last bit of walking, but closing my Welsh circuit is something that I've always pictured doing alone. That is how I've spent 95% of this trek and so it feels right to walk the last few miles that way too. However, to see the faces of many people who have supported me along this journey when I arrive home will be a fabulous end. I hope that if you've enjoyed my blog, donated, joined me for a day, or put me up for a night, you can make an appearance so that I can thank you in person. I'll save my overall reflections until tomorrow night, but people have played a much greater role in my wander than I expected, so I'm glad that I'll be able to finish it amongst some of the people who've made it as incredible as it has become.

Nos da, pawb. I'll see you all tomorrow, when I'm back at home and my Welsh Wander has come to an end. It's going to be an emotional day.

Day 63
Gladestry to Presteigne

This morning started perfectly: a cooked breakfast and nice conversation with Viv and Margaret. Their hospitality had been so fantastic and I hope we meet again soon. After a kind donation, Viv drove me down the road to meet my badminton friend Francis, and we were soon climbing rapidly to the very wet and misty summit of Hergest Ridge. Francis has walked this route a lot and so his knowledge of the local area is excellent. It was fascinating hearing stories and legends about the ridge, and I began to feel guilty for not having bothered to find out about or even walk this path, despite having lived only eight miles away from it for twenty years! *The Hound Of The Baskervilles* was based on a legend of a hound on Hergest Ridge, and as we neared the summit, we came across another site whose stories, both mythical and real, were very interesting. Legend says the Whetstone rolls off the ridge and down into the river on certain nights, before returning to its location on the grassy tump. In reality, it served as a trading post in the times of tuberculosis and plague outbreaks, when the people of Gladestry and Kington would communicate and trade by leaving things on the rock.

Geologically, the rock is just as fascinating. It's a lump of volcanic gabbro from a hill across the valley and is far too large to have been moved there by humans. Something much more powerful was at play. During the last ice age, a vast ice sheet covered much of Northern Britain all the way down to Mid Wales. Glaciers filled the valleys and the rate of erosion on the local rocks under the sheer weight of ice was rapid. Huge chunks were sheared off rock faces or toppled by freeze-thaw weathering, and the glaciers acted as conveyer belts, carrying the rocks along their slow, inexorable routes. As the ice melted and the glaciers retreated, the eroded debris was dropped where it stood, resulting in large chunks of rock that are alien to the area being found in strange places, much like the Whetstone today.

Following a quick descent, we arrived in Kington far too early, considering I was meant to be arriving at the golf club at midday and it was still not even 11 o'clock. To kill time, Francis and I stopped for a tea in a café, where we met Peter from Sydney. He was hiking the dyke, but was taking a day off today to see Presteigne's famous Judge's Lodging. A nice discussion ended with a kind donation and Francis sent me on my way towards the golf club that I have been a member of since I was a child. I'd expected a tough climb up to the club as it holds the title of being the highest golf course in England, but perhaps my legs were running on adrenaline as I reached the top in a little under 15 minutes.

On arriving at the eighteenth fairway, I saw Jenny Kelly waving an umbrella and expected to round the corner and see a few people waiting. What I got however, was a huge welcoming party of over 40 people! Family, friends, members of the golf club and rather touchingly, Callum, Dan and Max who were in the class that I taught for nearly two years, had all turned up to welcome me to the clubhouse. I was totally overwhelmed, and after being the focus of many photos, was taken into the clubhouse to eat and mingle. There are far too many people to name, but seeing each and every one of you was so special. Mum and Dad made speeches before putting me on the spot, at which point I rambled on for a little while and hoped that my gratitude towards everybody came across! A second cooked breakfast of the day went down a treat, and after speaking to everybody that had come to make the moment memorable, and laughing as the boys tried to walk while wearing Wilson, I was waved off on my last eight and a half miles. I'd been so moved by the number of people that had shown up and by the conversations we'd had, and my heart was as full as my bag as I walked across the first fairway and out of sight.

Climbing towards Rushock Hill, I was distracted by an amazing occurrence to my left. The rains of earlier had moved off and as the sun heated the ground, mist was rising at an impressive rate off the freshly-ploughed fields. The breeze was sweeping the mists along centimetres above the earth and they were swirling around the trees at the far end. I stood and watched for a few moments, admiring the beauty of the elements and was hit by a wave of realisation. I had only a few hours left of Welsh wandering and then moments like this would become much rarer. Vowing to take in every little detail of the landscape until I got home, I walked on to the crest of the hill to rejoin the actual Offa's Dyke earthworks for the first time since my first day back on the trail. There, on the waymarker, a feather was waiting for me. I looked to the sky, knowing that my grandma was looking down on me and urging me on towards the finish. The dyke was laid out along the ground like a huge rope to follow all the way home, so I walked along its top, totally lost in the moment.

I made good on my promise to myself during the next mile, taking in every detail of the beauty surrounding me. Nuthatches were flitting between elder trees whose leaves were beginning to turn deep red for autumn, and the rolling hills of home were dotted around haphazardly like they had been dropped into place accidentally. After crossing Herrock, I saw a rather special hill. This one was rather flat on top and not particularly high. It had two fields visible on its summit and was almost hidden behind a larger, wooded ridge in front. It wasn't anything great in comparison with other hills around, but it was home. I was seeing the top of our family farm for the first time since I walked away from it on 26th July. Without warning, a tear started to run down my cheek. Home, all of a sudden, felt very close indeed and I took a minute to savour the welcoming view before wiping my eyes and continuing the descent to Burfa.

After a dangerous-feeling road section around the sharp bends of the Walton road, I turned left by a sign for Presteigne and was confronted by another homely sign that nearly caused another tear to escape my eye. The ODP waymarker said 'Granner Wood – 1 mile'. This small but attractive pine woodland had been the location of my first steps on the Offa's Dyke Path nearly ten weeks ago. I had a little over a mile to go to complete my Welsh perimeter hike, and of course, a feather was stuck into the waymarker to make sure I got there safely.

I was lost in my own thoughts for that final mile. Flashbacks of my time on the path were only briefly interrupted by my urge to photograph the beautiful scenery, and I was soon within sight of the woodland where it all began. Still with well over an hour to go until I was due home, I tried to slow my legs down, but they weren't listening. They are used to my fast walking pace and had decided that having walked at that pace for hundreds of miles, that is how we'd finish the challenge too. I was just along for the ride. Thankfully, I soon met a lovely group of five walkers who were doing the dyke in the other direction. We shared stories, and I was envious of the remaining time they had left. Although I was desperate to arrive home, see my loved ones and finish the route, I also didn't want the challenge to be over. It has become my normal life. I wake up, pack Wilson, eat breakfast and walk all day, only stopping for food. To go back to staying in one place was going to be very hard indeed.

After wishing the group a wonderful next few days of walking, my legs propelled me forward to the finish line of my loop. I photographed the last waymarker (feather and all), crossed the Slough Road and touched the first one. I'm not ashamed to admit that I shed a few tears in that moment. I'd touched the rough wood of this sign at the start of my Welsh Wander, and it was now nearly over. I'd completed the whole circuit of Wales and there was no new ground left to see. For 1,096 miles, I've walked around the perimeter of my home country and learned so much about it, and myself, as I've travelled. They were tears that I couldn't attach to one emotion. There was a chunk of sadness, a pile of happiness, some relief, tiredness, love, loss – and running through them all were the millions of memories that I've made on the path. It was a special moment that I will savour forever.

I sat on the steps into Granner Wood for the next 20 minutes before the time came to head for home. A nice couple from Evenjobb were walking in my direction, so I joined them for a short way, chatting about the challenge and Snowdonia. I think that they came along at just the right moment to stop me getting too lost in my own thoughts. After parting, I set off down the Slough Road at pace hoping not to be late for my own homecoming! I soon reached the bottom of the hill and saw that my family had put out motivational signs, with pictures from my Wander, on the roadside for my final few hundred metres. The surprises kept on coming as I rounded the final bend and saw a huge crowd of people equal in size to the one at the golf club. They started clapping and cheering and I had to compose myself so that I didn't start blubbing! Before this challenge, I never cried, but the emotions of walking such a long distance are so intense that today it felt totally normal. I reached the bottom of the drive and didn't know where to look. There were so many faces of people that I know and care about, who had made the effort to walk up the road just to see a slightly smelly, bearded man walk home.

My family ran forward to hug me in turn and I felt the love and belonging that one only truly feels from being at home. My grandparents had decorated the drive with a wonderful homemade banner and bunting and my parents, with help from friends, had laid on a huge buffet underneath a couple of gazebos. The effort that had gone into the gathering took my breath away, and after many more photos, my next hour was spent trying to chat to everybody who had shown up. I was so touched that they had come and wanted to tell them all in person, so I hope I managed to get round everyone! Again, there are far too many people to name, but every single one of you made my homecoming so special and for that, I'll be forever grateful.

After a couple of hours, I noticed a white car which I vaguely recognised shoot up the drive. Dismissing my idea of who the owner might be quite rapidly, I continued chatting and then noticed a hooded man rounding the corner of the gazebos. With a grin on his face, Derek Brockway threw his hood back and walked over to greet me. I couldn't believe that he'd gone so far out of his way to come and see me at the end of a challenge that he has already helped to make so special. He kindly presented me with a signed copy of his book, *Great Welsh Walks*, and we spoke warmly about the last few days of Welsh wandering before being organised for various photos.

People began leaving in a slow trickle to start the walk back down the Slough Road as the evening grew darker and colder, until only a small group of us were left. Retreating indoors, we all found a perch around the living room and the conversation flowed until a knock at the door signalled the arrival of my good friends Matt and Adam. They'd kindly bought me a present and when I showed them into the lounge, their shock on seeing Derek sitting in one of our armchairs was quite comical! The conversations continued to flow freely and I had to stop and look around in amazement at one point. Our living room had never seen such a variety of people all at the same time. Mum, Dad, Em and I were often joined by Grandma and Grandpa, but the addition of my close friends Matt, Chad and Adam and then our beloved Welsh weatherman sitting in the armchair in the corner was quite bizarre! What was even stranger was that this group of people, whose connections to the family are very different, were all chatting so easily and it was ten o'clock by the time everyone started to make a move. The whole evening had been so lovely and it had ended in a very special way. Everyone exchanged hugs and we stood on the drive to wave people off one by one. Derek still had to drive back to South Wales and I was so touched that he had stayed with us for so long. He really is one of the nicest guys you could hope to meet, and had fitted straight in with my family and friends. I know that we'll stay in touch in the future.

I began this blog last night, but once two o'clock had come and gone, I decided to finish it today! There were so many wonderful moments to write about that to try and finish telling you about them while tired would have done them a disservice. I cannot say thank you enough to everybody who came to see me at my two homecoming gatherings. You made my last day so perfect, and I will treasure the memories for the rest of my life. As a bonus, the collection pots at both events raised a staggering amount of money! The golf club pot contained a total of £290 and the homecoming one made £215. Everybody's generosity has taken my total over £5,300, which, after originally setting a target of £1,100, is mind-boggling! So here begins my section of thank yous!

My Welsh Wander has been the single greatest experience of my life. I've seen so many breathtaking sights, had some incredibly special moments and battled through some tough ones too. Every day had something new and exciting to offer amongst the miles, and I've learned so much about myself and about my beloved home country. Wales is a land of beauty and brilliance. From the dramatic mountains of the north, to the rugged coastlines and bustling cities of the south, with the wide expanse of Cardigan Bay and ancient earthwork of Offa's Dyke linking the two, every area is special. Her history and natural, picture-postcard scenery have enchanted my imagination so many times in every day, and I have fallen even more deeply in love with her than I was before I began walking. The Welsh people have had a huge part to play in that too. The amount of kindness that I have received during my challenge has been out of this world and again, there are far too many people to name individually. For a solo hike, I cannot believe how huge a part people have played in my overall success and enjoyment. So many of my happiest memories from the last ten weeks include people, be they people who I've known for years or people who were total strangers before I started.

Thank you to everybody who gave me a warm bed for a night or more, with special mention to Valmai and her three sisters, who put me up for a total of ten nights, and to family and friends old and new who came to walk with me. Your hospitality and company made my challenge a lot easier and so much happier. Thank you to everybody who let me camp, or even stay in a chalet or their holiday cottage for free, and to everyone who fed me or went to buy me medicine while refusing to take payment. Your willingness to help a stranger or friend has restored my faith in humanity tenfold, and I'll think back to the kindnesses I've received when the opportunity arises for me to help others in the same way.

Thank you to the countless strangers who stopped on the

path to talk to me, and to the many people who had been so directly affected by Alzheimer's and were honest and open in sharing their experiences. Your decision to share your stories with me inspired a deep determination to complete this challenge, and was a huge part of why I stayed so positive in times that were particularly challenging. Thank you to Gareth, Menai and Guto for taking me in when I needed it most and for showing me how strong and genuinely lovely people can be. Thank you to Derek Brockway for getting behind my wander, walking with me and supporting me along the way. Your messages have been a real boost, and seeing you here at the end made the whole occasion even more special than I thought possible.

Thank you to my wonderful family for coming and visiting me, bringing me essential supplies and arranging little details behind the scenes. I couldn't have managed this walk without you and the effort that you'd put into arranging such a special homecoming was the icing on the cake. Seeing your pride at the end was a moment I'll remember for the rest of my life. I love you all so very much. Thank you to every single person who has sponsored me, either online or in the flesh. Your generosity has enabled me to raise over £5,300 for Alzheimer's Society; a cause which is very close to my family's heart. I know that you'll have helped so many people affected by all forms of dementia, and I know too that my grandad will be thanking you from his bed, and my grandma while looking down from above. The incredible total has kept rising every day and has instilled a certainty in me that I would succeed. You gave me the motivation to continue on days when only a fish would feel happy outdoors and my feet felt like they were more blister than skin.

And now for my final thank you. I always knew the isolation would be a challenging part of this trip. It was something that I expected to have a major impact on my mentality and overall success. I think one of the main factors of loneliness is when special things happen, but you have nobody to share them with. Despite the weeks spent walking totally alone and the many hours where I've not seen another soul, I've never felt that – because I've always been able to share the special moments with you. At the end of every day, I've sat in a quiet spot and told you everything that has made that day memorable, and that in itself has been one of the most special things about my Welsh Wander. So my last thank you is to you, the followers of my blog. Thank you for taking the time to read my ramblings from my ramblings, and thank you for sticking with me right until the end.

Nos da, pawb. I'll see you all again at some point in the future, I hope, because you are all now very special to me.

Postscript

When I set off from home at 7 a.m. on 26th July 2016, I felt like a young man going off on a slightly daunting adventure by himself. I would walk around Wales, some close friends and family could use my blog to track my progress, and I would hopefully raise £1,100 for Alzheimer's Society. When I returned home on 1st October 2016, I was met by a small army of people who had taken my little wander into their lives, my blog had received over 24,000 hits and I had raised over £5,300 in sponsorship. My blog hits would eventually climb to over 26,500 and my fundraising to £6,100 (£6,700 with gift aid).

Tom's Welsh Wander grew beyond all of my wildest dreams. It touched so many people in a way that I never thought possible, and in return, these people all inspired me to succeed. The blog gave me something to think about all day while walking, and whenever something happened that was worth including, I would jot it down in my phone and spend the next mile or so thinking about how I could word it. It became a friend in whom I could confide my every thought, feeling and emotion, and as a result, so did all of the readers. Their comments always gave me a little warmth in my heart and a little added drive to continue the following morning. Words cannot describe how special that little blog became to me, and I still visit it from time to time, holding on to those wonderful weeks spent exploring my home country. I hope you have enjoyed reading it as much as I enjoyed writing it!

Settling back into normal life proved to be as tough as I had feared. My family were wonderful, and gave me all the space I needed, but it felt like something was missing. I had happy moments when I would go out to meet friends, but when looking back a week later, I simply couldn't find any enthusiasm for what I'd achieved in the last seven days. In fact, I couldn't actually think of anything I had achieved. On my Wander, I could put a definite figure on how much progress I'd made, whether it be 32 miles in a day or 132 a week. I always had something to be proud of. When I stopped walking, I lost that, and it took a little while to find it again. A struggle that I hadn't expected was the stiffness in my legs and back. With hindsight, I should have walked more in those first few days at home, but I chose instead to take my chance to be lazy! My penance was muscles that were more stiff and aching than they had been in the entire 63 days of walking.

For the first month at home, I struggled to find a purpose for myself. I didn't feel ready to read through the blogs again yet, and took a trip up to Bangor to see Siân, visiting Wales' highest waterfall and a 4,000-year-old yew tree on the way to try and satisfy my thirst for continued discovery. We spent two days hiking in the mountains, which reminded me of the joys of walking all over again, and then I was treated to a very special moment in Caernarfon Castle. The poppies from the Tower of London were on display, cascading over the top of one of one of the towers and spilling out into the grassy courtyard. Crosses were being planted by members of the public to remember loved ones who'd fallen in battle and I planted one for my great, great grandfather, who died in the Somme.

It was while on top of one of the towers there that I experienced a moment so emotional that it snapped me out of my listless state. I was looking out over the Menai Straits section of my Welsh Wander with Siân by my side, when a choir gathered on the gravel directly below us and starting singing the Welsh National Anthem. Their rendition was beautiful, and as I gazed at parts of my walking route, tears started to flow behind my sunglasses. It felt like a celebration of what I'd achieved, and the outpouring of emotion was all I needed to stop desperately clinging to the freedom of those two months, turn the page in my life story and look ahead to the next chapter. As soon as I got home, I started editing my blog into the book that you are reading right now, and each day that I read would bring back a flood of happy memories.

I hope to walk another long distance trail in 2017, to once again experience the magic that comes from exploring new landscapes on foot every day. The thinking time and clarity that my challenge provided helped me decide that I wanted to start a new chapter in my life story, too. I have left the classroom behind to join a fantastic team of outdoor-activity instructors at Manor Adventure, Abernant Lake Hotel. It seems strange now sitting here with a great group of new friends downstairs, who I never would have met if it hadn't been for my Welsh Wander. With the lessons I learned on that trail, I feel more equipped to take on whatever might be thrown at me on the path of life.

Trekking Top Tips!

While walking, I learned a great many things that made my life on the trail easier. Some were my own discoveries and some were passed on to me by fellow walkers, but all were very valuable. The strains of walking such a long way are real, so anything you can do to make life a little easier is worthwhile. This section contains some lessons that I learned, in the hope that they can help you prepare for a big adventure of your own.

- **Buy boots that are half a size bigger than you would normally buy.** You don't want to be walking out of them, but if they feel snug in the shop, they will feel torturous once your feet begin to spread on Day 2. Extra socks can counter any looseness you have in your early training walks.
- **Pack light.** You need to decide how many luxuries you really need to make your trip enjoyable. I had romantic illusions of reading outside my tent, having a couple of clean shirts and plenty of clean boxers! In reality, I had no time to read (and if you do, it'd be far less weighty to download the Kindle or Kobo app to your phone!), and by Day 5, I was on my second pair of boxers and still hadn't changed my walking shirt. I culled 2 kg of kit from my bag when Mum visited that night, but my bag felt 10 kg lighter the next day. If you're not using it, it will feel very heavy indeed!
- **Download mileage charts to your phone.** Setting an achievable goal for the end of a day is vital, and long-distance guidebooks often don't have the detailed mileage information that you will require to do this.
- **Use your phone to photograph the relevant pages of your guidebook each morning (or download a digital copy).** It can be frustrating if you are on a poorly waymarked bit of

path and you keep having to take your bag off to get the guidebook out! It is, after all, hard to hold a book while you have a walking pole in each hand. It took me until midway through my wander to realise how much easier life would be if I just had to reach in my pocket for my phone to check my route. It's important to have the hard copy of the guidebook too though, just in case your phone dies!

- **Look after your tent.** From the very beginning, I was strict about this. I knew that if my tent became dirty and smelly, I would still have to live in it for ten weeks. Boots came off before I went into the inner section, and dirty clothes stayed in the outer section too. Once I had set up, there was no lounging around in the tent. It was straight in the shower (or to wash as best I could) so that everything inside stayed clean. If you make the effort, you'll have a nice canvas home for the duration of your challenge.
- **On rainy days, line your bag with a bin liner.** I carried a standard bin bag from the beginning, but rather stupidly thought my waterproof cover would be fine. A soaking wet sleeping bag on Day 26 proved this to be very wrong. From then on, my bag was always lined on rainy days.
- **Consider the weather when setting daily targets.** A rainy and windy day will slow you down a little, but you will find you are distracted by scenery less. Hot days require longer breaks and more refreshment stops and showery days will have you diving for your waterproofs often. It's important to think ahead and not set yourself too daunting a target – as I did on Day 8!
- **Don't plan too far ahead.** Lots of people asked if I had a schedule. I didn't. I wanted to see how I felt each morning and decide where to eat in the day, and where to sleep that night, over breakfast. It's far less stressful that way, and you have the freedom to stop and explore places that you want to spend more time in.

- **Set yourself short-term goals.** When I had a visit from somebody planned in the next week, I was usually happy. The end of your walk can seem like a lifetime away on down days. It helps to have something to look forward to within the next seven days of walking, because that never seems too far away.
- **Enjoy the little things.** There is beauty and enjoyment to be found in every day. Don't develop tunnel vision about a mileage target and forget to notice the patchwork of green fields, or the robin singing in the hedge, or the raindrops caught on a spider's web. If you notice these little wonders happening all around you, you'll be totally 'in the moment', as I liked to say. And that is the true secret to getting the most out of your hike: notice everything.
- **Put your phone on flight mode.** Not only does this make the battery last all day, possibly two, it makes you look up and enjoy your surroundings rather than wondering what's happening back at home. Finding Wi-Fi once a day was more than enough to keep me in the loop!
- **Prevention is better than cure.** This goes for a lot of things. If it's sunny, put on your sunhat, sunglasses and sun cream. If it's hot, drink plenty. If it starts to rain, get everything waterproofed as quickly as possible. If you feel a blister coming on, tape up that foot before it gets worse. I developed six blisters in my first week and walking became very painful. If you develop a blister, drain it with a sterilised needle at night, then tape it up the following morning. Compeed blister plasters worked well, but once the blisters are gone, it's far cheaper just to cover each problem area with Micropore tape every morning to prevent more forming. It's easier to stop a problem from developing than it is to try and fix it once it's too late.
- **Wild-camping is great, but not necessarily in between two 20-mile days.** At the end of a long, sticky and tiring day, you will crave a shower. I wild-camped a couple of times,

but soon realised that going to bed smelly and having to go into the woods to dig a hole in the morning is not a great set-up for your next day of walking. It was far nicer to seek out campsites, explain your challenge and stay somewhere with some little luxuries – such as hot water and a flushing loo! Some would rather wild-camp all the way, but you need to decide what is most important to you. For me, it was enjoyment.

- **If fundraising, a sign on your bag is worth its weight in gold.** Once Menai had made my first signs, my fundraising hit a new level. Some people noticed the writing when I walked past and called me back, but the biggest successes were in cafés and restaurants. I would make sure that I positioned Wilson where he could be seen, and countless people read my little notice on their way past.

- **Talk to people.** Even on my down days, when I wanted to just be invisible, I would make the effort to talk to people I passed. They would invariably pull me out of my misery. You learn so much from hearing people's stories and listening to their local knowledge. Your faith in humanity will be restored too. Most people are genuinely lovely, and will happily chat to you, offer help, donate to your fundraising or even give you a bed for the night. People were a huge part of my solo walk, so if you need help, simply ask someone. Very few will turn you away.

A Look Inside Wilson
(my backpack)

Since I arrived home, many people have asked what I carried with me on my Wander. Though everyone needs different things, I hope this rough guide can help you sort out the essentials from the luxuries.

Wilson himself
- Lowe Alpine TFC Kibo 65-litre rucksack

Camping
- Coleman Cobra 2-man tent
- Vango Trek self-inflating roll mat (later Mountain Equipment – much lighter but a little thinner)
- Vango Ultralite 600 sleeping bag
- Vango self-inflating pillow

Clothing
- Scarpa Mistral boots
- Berghaus RG Alpha waterproof jacket
- Berghaus Deluge waterproof trousers (full-length side zip for excellent ventilation on showery days)
- 4 pairs boxers
- 2 pairs trek socks (1 pair Bridgedale and 1 pair 1000 Mile)
- 4 pairs cotton socks to wear underneath the Bridgedales (after a few days, my clean evening pair became my hiking pair for the next day)
- 2 walking T-shirts
- Alzheimer's Society T-shirt
- clean evening T-shirt

- Montane changeable walking trousers/shorts (these stayed as my evening wear for the whole walk!)
- Mountain Equipment shorts (did all 63 days of walking!)
- North Face fleece
- Regatta wide-brimmed sunhat
- Bloc sunglasses
- Lifeventure Trek towel (large)
- PDQ closed-toe walking sandals (for the evenings – a bit heavier, but a lot more useful, than flip flops!)

Walking Kit

- 2 Mountain King walking poles (Essential when carrying a heavy bag. The extra support downhill and drive uphill was invaluable. They saved hundreds of ankle twists too, and fended off an angry German Shepherd.)
- 5 dry bags (1 for clothes, 1 for electricals, 1 for food, 1 for toiletries, 1 for fleece)
- guidebooks (I used the Cicerone *Walking Offa's Dyke Path* and *Walking the Wales Coast Path* books)
- compass
- whistle

Gadgets and Essentials

- money
- bank card
- driving licence (as identification)
- YHA membership card
- Just Giving and blog info cards x100 (Given out to people along the route. Earned me a lot in terms of sponsorship and followers!)
- 2 Aquapac waterproof phone cases (one used as wallet)
- phone and charger
- camera and charger (Though I used my phone for most photos, my camera is much more sophisticated and has

a much better zoom than my phone does. It was perfect for wildlife shots and sunsets, as well as the occasional distant interesting sight. Not an essential, but for a keen photographer, it was invaluable.)

- iPod and charger (Not an essential and rarely used as it cut out the sounds of nature. When I needed company, I played music quietly from my phone, so with hindsight, I wouldn't pack my iPod next time.)
- Anker portable charger (fully charged my phone twice before it needed a recharge)
- Nebo torch (used as my tent light when hung from the little hook in the highest point)
- penknife
- duct tape (great for repairing rips in waterproofs and fixing minor bag issues!)
- lighter (For sterilising needles used to drain blisters. Not pleasant, but you'll need to do it.)
- spare battery for torch
- small fold-up trowel (For when you have a call of nature out in the wild! I collected toilet paper from public loos as I needed top ups – just enough to cover emergencies.)

Medical and Toiletries

- first aid kit (plenty of plasters and blister plasters, steristrips, Micropore tape)
- deodorant (optional, but I preferred to smell a little like a civilised human being while walking through towns and cities)
- Kush soap bar (can be used in streams and the sea if need be as all ingredients are natural and harmless)
- soap leaves (for washing hands in streams etc.)
- travel wash (Does everything from clothes to food! I used it to wash my clothes in sinks.)
- toothpaste
- toothbrush

- nail clippers
- personal medication (for my Crohn's Disease)
- paracetamol
- foot oil (To reduce friction on your feet. Towards the end, Micropore tape was enough.)
- sun cream
- insect repellent
- Sudocrem
- Germolene foot cream (perfect for easing pain, especially blisters)

Food and Drink
- Lifestraw filter bottle (sent home at Portmeirion as I wasn't using it)
- 2 x collapsible, foldable bottles (Be organised and these will never run dry. Ask to fill them at pubs and cafés. Not one person said no to me!)
- Trail Mix (500 g to start. Good energy for snacking.)

Each little item that I carried became my friend. Your bag and everything inside it are your only constants on the walk, so you'll be surprised how attached to them you grow. I genuinely love everything that came with me on my Welsh Wander, to the point where I felt a little homesick when I saw a picture of my tent a month after finishing. It took three days to pluck up the courage to unpack Wilson for the final time! From your boots to your walking poles, your clothing to your roll mat, everything will be that little bit more special once you've returned home. You have a bond that won't ever be broken as you have survived your challenge together. Wilson now lives under my bed as I didn't want to shut him away in a cupboard. We still have the odd day out walking together, and will soon take on another big adventure.

The Final Mile

Thank you so much for sharing in my Welsh Wander. Editing the blogs and writing new sections has allowed me to relive the most wonderful experience of my life all over again, so I hope that you have found it both entertaining and informative, and that maybe I have inspired some of you to take on your own big adventure. If you want it enough, you only have to have the courage to take the first step.

Nos da, pawb!

Also from Y Lolfa:

Great Welsh WALKS

based on the
*Weatherman
Walking*
TV series

Derek Brockway
and Martin Aaron

y Lolfa

BBC Wales

£9.95

A Welsh Wander is just one of a whole
range of publications from Y Lolfa. For a full
list of books currently in print, send now
for your free copy of our new full-colour
catalogue. Or simply surf into our website

www.ylolfa.com

for secure on-line ordering.

TALYBONT CEREDIGION CYMRU SY24 5HE
e-mail ylolfa@ylolfa.com
website www.ylolfa.com
phone (01970) 832 304
fax 832 782